The Centrality of Christ in the Theology of Thomas F. Torrance

The Centrality of Christ in the Theology of Thomas F. Torrance

Some Dogmatic Implications

Paul D. Molnar

LONDON • NEW YORK • OXFORD • NEW DELHI • SYDNEY

T&T CLARK
Bloomsbury Publishing Plc
50 Bedford Square, London, WC1B 3DP, UK
1385 Broadway, New York, NY 10018, USA
29 Earlsfort Terrace, Dublin 2, Ireland

BLOOMSBURY, T&T CLARK and the T&T Clark logo are
trademarks of Bloomsbury Publishing Plc

First published in Great Britain 2024

Copyright © Paul D. Molnar, 2024

Paul D. Molnar has asserted his right under the Copyright,
Designs and Patents Act, 1988, to be identified as Author of this work.

For legal purposes the Acknowledgments on p. xii constitute
an extension of this copyright page.

Cover design: Gita Kowlessur

All rights reserved. No part of this publication may be reproduced or transmitted in any
form or by any means, electronic or mechanical, including photocopying, recording, or
any information storage or retrieval system, without prior permission in writing from
the publishers.

Bloomsbury Publishing Plc does not have any control over, or responsibility for, any
third-party websites referred to or in this book. All internet addresses given in this
book were correct at the time of going to press. The author and publisher regret any
inconvenience caused if addresses have changed or sites have ceased to exist, but
can accept no responsibility for any such changes.

A catalogue record for this book is available from the British Library.

Library of Congress Cataloging-in-Publication Data
Names: Molnar, Paul D., 1946- author.
Title: The centrality of Christ in the theology of Thomas F. Torrance : some
dogmatic implications / Paul D. Molnar.
Description: London : T&T Clark, 2025. | Includes bibliographical references.
Identifiers: LCCN 2024020715 (print) | LCCN 2024020716 (ebook) |
ISBN 9780567717955 (pb) | ISBN 9780567717962 (hb) |
ISBN 9780567717979 (epub) | ISBN 9780567717986 (pdf)
Subjects: LCSH: Torrance, Thomas F. (Thomas Forsyth), 1913-2007.
Classification: LCC BX4827.T67 M64 2025 (print) | LCC BX4827.T67 (ebook) |
DDC 230/.52092--dc23/eng/20240730
LC record available at https://lccn.loc.gov/2024020715
LC ebook record available at https://lccn.loc.gov/2024020716

ISBN:	HB:	978-0-5677-1796-2
	PB:	978-0-5677-1795-5
	ePDF:	978-0-5677-1798-6
	eBook:	978-0-5677-1797-9

Typeset by Integra Software Services Pvt. Ltd.
Printed and bound in Great Britain

To find out more about our authors and books visit www.bloomsbury.com
and sign up for our newsletters.

Contents

Preface		vi
Acknowledgments		xii
1	Conflicting Visions of Grace and Nature: Appraising the Views of Thomas F. Torrance and Karl Rahner	1
2	Appreciating How T. F. Torrance's View of Justification by Grace Alone Leads to a Proper Theology of Liberation	51
3	A Fine Point in Christology: Discovering Why It Is Important Not to Read the Missions of the Economic Trinity Back into the Immanent Trinity	127
Conclusion		185
Select Bibliography		194
Name Index		198
Subject Index		200

Preface

Today, it is generally acknowledged that Thomas F. Torrance was the most significant English-speaking theologian of the twentieth century. In my opinion, that is a well-deserved honor as, I hope, will be made abundantly clear in this book. This is a book that carries forward one of the key themes of my last book, *Freedom, Necessity, and the Knowledge of God: In Conversation with Karl Barth and Thomas F. Torrance* (London: T&T Clark, 2022). The key theme was that since Jesus Christ is indeed the incarnate Word of God, he must be both the *first* and the *final* Word in any properly theological theology. I proposed the view that if theologians allowed that to be the case, then everything they say about theology, beginning with Christology and the doctrine of the Trinity, and then leading to specific theological themes such as the issue of universalism, liberation theology, and knowledge of God, just to name three items, would be different. In this book, I will explore how this proposal affects the way grace and nature are conceptualized. Additionally, I will delve more deeply into what a proper liberation theology might look like. And finally, I will explore a fine point in Christology by focusing on how Torrance's understanding of Chalcedon offers a solid Christology linked to his trinitarian theology and avoids some serious christological errors as well. Strictly speaking, this is a constructive work in systematic theology with its main focus on Christology. That means I do not intend to offer a detailed development of Christology in any introductory sense. Instead, I will explore Christology with the help of Thomas F. Torrance as well as Karl Barth since both of them present a substantial evangelical view of Christology grounded in the main teaching of the Councils of Nicaea and Chalcedon. Their perspectives will contribute greatly to a serious study of Christology and its implications for other aspects of theology.

Chapter 1 focuses on Torrance's understanding of grace with a view toward explaining how, why, and with what implications he insists that grace cannot be detached from Christ the Giver of grace. In that chapter, I develop and present Torrance's view of grace in its identity with Jesus Christ, the Giver of grace, and then compare his view with the views of one of the twentieth century's most prominent Catholic theologians, Karl Rahner. I therefore explore and explain how several of Rahner's presuppositions and conclusions differ from the positions espoused by Torrance in order to illustrate that when grace is in fact detached from Christ the Giver of grace, then grace tends to be conceptualized as "a detachable and transferable divine quality which may inhere in or be possessed by the human being to whom it is given."

This is a rather widespread view of grace, and it leads to more than a few problematic conclusions. This is an extremely important issue because I will demonstrate that by detaching grace from Christ the Giver of grace, Rahner and those many who follow his method try to explain the meaning of grace, nature, revelation, faith, and the knowledge of God by focusing on us in our transcendental experiences. When Rahner's views are directly compared with the position of Thomas F. Torrance, one can clearly see the difference it makes when Torrance applies his view of the doctrine of justification by grace alone to theological anthropology, Christology, as well as to his view of grace, nature, revelation, faith, and knowledge of God. The results are at times startling and clear. His views consistently allow Jesus Christ himself to be his starting point and criterion for theological truth.

My ultimate aim in that first chapter is to suggest that if Protestant and Catholic theologians could agree to allow Jesus Christ in his uniqueness to be the starting point and criterion for true knowledge in these matters, important unifying implications would follow. For instance, genuine unity between the churches would naturally result because it would be Christ himself who is the Way, the Truth, and the Life (Jn 14:6), and not some other authority such as the moral law, or the teaching authority in the church, or even the Ten Commandments understood legalistically that would unite us, but God himself, as he meets us in his own self-revelation. So, instead of attempting to ground the truth of theology in our obedience to conscience or obedience to the moral law or some other external authority, the truth would be grounded in Christ himself and in him alone. From this it would follow that all Christians would be united in their acknowledgment of and recognition of the truth of God's being as we actually know God face to face with Christ.

For Torrance, it is because grace is not some "energizing principle" as understood in certain Hellenistic views that influenced Christian theology that he can make his claim that face to face with Christ we are face to face with God. This is a crucial point because this insight shapes his view of justification, which genuinely lets Christ occupy the center with the result that it is Christ's Person that determines his work and not the other way around. This approach to theology disallows nonconceptual knowledge of God, which is basic to Rahner's approach. Such a view leads to Rahner's view of the supernatural existential and to his view of anonymous Christianity. I will show exactly how and why those two ideas are indeed problematic in a properly functioning Christology. To accomplish this, I will not only discuss Torrance's view of truth and reality but I will contrast his view of cheap and costly grace with the views of the so-called "new theologians" John Robinson and Paul Tillich by showing how some of their key insights are replicated in the thought of Karl Rahner and in the thought of William V. Dych, who is a highly regarded interpreter of Rahner.

In Chapter 2, I specifically explore T. F. Torrance's view of justification by grace alone by revisiting his view of "cheap" and "costly" grace as that applies to God acting for us in his Word and Spirit. From this I explore the implications of this doctrine for discipleship by comparing his view of human freedom based on the freedom that is ours in Christ with the views of several prominent liberation theologians. For Torrance, liberation in the first instance means liberation from sin as self-will. That liberation comes to us through Christ alone, who lived a life of perfect obedience to God vicariously for our benefit. Thus, it is only in faith—which means knowledge of the truth, and includes conceptual and spiritual union with Christ through the Holy Spirit—that we are truly free to love God, who loved us while we were still sinners. And it is only on that basis that we become free to love others by fighting against oppression and for liberation from such oppression. In that way we would avoid any idea that it is up to us to "use" Jesus in order to advance our own social, political, or religious agenda which might include opposition to racism and sexism, to name just two items. In order to accomplish this, I will compare Torrance's thinking with the views of some liberation theologians to show what happens when it is mistakenly supposed that we first fight against all forms of oppression and out of that fight a proper liberation theology would emerge.

This chapter will unfold first by presenting Torrance's positive view of grace as that act of God for us in Christ which cost God the loss of his only Son on the cross and costs us all our attempts to live by relying in some sense on ourselves instead of on God alone. This chapter will include a discussion of how Torrance contrasted the ethical views of Bonhoeffer with the views of many of Bonhoeffer's contemporaries who were using his thought to argue for a "religionless Christianity" and "worldly holiness." Insightfully, Torrance argues against using God "as a prop" to support one's own view of religion precisely to avoid God's judgment, which applies to all people, even in their goodness, since it is only by God's forgiving grace that we may live in the freedom that comes through union with Christ. Thus, for Torrance taking justification seriously means that "the ground is completely taken away from [our] feet" and along with that would go the "prop-God" that belongs to any attempt to rely on ourselves and the moral law to be in right relation to God. Along with that Torrance maintained, with Bonhoeffer, that one's question would no longer be "How can I be good?" or "How can I do good?" but it would be "What is the will of God?" From this he consistently argues that we cannot substitute reliance on morality or religion for the real need to rely exclusively on Jesus Christ himself as the one who justifies and sanctifies us.

Then I will contrast his view with the views of a number of liberation theologians who think that the truth of liberation and of theology itself can be attained by our fighting against oppression and for liberation in the first instance. I argue that such an approach misses the all-important fact that liberation means that Christ is the Liberator, who liberates all of us from the sin which is identical with our free-will, which Torrance identifies as our self-will. I spell out the difference this starting point makes for a theology of liberation. I explain why Torrance so firmly rejects any idea of conditional salvation, why he consistently holds together the doctrines of the incarnation and atonement—why it was not the death of Jesus that constituted atonement but Christ as the Son of God "offering Himself in sacrifice for us." As Torrance insists, "Everything depends on *who* he was, for the significance of His acts in life and death depends on the nature of His Person." From this it follows that any focus on his benefits and not upon Christ himself will always lead to legalism or moralism and miss the actual meaning of justification and sanctification with some form of self-justification. Because Christ is the center in Torrance's theology precisely in this way, he insists that if we, as the sinners we are, use the moral law to determine our goodness before God, then what happens is that we rely on "moral awareness" which, he says, "tends to sever its connection with God … to establish an autonomous or semi-autonomous basis." Then people relate themselves to God "through duty to their neighbour" and also indirectly through the moral law. Precisely in that way they fail to relate themselves directly to God, who judges us and forgives us in Christ. That is itself another form of self-justification that separates us from God.

After presenting a thorough picture of Torrance's view of justification by grace through faith, I consider the implications of Torrance's position for the perspectives of several theologians who present versions of liberation theology. These include Elizabeth Johnson, who claims the symbol God functions, and we must make it function to overcome patriarchalism. Her argument clearly is a form of self-justification in that she thinks we can overcome the sin of patriarchalism by changing our language for God. However, we do not have that power since the name of God came to us from beyond us when God the Son became incarnate in history in Jesus of Nazareth and revealed God the Father to us. The idea that we have that power expresses just another form of self-reliance such that we are thrown back on ourselves to name God and overcome sin. It leads her to view conversion by claiming that conversion means that women need to tap into the power of themselves not only to name God but to overcome the problem of patriarchalism. That is the self-reliance that Torrance consistently and rightly opposed.

I also consider the views of Rubén Rosario Rodríguez, who thinks we can know the Holy Spirit from human works of liberation. I explain how and why that idea ends up separating the Spirit from the Word, which is impossible since they are *homoousios*. The result is his idea that "to participate in liberation is already, in a certain sense, a salvific work." I explain why this very idea embodies just the self-justification that a proper view of justification would want to avoid. Following this, I consider the views of Hanna Reichel, whose version of liberation theology involves a dialogue between constructive and systematic theology relying on the views of Marcella Althaus-Reid and Karl Barth. Here I explain that while she thinks that what they have in common is belief in a "wholly Other," she consistently misses Barth's important point that we cannot know who God is or the meaning of grace, faith, revelation, or even the love of God apart from specific recognition of the love of that meets us in his incarnate Son. For her, all of these categories become ways that we can relate with God by relying on our own experience, including queer experience, to understand Jesus as "bi-sexual" and God as a "queer God." Her analysis overtly smacks of projection so that instead of allowing God alone as the triune God, to shape her view of grace, she consistently understands grace from our supposed experience of grace which becomes her primary category for understanding theology. Her view that "there might be significant overlaps in the theology and material *realities* to which" Barth and Althaus-Reid "testify" leads her into a form of self-justification in spite of her attempt to avoid that. By reconstructing who God is based on queer experience, her position is in stark contrast with the actual views of Karl Barth, who insisted that any theology that is grounded in reason or experience betrays itself as a hypostatization of the human.

A last example considered in this chapter is James Cone's classic work, *A Black Theology of Liberation*. On the one hand, Cone makes some very appropriate statements about the centrality of Jesus Christ for all theology. On the other hand, he then claims that "it is necessary to investigate the meaning of his person and work *in light of the black perspective*." That second claim is the problem I analyze and reject because the moment Christ's person and work are investigated from a black perspective or any humanly constructed perspective, he ceases to be what Torrance called an "ultimate," namely, the ultimate. That means for Torrance there is no ground for believing in Jesus in his uniqueness other than Jesus himself. While no one can or should abandon their perspectives, they must also realize that no human perspective can be or become the starting point or criterion for the truth that comes to us in and from Jesus himself, who is the truth of God freeing us to know God and love God and, on that basis, to fight against all that threatens our humanity. In spite of his wish to keep Christ at the center of his theology,

Cone gives up the question of truth by claiming that "In the struggle for truth in a revolutionary age, there can be no principles of truth, no absolutes, not even God." From this he reasons that "truth for the black thinker arises from a passionate encounter with black reality. Though that truth may be described religiously, as God, it is not the God of white religion but the God of black existence. *There is no way to speak of this objectively; truth is not objective.*" It goes without saying that if Jesus really is the Way, the Truth, and the Life, then none of this is accurate because there cannot be another truth than this. And this particular truth is the truth that is objectively real and, as Barth claimed, is known with apodictic certainty in and from Jesus himself. Consequently, it is a serious mistake to claim that truth for blacks arises from an "encounter with black reality," with the implication that the truth of the Gospel actually could be different for whites than it is for blacks. Jesus himself is the criterion of true liberation and he sets all free from the sin of self-reliance, irrespective of their race or their human condition.

Finally, in Chapter 3, which is indeed a ground-breaking chapter, I discuss whether the Council of Chalcedon needs to be repaired in order to recognize and maintain the full and complete humanity of Jesus Christ as the incarnate Word. In that chapter I demonstrate that by employing such traditional notions as divine simplicity and impassibility, along with the concepts of *enhypostasis* and *anhypoastasis*, Torrance was able to achieve such a proper view of Christ's humanity. He accomplished that goal without changing the basic teaching of Chalcedon that Jesus was both truly divine and truly human without confusion, separation, or mixture of his two natures since his humanity was grounded in his being as the Word who became flesh. I contrast his understanding of these categories with the recent views expressed by Bruce McCormack as he claims that all four of these categories must be surrendered in their traditional form in order to recognize Jesus' true humanity as the humanity which he mistakenly claims is in some sense *constitutive* of his eternal Sonship. This chapter demonstrates that with McCormack's reduction of the *Logos asarkos* to the *Logos incarnandus*, he carries out his initial insight that the *Logos asarkos* is "an 'idol' by any other name" while simultaneously claiming that he does not reject the *Logos asarkos*, as Robert Jenson did. This leads to the bizarre notion that the second person of the Trinity "is eternally generated as divine-human relation" and that the second person of the Trinity was generated by the Father for the purpose of incarnation. These are views that were flatly rejected in the early church with the recognition that the God who meets us in his Word and Spirit is free in himself and never becomes dependent on anything external to himself, as he would if the Father's generation of the Son was contingent on the Son's future incarnation, suffering, and death.

Acknowledgments

I would like to thank Anna Turton, Publisher, T&T Clark (Theology), for her consistent assistance, support, and help in bringing this work to completion. She is a wonderful editor who is theologically astute and easy to work with. I would like to thank my good friend of many years Iain R. Torrance for his consistent support of my work on his father's remarkable theology. His friendship and theological insights have been invaluable to me over the course of many years now. I also would like to thank my good friend and colleague, George Hunsinger, for reading large sections of this work and for making incisive and helpful comments along the way. Our conversations over many years have been extremely helpful to me in thinking through key theological issues. I am grateful to my good friend Todd Speidell, Editor of *Participatio*, the Journal of the Thomas F. Torrance Theological Fellowship for reading sections of this new volume. His careful reading and theologically informed comments were and always remain very helpful. I would also like to thank my Graduate Assistant at St. John's, Alexander DeMarchena for his careful proofreading of the entire manuscript. This was no small task and his meticulous attention to detail was very helpful. Alex was also a wonderful conversation partner discussing the key themes of this book over the last couple of years. I would also like to thank my friend and colleague, David Haddorff for reading through Chapter Two, and making helpful comments regarding the text. I am grateful to the Journal of the Thomas F. Torrance Theological Fellowship, *Participatio*, for permission to reprint two previously published articles in revised form. They are "Conflicting Visions of Grace and Nature: Appraising the Views of Thomas F. Torrance and Karl Rahner," in *Participatio*, "The Priority of Grace in the Theology of T. F. Torrance" (2023), 3–59 and *Participatio*, "Torrance, Justification by Grace Alone, and 'Liberation Theology,'" in "The Priority of Grace in the Theology of T. F. Torrance" (2023), 101–50.

1

Conflicting Visions of Grace and Nature: Appraising the Views of Thomas F. Torrance and Karl Rahner

Among contemporary theologians, few are as clear or as consistent as Thomas F. Torrance in asserting and maintaining that grace, as he put it following St. Paul, is "actualised among men in the person of Jesus Christ."[1] Invariably, Torrance insists that grace cannot be detached from the Giver of grace, that is, from Jesus Christ himself. This simple statement has profound and wide-ranging implications. Torrance insists that grace is not "something which merely comes to the assistance of man in his own efforts for righteousness."[2] Instead, it is "the will of God to constitute man's life afresh on a wholly new basis and in a renewed world, to set him free from sin and Satan; to endue him with the Spirit, to make him the possessor of a supernatural life."[3] Among other things, Torrance noted that for Paul grace, as the gift of God, "is none other than the risen Christ who confronts men through the word of his Gospel. *Charis* is not here, therefore, in any sense a quality adhering to Paul, but a particular manifestation of the gracious purpose and power of Christ."[4] For Paul, grace, which is "the new supernatural order which breaks in upon men, but which manifests itself in their faith and in their Christian life," cannot be understood as "a transferred quality."[5] In other words, Torrance rejects any idea of infused grace. For Torrance, "Grace is not something that can be detached from God and made to inhere in

---

[1] Thomas F. Torrance, *The Doctrine of Grace in the Apostolic Fathers* (Eugene, OR: Wipf & Stock, 1996), 30. This volume was first published by Oliver and Boyd in 1948 and was Torrance's doctoral thesis written under the guidance of Karl Barth.
[2] Ibid.
[3] Ibid.
[4] Ibid., 31.
[5] Ibid.

creaturely being as 'created grace.'"⁶ This is the case because grace is identical with Christ himself as the active giver of grace.⁷

For Torrance, "Grace means the primary and constitutive act in which out of free love God has intervened to set our life on a wholly new basis, but also means that through faith this may be actualised in flesh and blood because it has been actualised in Jesus Christ."⁸ In his cross and resurrection, Jesus Christ becomes "our salvation, our righteousness, and our wisdom. Thus any attempt to detach grace in a transferred sense from the actual embodiment of God's grace in Jesus Christ is to misunderstand the meaning of the Pauline *charis* altogether."⁹ For Paul, Torrance insists, grace (*charis*) is not some energizing principle as it came to be understood due to Hellenistic influences in later Christian writings.

Rejecting this Hellenistic approach, Torrance opposed the idea that grace could be understood as "a detachable and transferable divine quality which may inhere in or be possessed by the human being to whom it is given in virtue of which he is somehow 'deified' or 'divinised.'"¹⁰ Torrance therefore rejects translating *theosis* as "deification" because he thinks that suggests a change in human nature. So he prefers to translate 2 Pet. 1:4 to say we are "partners of the Deity" but not "partakers of divine nature."¹¹ Understood in a properly christological and trinitarian way, there is no confusion of divine and human nature or divine and human activity because it is through our personal union with Christ that we share in his humanity, which is uniquely united to his deity by virtue of the hypostatic union. Thus, we are "partakers of the divine nature" through union with Jesus Christ.¹² In this context, Torrance thought Athanasius' statement that "He [the Word] became man in order to make us divine" was problematic. Noting that Georges Florovsky himself admitted that "The term *theosis* is indeed embarrassing" if it is conceptualized "in 'ontological categories'" because "man simply cannot become 'god,'" he

---

6 Thomas F. Torrance, "The Roman Doctrine of Grace from the Point of View of Reformed Theology," *Theology in Reconstruction* (London: SCM Press, 1965), 182.
7 See Thomas F. Torrance, *The Trinitarian Faith: The Evangelical Theology of the Ancient Catholic Church* (Edinburgh: T&T Clark, 1988; reissued in a Second Edition in the Cornerstone Series with a New Critical Introduction by Myk Habets, 2016), 24 and 140-1 and *The Christian Doctrine of God, One Being Three Persons* (Edinburgh: T&T Clark, 1996); reissued in a Second Edition in the Cornerstone Series with an Introduction by Paul D. Molnar, 2016, 21, 147. Because the Spirit cannot be separated from the Word, the gift of grace cannot be separated from the Holy Spirit either as the one who enables knowledge of the Father through his Son.
8 Torrance, *The Doctrine of Grace*, 33.
9 Ibid. Torrance adds: "To detach grace from the person of Christ and to think of it as acting impersonally upon man is inevitably to land in determinism. That was Augustine's mistake," ibid.
10 Torrance, *The Trinitarian Faith*, 140.
11 Torrance, *Christian Doctrine of God*, 95.
12 See Thomas F. Torrance, *Conflict and Agreement in the Church Vol. I, Order and Disorder* (Eugene, OR: Wipf and Stock, 1996), 110.

preferred, with Florovsky, to understand *Theosis* as "a personal encounter. It is the ultimate intercourse with God, in which the whole of human existence is, as it were, permeated by the Divine Presence."[13] Nonetheless, Torrance consistently rejected notions of "divinization" and "deification" to the extent that they implied confusion of Creator and creatures precisely by thinking of "grace as deifying man or heightening his being until he attains the level of a supernatural order" because such a view "appears to do docetic violence to creaturely human nature."[14]

Instead, for Torrance, "Christ Himself is the objective ground and content of *charis* in every instance of its special Christian use."[15] In the New Testament, grace (*charis*),

> refers to the being and action of God as revealed and actualised in Jesus Christ, for He is in His person and work the self-giving of God to men ... Grace is in fact identical with Jesus Christ in person and word and deed ... neither the action nor the gift is separable from the person of the giver, God in Christ.[16]

The connection between Christology and the doctrine of the Trinity is crucial in understanding Torrance's view of grace. Because Torrance thinks God is the content of his revelation to us in Christ, he maintains that "In Jesus Christ the Giver of grace and the Gift of grace are one and the same, for in him and through him it is none other than God himself who is savingly and creatively at work for us and our salvation."[17] Because God is the one who is savingly present in Christ, that also means that "The Holy Spirit is no less than the Son the self-giving of God, for in him the divine Gift and the divine Giver are identical. This is why the *homoousion* was applied to the understanding of the nature and identity of the Holy Spirit."[18] For these reasons, Torrance insisted that grace is never to be conceptualized as "a created medium between God and man" since as God's self-giving "in his *incarnate* Son in whom the Gift and Giver are indivisibly one," grace itself is "governed by the oneness of the Father and the Son," and therefore grace "cannot be regarded as a detachable and transferable divine quality which may inhere in or be possessed by the human being to whom it is given in virtue of which he is somehow 'deified' or 'divinised.'"[19]

---

[13] Torrance, *Christian Doctrine of God*, 96.
[14] Torrance, "The Roman Doctrine of Grace," *Theology in Reconstruction*, 180.
[15] Torrance, *The Doctrine of Grace*, 21.
[16] Ibid.
[17] Torrance, *The Trinitarian Faith*, 138.
[18] Torrance, *Christian Doctrine of God*, 147.
[19] Torrance, *The Trinitarian Faith*, 140.

With these important nuances and distinctions, Torrance could consistently maintain that our true humanity as it is in Christ is not dissolved in any way but intensified by being exalted in Christ to "share in God's life and glory."[20] However, because Torrance's Christology and trinitarian theology function seamlessly together, Torrance insisted that it is through the Holy Spirit, and not through anything we find in ourselves, such as our moral sense or our acts of will, that we know God and participate objectively in God. When thinking of our sharing in God's life and glory eschatologically, Torrance held that even now, we experience "communion in the consummated reality which will be fully actualized in us in the resurrection and redemption of the body."[21] That means at our resurrection we will not be transformed into another nature but that our human nature will become "imperishable." The point here, however, is that Torrance noted that in considering these matters, there is what he called "the danger of 'vertigo,'" because people tend to conceptualize this participation in the divine nature by identifying their own being with God's being in mystical or pantheistic fashion. Torrance adamantly opposes any such thinking because it would destroy the historical connection between the resurrection, ascension, and the historical Jesus as the one point in history where we have communion with the triune God and have hope for Christ's promised eternal life. Torrance thus held that "we share in the life of God while remaining what we were made to be, men and not gods."[22]

Torrance's rejection of infused grace is no small matter because it connects decisively with his view of truth. Specifically, Torrance insists that God "is himself the truth who reveals himself as he is and who remains faithful to what he reveals of himself."[23] Put directly, for Torrance, truth must be understood "as the truth which God is in his own eternal being, and the truth which he shines upon us from and through himself."[24] Following this line of thought, which he held was fundamental to patristic and early medieval theology, Torrance then maintains that:

---

[20] Thomas F. Torrance, *Space, Time and Resurrection* (Edinburgh: T&T Clark, 1998; reissued in Cornerstones Series with an Introduction by Paul D. Molnar, 2019), 135.

[21] Ibid., 136.

[22] Ibid.

[23] Thomas F. Torrance, "Truth and Authority: Theses on Truth," *Irish Theological Quarterly* 39 (3) (September 1972), 215–42, 224. This was originally a lecture presented to "L'Académie Internationale des Sciences Religieuses in L'Institut Catholique de Paris" on May 27, 1969. It was later reprinted in Thomas F. Torrance, *Transformation & Convergence in the Frame of Knowledge: Explorations in the Interrelations of Scientific and Theological Enterprise* (Grand Rapids, MI: Eerdmans, 1984), Chapter Ten, 303–32.

[24] Ibid.

Face to face with God, we are up against the ultimate truth of being in God's own self: it is only as we are cast upon him in this way, as the ultimate source of all truth who is not closed to us but who by his nature is open to us, that we may know him truly, for then, we know him under the immediate compulsion of his own being, in the power of his self-evidence.[25]

I mention Torrance's discussion of our knowledge of God as truth here to show exactly why it is such a major problem to conceptualize grace as infused grace. Torrance firmly maintains that theology, and in particular, knowledge of God and God's grace, can only be properly understood when *the truth of being* shapes our thinking. This means that we know God's being when in Christ, and through his Spirit, God makes himself known to us. We do not just know something about God metaphorically. We really know God in his eternal being as Father, Son, and Holy Spirit in faith. That means truth, as the truth of God, is grounded only in God and not in us and that if truth is condensed to what is conceptualized by us, then Kant's disjunction between idea and reality could not be overcome. The important point then is if grace is properly conceived, then there would be substantial agreement between Catholics and Protestants about the truth of who God is in himself and for us and who we are in Christ. That agreement would be reached based on *the truth of being* itself rather than being based on either our moral sense or our faith or our act of will or some external authority other than God himself. Understanding truth as grounded in the *being of God* rather than in us or some other external authority needs some explanation.

Thomas Aquinas and Anselm

Torrance helpfully explains what he means here by contrasting the views of Thomas Aquinas and Anselm. He begins by noting that for Anselm, "when we really know God we know that we know him under the compulsion of his being who he is and what by his nature he must be."[26] We thus know God truly "under the light of his truth which is his divine being coming to view and becoming in our understanding and knowledge of him what he is consistently in himself and in all his relations with us."[27] To clarify matters, Torrance here distinguishes between voluntary and involuntary objects of knowledge. The former refers to some object without will, such as one's hand. A hand is an

---

[25] Ibid.
[26] Ibid.
[27] Ibid.

object simply by being what it is. This object compels me to know it as it actually is precisely by being what it is. However, the latter refers to personal agents who can only be known to the extent that they allow themselves to be known to us by freely and willingly giving themselves to be known. Thus, knowledge in this case for medieval theologians involved "willing consent" because it involved "a moment of the will."[28] In this regard, Torrance refers to Duns Scotus to stress that even though such a moment of will is involved in others and in our knowledge of God and others, whenever that other reveals himself to me, "my mind still falls under the compulsion of what is there—and it is that which is finally compelling, and finally self-evidencing."[29]

Torrance states that it is the second point that is either omitted or forgotten in Thomist thought. He says that St. Thomas taught "that that to which the understanding gives assent does not move the understanding by its own power but by the influence of the will" so that our intellect is not sufficiently moved to assent "by its proper object, but through an act of choice, i.e. because it is enough to move the will but not enough to move the understanding."[30] This is a vital point because Torrance is here claiming that basing knowledge on choice or will detaches our understanding of the *truth of God* "even in the assent of faith, from the self-evidence of God in his own being and truth." Such a problematic approach means that faith then must rest on "moral grounds and operate only with an indirect relation to the *autousia* and *autexousia* of God."[31] And the key problem here is that this move creates a division between faith and the object of faith, which then "is occupied by an *authority other than the truth of being*."[32] That authority, of course, is filled by one's human act of will through some imagined infusion of grace. Torrance even wonders whether there is an element of "voluntarism" in Thomas' view of knowledge of God that would open the door to a kind of nominalism which Thomas certainly opposed theoretically.

Torrance's key point here, however, is crucial because he is claiming that this gap between faith and the being and action of God himself in his grace in Jesus Christ became the basis of Kant's separation of faith and its object. That encouraged the view that,

> because of the alleged non-evidence of its object [since we only know phenomena and not the noumenal] faith was moved to assent through the will, so that its understanding of God was made to rest on moral grounds. But once a gap is opened up in this way between the

[28] Ibid., 225.
[29] Ibid.
[30] Ibid.
[31] Ibid.
[32] Ibid.

understanding and its proper object and the will is allowed to move in to assist the understanding in giving assent, then sooner or later some form of the active intellect or active reason comes on the scene and there takes place a shift in the basic notion of truth.[33]

What then was that shift, and what was the result with regard to grace and knowledge of the truth of God through his self-revelation? Torrance's answer is instructive. He says this shift led to the idea that truth came to be understood more as the connection between our understanding and our intellect than as a connection between our intellect and reality itself. This shift in thinking, Torrance believes, occurred in medieval thought and can be seen today in both Protestant and Catholic thought. Torrance maintains that this approach to knowledge of the truth finally suggests that we are the ones who "control and manipulate what we know, and as Kant used to say, make it the object of our thought."[34] He notes that in Roman Catholic thought, this thinking can be seen in "Roman phenomenological theology, in which theology tends to be converted into some form of theological anthropology."[35]

---

[33] Ibid., 226.
[34] Ibid.
[35] Ibid. Rahner's theology certainly fits into that category as he claims that "The question of man and its answering may not be regarded ... as an area of study separate from other theological areas as to its scope and subject-matter, but as the whole of dogmatic theology itself," Karl Rahner, *Theological Investigations* 23 vols. (hereafter TI). TI 9 *Writings of 1965-1967*, trans. Graham Harrison (New York: Herder and Herder, 1972), 28. Among other things this leads Rahner to maintain that "anthropology and Christology mutually determine each other within Christian dogmatics if they are both correctly understood" (ibid.). From this he concludes that "not only is it important for a true Christology to understand man as the being who is oriented towards an 'absolute Saviour' both *a priori* and in actuality, (his essence having been elevated and set in this direction supernaturally by grace), but it is equally important for his salvation that he is confronted with Jesus of Nazareth as this Saviour—which cannot, of course, be transcendentally 'deduced'" (ibid., 29–30). Torrance rejects all three of these ideas because for him the logic of grace is identical with Jesus himself and cannot be detached from him. And for Torrance there is an irreversible relation between grace and our response to Christ in faith. Moreover, we do not have any *a priori* on the basis of which we can know Christ and God himself because the condition of the possibility for that knowledge is the action of the Holy Spirit uniting us to Christ and thus to the Father. Finally, while Rahner claims he is not deducing salvation from his *a priori*, that is in fact what he does, because he misses one of the crucial points of Christology, namely that incarnation and atonement cannot be separated. Thus, what is revealed by the cross is that we, as fallen sinners, are not oriented toward Christ as the savior but are opposed to him and need to experience his judgment and grace by taking up our cross and following him alone to know God through Jesus himself. From our encounter with Christ, we learn that on our own we are enemies of grace and become true children of God by not relying on ourselves at all and turning to Christ alone as our savior. Cf. Jn 1:11-13, "He came to what was his own, but his own people did not accept him. But to those who did accept him he gave the power to become children of God, to those who believe in his name, who were born not by natural generation nor by human choice nor by a man's decision but of God."

Torrance further states that, in his view, "the movement in Roman theology from Maréchal to Rahner which brings St Thomas and Kant together, instead of overcoming Kantian phenomenalism serves rather to bring out the latent phenomenalism in Aquinas, and thus accentuates the retreat from the truth of being."[36] This problematic attempt to bring St. Thomas and Kant together in this way is an enormously important point because Torrance thinks the transcendental Thomists did indeed retreat from the *truth of being* by grounding their theology in transcendental experience.

Here it is worth considering Torrance's critique of transcendental Thomism as it relates to his understanding of truth and, thus, of God's grace. He says if we follow Anselm's approach, which held that faith cannot know the being of God without concepts, then theology would operate properly by allowing *the truth of being* rather than our moral acts or acts of will to shape our understanding of the truth of God and God's grace. That is why he believes that when the truth of being is considered "in light of the teaching of St Anselm, it becomes very apparent that the root difficulty lies in the admission of a *non-conceptual element* in our basic knowledge of God."[37] For Anselm "we cannot have experience of Him or believe in Him without conceptual forms of understanding—as Anselm used to say: *fides esse nequit sine conceptione*."[38] It is just because for Anselm "it is through his Word and Spirit" that we know God "in his own Being and according to his own nature" that he "could reject a non-conceptual relation to God."[39] Anselm's view cuts the ground out from under the Protestant liberalism of the nineteenth century that continues today in the form of Neo-Protestantism. It also cuts the ground out from under the transcendental Thomist view, which Torrance maintains does not really overcome Kant at all because it grounds knowledge of the truth in some sense in us and our intellectual actions that supposedly respond to God, but actually are responding to the God which we equate with our nonconceptual transcendental experiences of reality.

Torrance is direct: "There can be no knowledge of God, no faith [which for Torrance and Calvin means knowledge of the truth], which is not basically conceptual, or conceptual at its very root, and therefore there is no non-conceptual gap between God's revealing of himself and our knowing of him."[40] Thus, our human concepts "which arise in faith under the creative impact of the speech of God are grounded beyond themselves in the *ratio*

---

[36] Ibid.
[37] Ibid., 226.
[38] Thomas F. Torrance, *God and Rationality* (London: Oxford University Press, 1971; reissued Edinburgh: T&T Clark, 1997), 170.
[39] Torrance, *Truth and Authority*, 228.
[40] Ibid.

veritatis of the divine Being."⁴¹ The point here is crucial. It means that unless the truth of God's own being determines the truth of theology and of our knowledge of grace, then a supposed "non-conceptual" relation to God which always breaks the connection between our concept and God's actual being as the triune God will have to mean that "instead of terminating upon God himself as their rational ground, our concepts bend back and terminate upon our own consciousness, so that in the last analysis it is our own self-understanding which is the criterion of their truth or falsity: they never get beyond what the medievals called the *ojbecta mentis*."⁴²

Let me make several more key points here. First, the nonconceptual element in knowing God not only does not overcome Kant but it always leads to a kind of subjectivism. Torrance certainly knows that when we understand reality by understanding the truth of being and not just our conception of the truth of being, then there is also a "subjective counterpart" to that knowledge. Obviously, this is the case since it is we "who conceive, think, formulate and our knowledge of God grounded upon his own self evidence is not cut off from the fact that it is, *deo dante et deo illuminante, our* knowledge of him."⁴³ Importing some nonconceptual element into knowledge of God at this point, however, leaves out the decisive fact that true knowledge comes *only* from God encountering us in his grace and love as he meets us in Christ himself. Second, allowing this nonconceptual element into the picture leads to the problematic view of Thomas that since "the object [God] is not sufficiently compelling of itself to our understanding," we then would need "some kind of *lumen infusum* or some kind of *gratia infusa* or indeed *fides infusa*, which then comes, as it were, from behind in order to enable us to assent to the truth in spite of its non-evidence."⁴⁴

This approach, Torrance astutely claims, leads toward fideism and authoritarianism because for this view, assent to the truth requires "submission of the will to what is not evident to the mind rather than through a direct yet willing assent to the truth of being."⁴⁵ Here the nonconceptual element in knowledge of God is overcome, Torrance says, "through an infused grace motivating assent." Torrance claims that "sooner or later, however, that roundabout way is bound to collapse, and then thought breaks apart, and tension arises between authoritarian pronouncements of truth and the

---

⁴¹ Ibid.
⁴² Ibid., 229–30.
⁴³ Ibid., 226–7.
⁴⁴ Ibid., 227.
⁴⁵ Ibid.

consciences of the faithful."[46] The result in Roman Catholic theology is that "both the theologians of the Curia and the advocates of 'the new theology' still rely on St Thomas's analysis and solution of the problem" so that neither side has sufficiently thought through the problem here by allowing the "*truth of being*" rather than something in us to shape the meaning of God and God's grace.

The Logic of Grace and the Logic of Christ

Third, let me make more of a direct connection with Torrance's view of grace to illustrate his reasoning. In his important book, *Theological Science*, Torrance speaks of the logic of grace and claims that since that is the way the truth of God has come to us in history, our thinking about God and God's grace must allow all our ideas about God and revelation to "reflect the movement of Grace."[47] Recall that for Torrance one cannot separate grace from the Giver of grace, namely, Christ himself. With that in mind, Torrance maintains that there is an "unconditional priority of the Truth as Grace and the irreversibility of the relationship established between the Truth and us."[48] This priority of grace makes perfect sense when you consider Torrance's insistence that knowledge of the truth, as knowledge of God, cannot be detached from *the truth of being* and thus cannot be grounded in some supposed nonconceptual relation to God. Any such idea detaches grace from the Giver of grace and locates it in us.

It is important to note that for Torrance, knowledge of the Truth, which follows the logic of grace, "requires acts of obedience on our part." Of course, he does not mean obedience to our conscience or obedience to church authority; those alternatives would shift the weight from obedience to grace in its identity with Christ to other external factors grounded in us or the church. Torrance says obedience involves decision and makes an interesting distinction. He claims we do not need to make a decision when we say $2 \times 2 = 4$ because such a statement is simply timeless and necessary; that is not something that "becomes true, and has to operate in order to be true. No choice, no decision is involved. The conclusion is necessary; it is not reached through a free act."[49] The truth of theology cannot be understood this way because the truth of theology can only be grasped in the decision of faith.

---

[46] Ibid.
[47] Thomas F. Torrance, *Theological Science* (Oxford: Oxford University Press, 1978), 214.
[48] Ibid.
[49] Ibid.

Here Torrance makes another crucial point that is missed by all of those who speak of faith in a general sense as faith in a higher power or faith in something greater than us, or faith in a supreme being. That is not at all what he means because he is claiming faith, as knowledge of the truth, must reflect the unconditional priority of grace and thus the irreversible relation between the triune God of revelation and us.

Another decisive point Torrance makes is to insist that we must not "think of faith or decision as an organ for perception or as a means of 'making real' the truths of the Gospel."[50] Such a view annihilates the common concept of faith as faith in a higher power. Torrance says, "personal decision or the act of believing by itself tells us nothing. The act of faith reposes upon the prior act of Christ, a final decision made by Him on our behalf. Our decision for Christ answers to His decision for us, and relies upon it as its objective ground."[51] Because our personal decision is based on God's decision for us in Christ, "our act of faith is grounded on God's decision of Grace to give Himself to us and to choose us for Himself." In other words, it is grounded in election, which for Torrance refers to "the prevenient movement of God's love that is so incarnated in Jesus Christ that in Him we have both the pure act of divine Grace toward man and the perfect act of man in obedient response toward God's Grace."[52]

In his life of perfect obedience, Christ himself:

> has appropriated God's Grace for us, because from beginning to the end of His incarnate Life He stood in for us and not only gave an account to God for us, offering our response to the Father, but actualised in Himself the Truth of God translating it into His human life, that we may know the Truth in and through Jesus Christ.[53]

For these reasons, our personal act of faith, that is, our personal decision, is thus based on his actions for us. Therefore, "we do not relate the truths of the Gospel to one another by our decision, but in and through our faith we discern how the truths are already related in the decisive movements of the Grace of God in Jesus Christ."[54] That is why everything said in theology must reflect this unconditional priority of God's grace to be faithful to

---

[50] Ibid., 215.
[51] Ibid.
[52] Ibid.
[53] Ibid.
[54] Ibid.

the truth: "It is the logic of Grace that shapes the inner form of every true theological statement."[55]

It will be noticed here that for Torrance, one cannot detach the logic of Grace from Christ himself and thus one cannot know God truly apart from Christ. So, he also speaks of the Logic of Christ as well as the Logic of Grace. And what he says is extremely revealing. First, he says the logic of Christ is "the other side of the Logic of Grace."[56] Second, he begins his consideration by saying that he is not trying to impose a viewpoint on his theology, but, rather, he wishes to understand its "material content" by letting it reveal itself as he directs his questions toward it. Third, when this is done correctly, then, Torrance asserts, "we are directed to Jesus Christ, to the Incarnation, to the hypostatic union, the unique togetherness of God and man in Christ which is *normative for every other relationship between man and God*."[57] Fourth, Torrance then insists that the hypostatic union must not be understood statically but as the union of God and humanity in Christ "in the one Person of the Son running throughout all His historical life from His birth to his resurrection."[58] That, Torrance says, is the center from which we may consider the doctrine of the Trinity, that is, "of the Father and of the Holy Spirit as well as the Son, and therefore of creation as well as redemption."[59] All other doctrines have their proper place and truth "by reference to this central point in Jesus Christ."[60]

Justification by Grace through Faith

Having said this, it is not at all surprising that when he considered the doctrine of justification, Torrance held that,

> Because God has concluded us all under His mercy and justified us freely through grace, all men are put on the same level, for whether they are good or bad, religious or secular, within the Church or of the world, they all alike come under the total judgement of grace, the judgement

[55] Ibid., 216.
[56] Ibid.
[57] Ibid., emphasis mine.
[58] Ibid.
[59] Ibid.
[60] Ibid., 216–17.

that everything they are and have is wholly called into question simply by the fact that they are saved by grace alone.[61]

These remarks are loaded and comprehensive because Torrance is claiming that we cannot rely on our goodness or our religious consciousness, or any authority other than the grace of God, which meets us in Christ as judgment (by calling into question *all* our attempts at self-reliance) and mercy (by freeing us to live in obedience to Christ alone). That is why he says grace is costly for God and for us. It is costly for God because "it is grace through the blood of Christ." But it is costly to humanity because "it lays the axe to the root of all [our] cherished possessions and achievements, not least in the realm of [our] religion, for it is in religion that man's self-justification may reach its supreme and most subtle form."[62]

Torrance explains that when the Reformers spoke of justification by faith alone, they meant by grace alone. However, the notion of justification by faith is ambiguous because it could be and eventually was interpreted to mean that faith was quickly turned into a justifying work. That, for Torrance, is a disaster because it is not by our faith that we are saved but by the object of faith, namely, Christ himself and Christ alone. Whenever it is thought that "men and women are justified by God's grace *if* they repent and believe," then the unconditional love of God is compromised with some notion of "*conditional grace*," which, Torrance says, "permeated Protestantism, Lutheran Pietism, and the Federal Theology of the Calvinists, Puritanism and Anglicanism alike."[63] He thinks that for Roman Catholics, we first need "an infusion of supernatural grace," which we receive "*ex opere operato*," without any cooperation on our part. But once that infusion takes place, we can cooperate with grace and merit more grace.

Torrance rejects this idea of merit as Pelagian because it carries with it the notion that we can rely on what we do to be saved when, in fact, salvation comes freely to us only as Christ himself empowers that freedom through union with him in faith. Insightfully, Torrance notes that when righteousness was thought to be "offered to us by God under the condition of faith," then the Gospel is distorted and "a new legalism resulted."[64] Consequently, once "justifying faith" is turned into a work that we must do to become righteous in relation to God and our neighbors, then that in itself represents a legalizing of the Gospel of free grace. To avoid such legalizing, faith must be seen to

---

[61] Torrance, *God and Rationality*, 56.
[62] Ibid.
[63] Ibid., 57.
[64] Ibid.

be grounded on Christ's own active obedience and his complete sufficiency for our justification. Only then can we maintain the "unconditionally free proclamation of the Gospel."[65]

Torrance could not be clearer. He insists, "It is not faith that justifies us, but Christ in whom we have faith."[66] This means that if ever one holds that "people will not be saved *unless* they make the work of Christ real for themselves by their own personal decision, or that they will be saved *only if* they repent and believe," then that thinking makes Christ's own work "conditional upon what the sinner does."[67] That is a disastrous view of the Gospel because it "throws the ultimate responsibility for a man's salvation back upon himself."[68] That is not good news. That is bad news because, even in our goodness, we are sinners at enmity with God by virtue of our attempts to be self-reliant independently of grace. However, we need God's unconditional forgiving grace to live in freedom before God and others. While Christ's work for us calls for repentance and obedience, that cannot imply that we "can be saved on condition that [we] repent and believe" because this conditional view always shifts the emphasis "from 'Christ' to 'me', so that what becomes finally important is 'my faith', 'my decision', 'my conversion', and not really Christ himself."[69]

Bultmann's Subjectivism

For Torrance, the ultimate negative example that shifts the emphasis from Christ to us is Bultmann's idea that we are saved by our existential decision, which then takes the place of Christ. Luther believed there was nothing we could do to escape our "in-turned, self-centred self"; he thus refused to hold that the truth of our justification could be equated with what the Gospel means to us. That is because faith "rests entirely on the objective fact proclaimed by the Gospel that Jesus Christ was put to death for our trespasses and raised for our justification."[70] Bultmann distorted this by claiming that all New Testament statements about what Christ has done for us must be "transposed to speak only of what *He means for me*."[71] It is certainly true

---

[65] Ibid., 57–8.
[66] Ibid., 58.
[67] Ibid.
[68] Ibid.
[69] Ibid.
[70] Ibid., 59.
[71] Ibid.

that what Christ has done has meaning for me and for everyone else. But Torrance says that this objective action of Christ dying on the cross and being raised from the dead for us and our salvation is exactly what Bultmann ends up denying. He drops the objective events that occurred in Christ for us and substitutes what he considers its meaning for us. So, Torrance says, for Bultmann, the meaning of the Gospel is not found in the death of Christ on the cross, which, in itself, has no meaning for us, but in the preaching of the apostles about that event, which we then apply to ourselves. Bultmann shifts the weight from the objective actions of Christ for us to the meaning we construct from our hearing of the Gospel. For Bultmann I must "be prepared to give up any attempt at the kind of security that finds for faith an objective act of God in history, and take the road of radical decision in which I work out the meaning for myself in the present."[72]

With this thinking, Bultmann snaps the connection between faith and what Christ actually has done objectively for us because, for him, faith is faith in "man's own human act, his existential decision, the process by which he gives meaning to the *kerygma* for himself in the present." Torrance unequivocally rejects this thinking because "whenever we take our eyes off the centrality and uniqueness of Jesus Christ and His objective vicarious work, the Gospel disappears behind man's existentialized self-understanding, and even the Reality of God Himself is simply reduced to 'what He means for me' in the contingency and necessities of my own life purpose."[73] Torrance perceptively noted Bultmann's mistake, asserting that,

> The difficulty of Bultmann's position becomes clear when we find that even the fatherhood of God becomes problematic. In *Jesus Christ and Mythology* (p. 69), Bultmann says, "in the conception of God as Father the mythological sense vanished long ago", but he says that we can speak of God as Father in an analogical sense. However, he also says that "we cannot speak of God as he is in himself, but only of what he is doing to us and with us" (*op. cit.* p. 73). We cannot make general statements about God, only existential statements about our relation to him. "The affirmation that God is creator cannot be a theoretical statement about God as *creator mundi* (creator of the world) in a general sense. The affirmation can only be a personal confession that I understand myself to be a creature which owes its existence to God" (*op. cit.* p. 69). Statements about God are not to be understood as objective (that is mythology)—they have to be understood as existential statements (*op. cit.* p. 61ff).

[72] Ibid.
[73] Ibid., 60.

> But if we can say nothing about God in himself or about what he does objectively, can we still give any content to his actions in relation to ourselves, and can we really say anything at all of God, even in analogical language? Can Bultmann discard what he thinks of as mythological and still retain the analogical?[74]

Notice that objectivity here means for Torrance that we must be able to speak about God in himself and not just about what we think God is doing for us because the latter view reduces the immanent to the economic Trinity. That's what Bultmann did by saying we cannot say anything about God in himself. Torrance rightly holds that we need to recover the fact that Christ himself is the one who gives meaning to our justification and sanctification. He says, "everything is interpreted by reference to who He was and is. After all, it was not the *death* of Jesus that constituted atonement, but Jesus Christ the Son of God offering Himself in sacrifice for us. Everything depends on *who* He was, for the significance of His acts in life and death depends on the nature of His person."[75] Bultmann's approach undermines this view of Jesus' death because in Torrance's estimation, for Bultmann, God "is present and active in the death of Jesus Christ in no other way than he is present and active in a fatal accident in the street."[76]

For Torrance, because you cannot separate the gifts of eternal life and knowledge of the truth that are ours in Christ from Christ himself, all our personal relations can only be rightly understood from the "unique relation of divine and human natures in the One Person of the Son."[77] Consequently, we can only grasp "the interior logic of theological thinking" from "the inner life and being of Jesus Christ, in the hypostatic union."[78] This is a logic "that is in Christ before it is in our knowledge of Him."[79] Do not allow this remark to slip by unnoticed. It is a decisive remark because with this statement, Torrance is holding fast to his belief that there is no possibility at all of any *a priori* understanding either of Jesus Christ or of Christology and thus of God himself. Thus,

> We cannot know Christ *a priori*, but only after and only in his action, but in *his* action. Thus to assert that we know the deity of Christ *a*

---

[74] Thomas F. Torrance, *Incarnation: The Person and Life of Christ*, ed. Robert T. Walker (Downers Grove, IL: InterVarsity Press, 2008), 287–8.
[75] Torrance, *God and Rationality*, 64.
[76] Torrance, *Theology in Reconstruction*, 277.
[77] Torrance, *Theological Science*, 217.
[78] Ibid.
[79] Ibid.

posteriori is not to say that it is an *arrière-pensée*! The Divinity of Christ can be no after-thought for faith but is its immediate asseveration in the holy Presence of the Son of God. After-thoughts as such are bound to degenerate into value-judgements, and thence into doubt and even disbelief.[80]

We know Christ only as he gives himself to be known and thus only *a posteriori*. That is why Torrance insists that "We cannot earn knowledge of Christ, we cannot achieve it, or build up to it. We have no capacity or power in ourselves giving us the ability to have mastery over this fact."[81] This is because "we know him in terms of *himself*. We know him out of pure grace as one who gives himself to us and freely discloses himself to us."[82] Christ gives himself to us "by his own power and agency, by his Holy Spirit, and in the very act of knowing him we ascribe all the possibility of our knowing him to Christ alone, and none of it to ourselves."[83]

So, when we know Christ, we apprehend the "logic that inheres ontologically and personally in Him but which is reflected noetically and sacramentally in us in the conformity of our life and thought to Him and in the directing of them through Him to God the Father."[84] Torrance is very clear that he does not want to make the hypostatic union into some "ideological truth" which we can wield at will because, like all theological concepts, that concept does not have the truth in itself. Its only function is to point us to Jesus Christ "who meets us as very God and very Man in one Person, who is Lord over all our knowing of Him and must remain Lord over all our articulation and formulation of the truths He communicates to us."[85] For this reason, Torrance asserts, "we must hold together 'the logic of Grace' and the 'logic of Christ', for it is only in the freedom of His Grace that God's truth has come into our midst and assumed human nature into union with Himself, thus establishing the hypostatic union."[86]

---

[80] Thomas F. Torrance, *The Doctrine of Jesus Christ* (Eugene, OR: Wipf and Stock, 2002), 22. With this remark Torrance was rejecting the approach of Albrecht Ritschl (1822–89) and those who embrace his method.
[81] Torrance, *Incarnation*, 2.
[82] Ibid., 1–2.
[83] Ibid., 2.
[84] Torrance, *Theological Science*, 217.
[85] Ibid.
[86] Ibid.

Enhypostasis/Anhypostasis

From here, Torrance employs the two important theological categories of *enhypostasis* and *anhypostasis* to explain the function of grace in Christ. The hypostatic union can only be properly understood therefore "as the expression of the act of divine Grace and the irreversible relation between God's Grace and man."[87] He says, "*Anhypostasia* asserts the unconditional priority of Grace, that everything in theological knowledge derives from God's Grace, while all truths and their relations within our thinking must reflect the movement of Grace." Then he says, "*enhypostasia* asserts that God's Grace acts only as Grace. God does not override us but makes us free."[88] The fact that God makes us free and does not override us is an enormously important point that is sometimes misunderstood by commentators on Torrance who think that his emphasis on Christ leaves no room for us and our free decisions and actions. It is quite the contrary. It is just because his humanity is the humanity of the Word and cannot be separated from his being as the Word incarnate that he acts in human freedom spontaneously in relation to God and us. Torrance claims he brings us into union with himself so that we can share in his life and love. It is in this way that,

> He sets us on our feet as persons in personal relation with Him, affirming and recreating our humanity in communion with Him; He bestows His love freely upon us and asks of us the free love of our hearts; He takes our cause upon Himself and makes provision for true response on our part as we are allowed to share in the human life and response of Jesus to the Father.[89]

In Torrance's view then, the doctrine of "*enhypostasia* asserts the full unimpaired reality of the humanity of the historical Jesus as the humanity of the Son of God" and also "affirms in our theological knowledge full and unimpaired place for human decision, human response, and human thinking in relation to the Truth of God's Grace."[90]

As we know Christ, we are conformed to him in thought and action so that it is "only in conformity to the movement of Grace in Jesus Christ as the Way, the Truth and the Life, that we may discern the interior logic of

---

[87] Ibid.
[88] Ibid.
[89] Ibid., 218.
[90] Ibid.

theological knowledge."⁹¹ As grace "from beginning to end," therefore, "it is Christ the Truth who adapts us to Himself" so that it is through union with him in his "own perfect humanity, that He both affirms our humanity and imprints upon it the pattern of His own life. That is the logic that is in Christ before it is in our knowing."⁹² In our faithfulness to him, as he reveals himself to us as "God and Man in one Person, there arise analogical forms of personal life and understanding within us" and that is the "interior logic of theology."⁹³ Torrance thinks that Christ is the material logic here, and all our formal logic must be subordinated to him. Unless that happens, we will simply read logical necessities into Christ and into the nature of grace and of God himself.

Comparing Rahner and Torrance

Now, let us compare Torrance's reflections on grace and knowledge of God with the views of Karl Rahner by assessing their views of grace and nature in relation to Christology and the doctrine of God. At one point, Torrance thought Rahner could help bring Catholic and Protestant theology together by beginning theology exclusively with the economic trinitarian self-revelation.⁹⁴ But Torrance later came to see more clearly than he did when

---

⁹¹ Ibid.
⁹² Ibid.
⁹³ Ibid.
⁹⁴ See Thomas F. Torrance, *Trinitarian Perspectives: Toward Doctrinal Agreement* (Edinburgh: T&T Clark, 1994), Chapter 4. Torrance summarized the results of a Colloquium that discussed Rahner's trinitarian theology in 1975. He wrote: "The basic approach by Karl Rahner from God's saving revelation of himself as Father, Son and Holy Spirit in history, pivoting upon God's concrete and effective self-communication in the Incarnation, has the effect of making the Economic Trinity the norm for all our thought and speech about God, and therefore of destroying the isolation of the treatise *On the Triune God (De Deo Trino)* from the treatise *On the One God (De Deo Uno)*," 77–8. With such a method there is the possibility of "rapprochement between Roman Catholic theology and Evangelical theology, especially as represented by the teaching of Karl Barth," ibid. I have demonstrated in detail that while Torrance's statement here is correct, the fact of the matter is that Rahner's transcendental theology does not explicitly, decisively, and consistently begin with God's self-revelation in Christ (the economic Trinity), but rather with our supposed experience of revelation in the depths of our existence which he then attempts to connect with Jesus Christ and knowledge of the Trinity. That is why he thinks natural theology and revealed theology and Christology and anthropology exist in a mutually conditioning relationship. See Paul D. Molnar, *Divine Freedom and the Doctrine of the Immanent Trinity: In Dialogue with Karl Barth and Contemporary Theology 2nd Edition* (London: Bloomsbury T&T Clark, 2017), 74–88, 207–61, 323–36, 358–78. It is that mutual conditioning that Torrance consistently rejected by insisting on the irreversibility of grace and our experience of and knowledge of God's self-revelation and of the Trinity. Even in his hopeful summary of the judgments of the Colloquium on

he criticized Rahner for not consistently allowing the economic Trinity to determine his thought that there were serious problems in Rahner's approach. While Rahner formally held that proper view of beginning only with the economic trinitarian self-revelation, and while that view would have had a unifying effect, his actual method allowed him to read logical necessities back into the Trinity. It is the failure to allow the material content of theology, namely, Jesus Christ (theology's material logic), to be his sole starting point and criterion for theology that creates difficulties and inconsistencies in Rahner's thinking. My hope in this chapter is to show that there can only be a genuine unity between the Reformed views of Torrance and the Roman Catholic views of Rahner if and to the extent that both theologians allow the logic of grace to be determined by the logic of Christ.

In a chapter on "Grace and nature" in his book on Rahner, William V. Dych, who is a highly regarded interpreter of Rahner, begins discussing Rahner's views by noting that in his discussion of God's hiddenness Rahner explains that his philosophical and speculative knowledge proceeds "from a conviction of faith, that is from a strictly theological proposition."[95] What is Rahner's theological proposition? Rahner says that the theological proposition that "forms the basis of all the reflections which are contained in [his] essay" is that "God himself and nothing else is our eternal life, however he may be understood by us here and now."[96] Thus, for him, philosophy

---

the Trinity, Torrance noted the problem in Rahner's thought: "The main difficulty we have had with Rahner's treatise is with the way in which he has posed and framed the following axiom: 'The "Economic" Trinity is the "immanent" Trinity and the "Immanent Trinity" is the "Economic Trinity"', and with the way in which he has set out the transition from the Economic Trinity to the Immanent Trinity, and grounded the former in the latter, for in spite of the relation of *identity* between the Economic and the Immanent Trinity as immanent, that is, as it is in God, in such a way that it precinds [sic] from God's free self-communication, and so a moment of abstraction appears to be introduced between what God is in himself and the mode of his self-revelation and self-communication to us" (79). That abstraction occurs precisely because of Rahner's choice to begin his reflections with our supposed transcendental experiences which for him include everyone's unthematic, nonobjective, and nonconceptual knowledge of God, instead of exclusively with Jesus Christ himself. That is why Rahner could say: "Revealed theology has the human spirit's transcendental and limitless horizon as its inner motive and as the precondition of its existence" (TI 9, 34). Torrance would reject this assertion claiming that revealed theology is grounded only in Christ and not at all in our transcendental experience as its precondition; the only precondition for revelation is the fact that Christ empowers us through his Spirit to be one with him and to know God the Father through union with him.

[95] William V. Dych, S. J., *Karl Rahner* (Collegeville, MN: The Liturgical Press, 1992), 32. Dych is referring here to Rahner, TI 16, "The Hiddenness of God," 235.
[96] Rahner, TI 16, 236.

serves theology by making "the primary theological statement intelligible."[97] How does Rahner proceed?

He says, "'*The* Truth' occurs in the basic experience of the mystery itself."[98] Rahner continues by explaining that,

> the essence of knowledge lies in the mystery which is the object of primary experience and is alone self-evident. The unlimited and transcendent nature of man, the openness to the mystery itself which is given radical depth by grace does not turn man into the event of the absolute spirit in the way envisaged by German idealism ... it directs him rather to the incomprehensible mystery, in relation to which the openness of transcendence is experienced.[99]

What is that mystery? For Rahner, that mystery is, as he has already said, God. But it will be recalled that he says it is God "however he may be understood by us here and now." And that is the problem. This approach to truth and to knowledge of God is presented without any specific reference to Jesus Christ as *the* Truth, and indeed as the Way, the Truth, and the Life as Torrance claimed from the start of his understanding of the Truth as discussed above. So Rahner then contends that,

> in forming any concept, he [the human person] understands himself as the one who reaches out beyond the conceptual into the nameless and the incomprehensible. Transcendence grasped in its unlimited breadth is the a priori condition of objective and reflective knowledge and evaluation. It is the very condition of its possibility ... It is also the precondition for the freedom which is historically expressed and objectified.[100]

Rahner explains that knowing this mystery means we are "addressed by what no longer has a name, and it is relying on a reality which is not mastered but is itself the master. It is the speech of the being without a name, about which clear statements are impossible."[101]

---

[97] Ibid.
[98] Ibid.
[99] Ibid.
[100] Ibid., 236–7.
[101] Ibid., 237.

Rahner even claims that,

> The origin and goal of knowledge in the mystery is one of its constituent elements. In an unthematic way this is experienced in day-to-day knowledge and may be called "primary" in the sense of the a priori condition of possibility of all knowing, even though it only becomes thematic in a secondary sense through subsequent reflection upon its own a priori presuppositions.[102]

For Rahner, then, it is "the unfolding of the mystery itself, from the *one* truth" that one experiences in this way. And the "presence of the one truth is of course unthematic, since it exists in the first instance as the condition of possibility of spatio-temporal and categorial-historical experience."[103] Rahner claims this is the event of spirit and is indeed an experience of what he calls the *deus absconditus* (the hidden God). Thus, "knowledge is primarily the experience of the overwhelming mystery of this 'deus absconditus.'"[104] From this it follows that "divine revelation is not the unveiling of something previously hidden" but it refers "to the fact that the 'deus absconditus' becomes radically present as the abiding mystery."[105] So, revelation does not mean that "the mystery is overcome by gnosis bestowed by God." Rather, "it is the history of the deepening perception of God *as* the mystery."[106]

Enough has been said here to see some clear contrasts between Rahner's view of the truth and of God as mystery and Torrance's view of God as truth and mystery. In this chapter, I wish to focus primarily on the knowledge of God's grace in its identity with the Giver of grace. But before exploring this view in relation to Rahner's specific views of grace, it is important to see that Rahner embraces several ideas that Torrance specifically and with good reason rejected. First, Rahner embraces what he calls "unthematic" or nonconceptual knowledge of God as mystery. This conception of mystery as nonconceptual is what he means when he speaks of "transcendental revelation." That approach leads him to conclude that our knowledge of God develops from the transcendental experience of the "nameless." That is why Rahner could say knowledge of God is an *a priori* knowledge of mystery which everyone in their experience of self-transcendence knows unthematically. It refers "to a knowledge which is both transcendental *and* unavoidable and

---

[102] Ibid.
[103] Ibid.
[104] Ibid., 238.
[105] Ibid.
[106] Ibid.

is always sustained by the offer of God's self-communication in *grace*."[107] Consequently, for Rahner, "the doctrine of the *natural* knowability and knowledge of God is not a knowledge which appears in isolation, but one element, only subsequently isolated, in a single knowledge of God, authorized by him in its direct relation to him, which, when it is accepted, is already faith."[108]

Notice the progression of thought here. Rahner moves from our transcendental experiences of the nameless to the idea that everyone has nonconceptual or unthematic knowledge of God as mystery and then to the idea that we have an obediential potency for revelation and a supernatural existential. That is why he can claim that even natural knowledge of God is true knowledge of God. Thus, everyone has unavoidable knowledge of God as a nameless mystery and that is the *a priori* for understanding God, revelation, grace, and faith itself for Christians. However, the obvious problem here is this: Rahner assumes that natural knowledge of God as absolute being is the same as knowing God in faith.[109] It is not because faith, by its very nature, is directly tied to Jesus Christ, who is the object of faith. There is no mention of Christ in Rahner's statement about faith here. Of course, Rahner wishes to tie knowledge of God to salvation and thus to Christ. But he is unable to maintain the irreversibility of the object of faith (Christ) and us as the subjects experiencing that faith. Thus, he can say:

> a theological object's significance for salvation (which is a necessary factor in any theological object) can only be investigated by inquiring at the same time as to man's *saving receptivity for* this object. However, this receptivity must not be investigated only "in the abstract" nor merely presupposed in its most general aspects. It must be reflected upon with reference to the concrete object concerned, which is only *theologically relevant* as a result of and for the purpose of this receptiveness for

---

[107] Rahner, TI 9, 135.
[108] Ibid., 135–6.
[109] This is why he can say "The experience of the self is the condition which makes it possible to experience God. The reason is that an orientation to being in the absolute, and so to God, can be present only when the subject (precisely in the act of reaching out towards being in the absolute) is made present to himself as something distinct from his own act and as the subject of that act" (Rahner, TI 13, 125). It is striking in the piece cited here, "Experience of self and experience of God," that Rahner never mentions the need for reconciliation, forgiveness, revelation in its identity with Christ, or the need for a specific act of the Holy Spirit to know God specifically as the eternal Father, Son, and Holy Spirit. That is because he thinks he can speak of God as mystery and as the infinite and absolute and then connect that view with the Trinity. It cannot be done without undermining our actual knowledge of the immanent Trinity through an encounter with the economic Trinity.

salvation. Thereby the object also to some extent lays down the conditions for such receptiveness.[110]

It will be noticed here that Rahner claims we have a saving receptivity for God and God's grace. For Torrance, as we have seen, our actual encounter with Christ discloses that we have no such receptivity and that our reception of revelation is the work of the Holy Spirit uniting us to Christ. For Rahner, our saving receptivity is subjective and can be understood by exploring our subjectivity. Torrance rejects that approach all along the line because for him it is *exclusively* the object of faith that determines the truth of our theological knowledge. And that truth is identical with Jesus Christ, the incarnate Son of the Father. Finally, Rahner wants objective knowledge here, but he says only that the object "to some extent lays down the conditions for" reception of such knowledge. If that is in any sense true, then that idea in and of itself has already compromised the sovereignty of God's grace and love by inadvertently advocating some idea of conditional salvation. With these assumptions Rahner is eventually led to conclude that self-acceptance is the same as accepting God and Christ. It is not. A closer look at Torrance's view here will be helpful.

For Torrance, as we have seen, knowledge of God comes to us from Christ himself through the power of the Holy Spirit such that we know God's name precisely as the eternal Father, Son, and Holy Spirit. In other words, the triune God is not nameless, as Rahner alleges. And knowledge of God does not derive from a general experience of mystery which we can know *a priori* as Rahner also claims. God has a name and that is made known by grace (through Christ), and thus in faith as we recognize that we are made righteous by what he has done and does for us as the savior of the world. Of course, it is not our faith that grounds that knowledge but the object of faith. That is why Torrance consistently links our knowledge of God to the doctrine of justification, claiming that what is required is a recovery of

> an understanding of justification which really lets Christ occupy the centre, so that everything is interpreted by reference to who He was and is ... we must allow the Person of Christ to determine for us the nature of his saving work, rather than the other way round. The detachment of atonement from incarnation is undoubtedly revealed by history to be one of the most harmful mistakes of Evangelical Churches.[111]

---

[110] Rahner, TI 9, 35–6.
[111] Torrance, *God and Rationality*, 64.

Grounding his knowledge of God in Jesus Christ as the revelation of God for us, Torrance disallows any sort of unthematic or nonconceptual approach to knowing God and salvation because, as noted above, he follows Anselm and claims that we cannot have experience or knowledge of the Christian God without concepts.[112] By ascribing unthematic knowledge to everyone, Rahner undermines objective knowledge of God as the eternal Father, Son, and Holy Spirit and opens the door to his notion of anonymous Christianity. For Torrance, there is no such thing as anonymous Christianity because to be a Christian means to accept Jesus Christ as the Truth and to take up our cross and follow him. And none of that can be done without a specific concept of who he was and is and what he has done and is doing as the one Mediator here and now.

Thomas F. Torrance, Karl Rahner, John Robinson, and Paul Tillich

This grounding our knowledge *conceptually* in Christ is an exceptionally important point because grounding knowledge of God and of Christ in some unthematic experience, Torrance believes, will always lead to some form of subjectivism as in the thinking of John Robinson and Paul Tillich, who could be considered liberal Protestant counterparts of the Roman Catholic Rahner. Nonconceptual knowledge of God begins for Rahner with an experience of the nameless that leads him to a view of mystery that he calls God, no matter how that is understood. That approach clearly leaves open the possibility of naming God in various ways other than as Father, Son, and Holy Spirit. By contrast, Torrance insists that when we speak of God as "person," then "the kind of 'person' that is meant is determined by who God is, and so we speak of God as *the* Person, and indeed the source of all personal existence."[113] However, Torrance then insists that when we speak of God as "person," that notion of person when "used of God must be *ontologically* derived from God's own nature, and therefore from the Trinity, and *not logically* worked up from general ideas we already hold on other grounds."[114] As I have discussed

---

[112] For a full discussion of Torrance and Rahner on nonconceptual knowledge of God, see Paul D. Molnar, *Freedom, Necessity, and the Knowledge of God: In Conversation with Karl Barth and Thomas F. Torrance* (London: T&T Clark, 2022), Chapter Four.
[113] Torrance, *God and Rationality*, 80.
[114] Ibid.

in detail elsewhere,[115] the issue here is illustrated in the thinking of those who wish to rename God as mother, lover, and friend, She Who Is, or even as holy mystery with Rahner instead of exclusively as Father, Son, and Holy Spirit.

On this basis, Torrance says all our statements about God must be traced back to the Trinity and not to any general ideas of mystery or of the nameless. That is why he firmly rejects John Robinson's attempt to rethink God in pictures "deemed relevant to 'secular' man, which *we* must put in the place of the old image of God."[116] Such thinking presents God as the ground of our being. But that is to think "out of a centre in the depth of man rather than out of a centre in God himself" and that, Torrance says, is mythology and not theology.[117] Torrance complains that thinking of God in this fashion presents us with a God who cannot interact with us in any causal way. This is the case because for Robinson, God "cannot be other than what Robinson always and actually is in the depth of himself."[118] This approach by Robinson, Torrance insists, makes his position worse than straightforward deism because "he is unable to distinguish God 'out there' rationally as objectively and transcendently other than the depths of his own being, and so he is thrown back upon himself to give content to his notion of God, as what is of ultimate concern *for* him in the depth and significance of his own being."[119] That God, Torrance says, is nothing other than "the 'God' he wants" instead of the true God. It is a "God" that he can use "for his own ends and satisfactions."[120] That, Torrance asserts, is an idol.

The same thing happens to Paul Tillich, who believes that if you do not like the traditional name for God, then you can follow the pattern of the "so-called 'psychology of depth,'" which leads us from "the surface of our self-knowledge ... into our depth."[121] While this psychology of depth "cannot guide us to the deepest ground of our being and of all being, the depth of life itself," the name of this "infinite and inexhaustible depth and ground of all being is *God*."[122] Tillich says that is what the word "God" means. From this, he concludes that "if that word has not much meaning for you, translate it, and

---

[115] See, e.g., Molnar, *Divine Freedom and the Doctrine of the Immanent Trinity, Faith, Freedom and the Spirit: The Economic Trinity in Barth, Torrance and Contemporary Theology* (Downers Grove, IL: IVP Academic, 2015), and *Freedom, Necessity, and the Knowledge of God*.
[116] Torrance, *God and Rationality*, 80.
[117] Ibid.
[118] Ibid., 81.
[119] Ibid.
[120] Ibid., 81–2.
[121] Paul Tillich, *The Shaking of the Foundations* (New York: Charles Scribner's Sons, 1948), 56–7.
[122] Ibid., 57.

speak of the depths of your life, of the source of your being, of your ultimate concern, of what you take seriously without any reservation."[123] Notice how close Tillich's view of God is to that of John Robinson. Both theologians equate knowledge of God with knowledge of our own depth and the ground of being conceived in light of that experience. From that, they reckon that by speaking of our depth, and ultimate concerns, we speak of God.

However, given Torrance's insistence that knowledge of God must be grounded in the nature of God as the eternal Father, Son, and Holy Spirit, this amounts to subjectivism and mythology on the basis of which Robinson and Tillich are out for what Torrance called "*cheap grace*, i.e. the 'God' *they* want, one to suit themselves and modern 'secular' man, rather than the God of *costly grace* who calls for the renewing of our minds in which we are not schematized to the patterns of this world but are transformed in conformity with His own self-revelation in Jesus Christ."[124] In other words, both theologians neglect Jesus Christ and his message, "where He asks them to renounce themselves, take up the cross and follow Him unreservedly all along the road to crucifixion and resurrection."[125]

Second, because Rahner begins his theology with experiences of self-transcendence and with a general concept of mystery linked to his view of the nameless, he then is led to believe, as Dych notes, that grace cannot be seen in some extrinsic way such that "grace appears ... as a mere superstructure ... imposed upon nature by God's decree."[126] Rahner wanted to follow the "new theology" and hold that the human desire for God is both "truly human," and at the same time it is "an intrinsic part of human nature," and yet it is still grace. The new theologians, especially Henri de Lubac, wanted to conceptualize grace by linking the human desire for God with grace. However, de Lubac did not clearly distinguish grace from nature, and thus, for Rome, the new theologians did not "do justice to the sovereign freedom of God's grace."[127]

For Rahner, if grace is merely an "extrinsic addition to human nature ... then the whole realm of the human as such seemed to be deprived of any ultimate meaning."[128] Rahner was dissatisfied with Vatican I, which considered the relation of nature and grace in the context of knowledge of God by asking, "how the natural knowledge of God is related to the

---

[123] Ibid.
[124] Torrance, *God and Rationality*, 82.
[125] Ibid.
[126] Rahner, cited in Dych, 33.
[127] Ibid.
[128] Ibid., 34.

supernatural knowledge of revelation." This Council simply taught that "they cannot contradict each other because they both have the same source in God."[129] Rahner thought this view did not appreciate that there was a deeper unity of our natural knowledge and graced knowledge. In any case, Dych points out that Vatican II discussed the relation of nature and grace in the context of history rather than of knowledge of God. So, Dych says Vatican II maintained the "absolute freedom and gratuity of God's grace, but at the same time [wished] to see it as a universal possibility for every person."[130] Discussing the relation between nature and grace in the context of history rather than in the context of knowledge of God is the context within which Rahner worked out his view of grace and nature. Interestingly, Dych concludes by asking, "What concept of grace would allow it to be utterly free and gratuitous and at the same time an intrinsic part of all history?"[131] Please notice that in all of this discussion of grace thus far in both Rahner and Dych, there is no mention of the need for justification or the need for Jesus Christ as the Giver of grace or the need to look beyond ourselves. That is the case because both theologians are attempting to explain the relation between grace and nature by focusing on our depth experiences and our supposed historical experiences of grace, which are presumed to be part of human transcendental experience.

It is here that Rahner presents a view that is more closely aligned with the problematic thinking of John Robinson and Paul Tillich than it is with a view that does not detach grace from the Giver of grace. Instead of focusing on Christ as the center, as Torrance clearly did, Rahner, relying on the thought of Heidegger, focuses on our depth experience by asking,

> *must* not what God decrees for man be *eo ipso* an interior ontological constituent of his concrete quiddity "terminative", even if it is not a constituent of his "nature"? For an ontology which grasps the truth that man's concrete quiddity depends utterly on God, is not his binding disposition *eo ipso* not just a juridical decree of God but precisely what man *is*, hence not just an imperative proceeding from God but man's most inward depths?[132]

These assertions are clearly problematic when compared to the views of Torrance. Why? Because Rahner does not turn to the objective knowledge

---

[129] Ibid.
[130] Ibid., 35.
[131] Ibid.
[132] Rahner, TI 1, 302.

of God that meets us in the crucified and risen Lord to understand the gratuity of God's grace. Instead, in a manner similar to Schleiermacher, who thought that knowledge of God started with the human feeling of absolute dependence on God, Rahner attempts to explain the nature of grace by referring to our human "quiddity," which he says depends upon God. From this he presumes that since this decree of God is what we are in our humanity as dependent on God, it is "not just an imperative proceeding from God but man's most inward depths." Here, Rahner equates our experiences of depth with knowledge of God and relationship with God. That is the main problem in his entire approach to this issue.

While Torrance refuses to separate incarnation from atonement because it is in the incarnation that the Incarnate Word put us into right relationship with God through his own vicarious life of obedience to the Father, Rahner, with Tillich and Robinson, ignores the problem of sin with this approach as well as the need for reconciliation *in order* to know God and God's grace in its identity with Christ. Put bluntly, by focusing on our humanity as it is presumed to be geared toward grace, Rahner never even mentions what, for Torrance, was a crucial point. That point is that while God created us for fellowship with him, the problem of sin intervened and has left us at enmity with God so that our free-will is our self-will. And for Torrance, we have no way of escaping this predicament. Thus, even in our moral goodness, we are not able to be in right relationship with God. It is only when we live our justification by grace as this justification is objectively ours in Christ that we give up all self-reliance and live in fellowship with God as God intended and intends. This thinking also applies to natural knowledge. So, when Vatican I asserted that there cannot be any contradiction between natural knowledge of God and revealed knowledge because God is the source of both, the whole problem of sin and the need for reconciliation *before* we can know the truth of God is bypassed. Natural knowledge is possible because we are God's creatures. But to say that natural knowledge of God is not in conflict with the true God who meets us in his justifying grace through faith is a mistake because no natural knowledge of God is unequivocally bound to the knowledge of the Father that comes to us from the Son and by the Holy Spirit.

In any case, because of this approach, Rahner then makes a claim that Torrance directly rejected, namely, that the divine decree of which he spoke "necessarily entails an ontological change in human existence."[133] In Rahner's understanding, uncreated grace and created grace mutually condition each other so that God's relation to us through uncreated grace means that God

---

[133] Dych, 36.

communicates himself to us in the power of the Holy Spirit. But that, Rahner says, "implies a new *relation* of God to man. But this can only be conceived of as founded upon an absolute entitative modification of man himself, which modification is the real basis of the new real relation of man to God upon which rests the relation of God to man."[134] And for Rahner, "this absolute entitative modification and determination of man is created grace."[135] Further, Rahner maintains that "Grace, being supernaturally divinizing, must rather be thought of as a change in the structure of human consciousness."[136] Recall that Torrance rejected the Hellenistic view of grace as a "detachable and transferrable divine quality which may inhere in or be possessed by the human being to whom it is given in virtue of which he is somehow 'deified' or 'divinised.'"[137] Such deification, in Torrance's view, suggests a change in human nature. The key problem with this idea is that it then leads one to think grace can be understood by focusing on human nature instead of turning to Christ, who enables us, as fallen creatures, to be in union with God through Christ's forgiving grace and not otherwise. So, for Torrance any changes in us are those which can be seen as the conforming of our lives and activity to the logic of grace by taking up our cross and following Jesus.

This issue of focusing on changes in us instead of on Christ, in and through whom we are changed, is no superficial problem because Rahner claims that as humans, we are "inwardly other in structure than [we] would be if [we] did not have" God as our supernatural end which we experience in our desire for mystery.[138] So, to safeguard the gratuity of God's grace without the notion of pure nature, Rahner thinks that grace should be understood as a "supernatural existential."[139] This is a disastrous proposal. On the one hand, it leads to the notion that we have an obediential potency for God notwithstanding the Fall. On the other hand, it encourages the assumption that we know the true God through natural theology. In order to avoid extrinsicism, this assumption leads Rahner to make statements that certainly appear to ascribe grace and revelation to us directly in our transcendental experiences. Ascribing grace and revelation directly to us this way opens the door to Pelagianism and to ideas of self-justification.

---

[134] Rahner, TI 1, 324.
[135] Ibid.
[136] Rahner, TI 5, 103.
[137] Torrance, *The Trinitarian Faith*, 140.
[138] Rahner, TI 1, 303.
[139] Ibid., 302.

Supernatural Existential

Let me address what is meant by the supernatural existential by starting with the words of William V. Dych. He asks: "What concept of grace would allow it to be utterly free and gratuitous and at the same time an intrinsic part of all human history?"[140] Notice how very different this question is from the approach taken by Torrance. Recall that for Torrance, grace, as God's gift, "is none other than the risen Christ who confronts men through the word of his Gospel. *Charis* is not here, therefore, in any sense a quality adhering to Paul, but a particular manifestation of the gracious purpose and power of Christ."[141] First, Dych, with Rahner, is rightly trying to recognize and maintain the freedom of God in relation to us. Second, he does so not by turning to the freedom of grace actualized for the human race in the history of Israel and uniquely in Jesus Christ, as Torrance did. Instead, with Rahner, he universalizes grace and then thinks of it as "an intrinsic part of all human history." According to Torrance, God's grace is active in all human history. But that grace cannot be conceptualized as an intrinsic part of all human history without detaching it from God's actions in his Word and Spirit.

According to Dych, Rahner conceptualizes God in a way that gives creation and humanity "a supernatural end and this end is first 'in intentione.'" And if this is so, then humanity, and the world itself, "*is* by that very fact always and everywhere inwardly other in structure than he would be if he did not have this end."[142] However, while the "new theologians" thought this inner reference "of man to grace" was "a constituent of his 'nature' in such a way that the latter cannot be conceived without it, i.e., as pure nature," Rahner thought this

---

[140] Dych, 35.
[141] Torrance, *The Doctrine of Grace*, 31.
[142] Dych, 36. Rahner, TI 1, 302–3 and *Foundations of Christian Faith: An Introduction to the Idea of Christianity* (hereafter FCF) trans. William V. Dych (New York: Seabury, 1978), 128. Rahner carefully notes that God's self-communication is the "necessary condition which makes possible an acceptance of the gift" so that "this acceptance must be borne by God himself. God's self-communication as offer is also the necessary condition which makes its acceptance possible," FCF, 128. But because Rahner focuses on the human subject with his analysis, he detaches the gift (grace as God's personal self-communication) from Christ the Giver and then says, "God's self-communication must always be present in man as the prior condition of possibility for its acceptance. This is true insofar as man must be understood as a subject who is capable of such an acceptance, and therefore is also obligated to it … God's self-communication must be present in every person as the condition which makes its personal acceptance possible," ibid. The obvious problem here from Torrance's perspective is that since it is God alone who enables us to hear his Word and participate in his own self-knowledge and love as the eternal Father, Son, and Spirit, that fact eliminates any idea that God's self-communication is present in everyone because it is present only in those who are living by grace alone and thus relying on Christ alone.

approach made it impossible to give a complete definition of "pure nature."[143] Rahner wanted to offer a proper view of "nature without grace" in order to preserve the gratuity of grace. And his way of doing that was with his idea of the "supernatural existential." Then he could say that nature is a remainder concept when it is subtracted from the supernatural existential.[144] But, as noted above, this was bound to be a failure because the whole approach had already universalized grace as an intrinsic part of all human history.

Here is what Rahner thinks regarding the supernatural existential. First, he thinks of revelation itself as, in some fashion, identical with our transcendental dynamisms. Hence, Rahner conceives the universal offer of grace as "always and everywhere and primarily to the transcendentality of man as such," which is accepted and justifying "when this transcendentality of man is accepted and sustained by man's freedom." Indeed, Rahner believes that "the universality of the factuality of grace from the outset [is] ... an existential of man's transcendentality as such."[145] According to John P. Galvin, the supernatural existential refers to "our being in the world, or our being with others ... this existential ... is not given automatically with human nature, but is rather the result of a gratuitous gift of God ... Because of the supernatural existential, grace is always part of our actual existence."[146] From Torrance's perspective presented above, we can easily see the problems embedded in this thinking. Rahner has here conceptualized grace as an infused offer intrinsic to us in our transcendental experiences. This very move destroys the freedom of grace by detaching grace from the active love of God, which comes to the world and to us from the crucified and risen Lord and from him alone, as he is attested in both the Old and New Testaments.

Second, Rahner then presents a view of *conditional* salvation, which Torrance flatly rejected because it throws the weight of salvation back on us sinners who are utterly incapable of escaping the self-will that makes us turn to ourselves for knowledge of the truth in the first place. Third, these remarks demonstrate no recognition of the seriousness of sin with the assumption that we have the freedom to accept the "offer" of grace when, in fact, that freedom must come to us as an act of the risen Lord himself in the power of his Holy Spirit. Thus, for Rahner, the universal offer of grace is accepted and justifying "when this transcendentality of man is accepted and sustained by man's freedom." Rahner does mention the problem of sin, but he does not

---

[143] Dych, 36.
[144] Rahner, TI 1, 313–14.
[145] Rahner, TI 18, 182. See also, FCF, 129.
[146] John P. Galvin, "The Invitation of Grace," *A World of Grace: An Introduction to the Themes and Foundations of Karl Rahner's Theology*, ed. Leo J. O'Donovan (New York: Crossroad, 1981), 72–3.

see it the way Torrance does because he thinks that, despite original sin, we have the freedom to accept God's offer of grace by virtue of our supposed obediential potency for revelation and our supernatural existential. So, he visualizes God's closeness to us as a "holy mystery," which:

> is also a hidden closeness, a forgiving intimacy, his real home, that it is a love which shares itself, something familiar which he can approach and turn to from the estrangement of his own perilous and empty life. It is the person who in the forlornness of his guilt still turns in trust to the mystery of his existence which is quietly present and surrenders himself as one who even in his guilt no longer wants to understand himself in a self-centered and self-sufficient way, it is this person who experiences himself as one who does not forgive himself, but who is forgiven.[147]

Notice here that Rahner speaks of guilt and forgiveness not by explicitly focusing on the cross and resurrection of Jesus Christ in and through which we are judged and forgiven by his personal actions on our behalf. Instead, his focus is on "a transcendental experience of the absolute closeness of God in his radical self-communication."[148] Consequently, Rahner never notices what for Torrance was a key point, namely, that our free-will is disclosed in Christ as our self-will, which we cannot escape without actually turning to Christ and living by grace alone. Rahner thus argues that:

> When a person in theoretical or practical knowledge or in subjective activity confronts the abyss of his existence, which alone is the ground of everything, and when this person has the courage to look into himself and to find in these depths his ultimate truth, there he can also have the experience that this abyss accepts him as his true and forgiving security.[149]

Unfortunately, while Rahner says he wants to abandon human self-sufficiency, it is here that self-sufficiency rears its ugly head. He tells us to look into ourselves to find in our depth experiences the ultimate truth. But the whole point of recognizing grace in its identity with Christ is that he himself *is* the *ultimate truth* who alone can disclose the depth of sin and the nature of his unconditional free love of us in spite of that sin. Rahner thinks by experiencing some sort of an abyss, we experience some forgiving

---

[147] Rahner, FCF, 131.
[148] Ibid.
[149] Ibid., 132.

security. But in that way, he espouses exactly what Torrance rejects, namely, conditional salvation. Rahner's espousal of conditional salvation is evident in his claim that we can only experience the forgiveness that he has in mind by having the courage to look into ourselves to find the ultimate meaning of truth. That, for Torrance, makes forgiveness dependent on our courage to look into ourselves. He would regard that view of grace as the cheap grace espoused by Bultmann, Tillich, and Robinson. This claim illustrates that, relying on ourselves, we cannot escape the sin of self-reliance and self-will at all because salvation and God's forgiving grace do not depend on us having the courage to look into ourselves. These are unconditionally given in Christ himself and his vicarious life of perfect obedience on our behalf and can only be found in him by looking beyond ourselves toward him. And we can do that only as the Holy Spirit actualizes in us the objective reconciliation accomplished for the human race by and in Christ himself. In other words, we can only take up the cross and follow him.

There can be no doubt here that Rahner is speaking of sin, forgiveness, and grace by referring us to ourselves in our experiences of depth. This approach completely side-steps the fact that it is only through Christ's atoning life of perfect obedience to the Father that we can know the true meaning of sin as well as the meaning of salvation through Christ alone and thus by grace alone through faith. It is no accident that Christ is not explicitly mentioned a single time in Rahner's analysis here. This failure to mention Christ explicitly occurs because he has conceptualized the meaning of sin, freedom, salvation, and forgiveness all in general terms based on our transcendental experiences such as experiences of "death," "radical authenticity," and "love."[150]

For Torrance, we need to be *made free* for grace through the act of Christ himself here and now. Apart from conceptual and ontological union with Christ in faith, our free-will is and remains our self-will. No wonder Rahner can conclude that self-acceptance is the same as accepting Christ when he claims, "Anyone who accepts his own humanity in full ... has accepted the Son of Man."[151] Such thinking leads directly to his view of anonymous Christianity, which is essentially a Christianity without Christ. Thus, Rahner advocates what he calls "existentiell Christology" and concludes that an anonymous Christian has a "real and existentiell relationship" to Christ "implicitly in obedience to his orientation in grace towards the God of absolute, historical presence and self-communication. He exercises this obedience by accepting his own existence without reservation."[152] By contrast, Torrance maintains

---

[150] Rahner, FCF, 132.
[151] Rahner, TI 4, 119.
[152] Rahner, FCF, 306.

that when confronted by revelation in its identity with Christ, we are called to take up the cross and follow him since he is our salvation. This major difference between the two theologians stems directly from the fact that Rahner turns toward us in our transcendental experiences to explain the meaning of grace and nature and only then towards Christ. By contrast, Torrance turns exclusively toward Christ, who alone justifies sinners, thus enabling a true understanding of grace and nature. For Torrance, once again, the relationship between Christ and us and thus between grace and nature is an irreversible relationship in which our experiences do not condition or determine in any way the unconditional love of God that comes to us in Christ.

Let me illustrate from another perspective what Rahner has given us here. Listen to the words of William V. Dych. He says Rahner used the word "existential" following Heidegger to analyze human existence by designating "those components which were constitutive of human existence." These components distinguished human beings from other beings. From this, he concludes that "if God created human beings precisely for the life of grace, then the offer and the possibility of grace is given with human nature itself."[153] Notice what is missing here. Torrance thinks Christ is the "personalizing Person" who enables us to be children of God and thus to be truly human as God's good creatures by judging us and forgiving us personally. By ascribing the offer and possibility of grace to us in our human nature itself, the problem of sin is simply ignored. We are told that if God created us to share in his own life (which he did), then that must mean that both the offer and possibility of grace is already given to us as part of our human nature as theologically understood within history.

However, after the Fall, our human nature was marked by sin and death and did not possess the offer and possibility of grace in itself. Our human nature was restored for us by being brought into right relation with God by God's grace in the life, death, and resurrection of Jesus Christ. And that means the possibility and reality of grace cannot be detached from Christ, the Giver of grace, and ascribed directly to us in our fallen human nature. Dych, with Rahner, thinks that "Creation is intrinsically ordered to the supernatural life of grace as its deepest dynamism and final goal."[154] It is true that creation needs God's grace to be what it was meant to be but is not, because of original sin. However, for Torrance, to claim that any of our dynamisms is identical with our movement toward our final goal, which is supposed to be the supernatural life of grace, is a flat confusion of nature and

---

[153] Dych, 36.
[154] Ibid.

grace. It is precisely what Torrance rejected in rejecting the views of John Robinson, Rudolf Bultmann, and Paul Tillich.

There is no doubt here that Dych and Rahner have confused nature and grace. Dych writes: "The offer of this grace, then, is an existential, an intrinsic component of human existence and part of the very definition of the human in its historical existence."[155] By contrast, if with Torrance, we do not detach grace from the active mediation of Christ himself through the power of his Holy Spirit, who is always the Giver of grace, then grace, as God's action of love for us in Christ, is not and never becomes a "component of human existence" so that it is "part of the very definition of the human in its historical existence."[156] So, for Torrance, the offer and possibility of grace meet us only in an encounter with the Word of God, which comes to us in Christ. To live by grace is to accept Christ as the Lord and Savior of the world; it cannot mean simply self-acceptance in our supposed innate movement toward absolute being or what Rahner calls "holy mystery," and then equates with the Trinity. The difference here is that Torrance conceptualizes God's self-communication in Christ in its identity "with God himself in his own eternal Being" with the result that "the Gift and the Giver are one" so that in him we encounter God as he is in himself and also toward us.[157] Rahner and Dych conceptualize God's self-communication as a universal "existential" that is given directly to everyone in their depth experiences or experiences of self-transcendence.[158] That thinking detaches grace from Christ, the Giver of grace, and cuts us off from God in his eternal oneness as Father, Son, and Holy Spirit, both noetically and ontologically.

On the one hand, Rahner thinks that "nature has a certain affinity for grace," which essentially means an "affinity for the supernatural existential."[159] This affinity, he believes, is the "concrete mode in which human nature was created and actually exists as a result of God's intention in creating it."[160] Because of this, "'Pure nature' is an abstract possibility, not a reality. Hence ... the supernatural existential wants to affirm something about the reality of grace, namely, that it is a constituent part of our historical human existence."[161] Dych explains that this implies first that the terms "supernatural" and "existential" affirm "that grace is utterly free and gratuitous and at the same time that it is utterly intrinsic to human nature and human existence." Consequently, "the

---

[155] Ibid.
[156] Ibid.
[157] Torrance, *Theology in Reconstruction*, 182.
[158] Dych, 36–8.
[159] Ibid., 37.
[160] Ibid.
[161] Ibid.

offer of grace is part of being human."[162] On the other hand, the supernatural existential allows us to understand "God's gracious presence in human existence as an existential" such that God's presence is seen as "universal." Because it is a "transcendental determination" that "permeates and pervades all of human existence" it is "not confined to one compartment of human life or to particular times and places, but touches everything human."[163]

Dych's presentation here is certainly an accurate interpretation of Rahner's theology as Rahner claims that God's self-communication "radicalizes" our transcendental experiences so that "the original experience of God even in his self-communication can be so universal, so unthematic and so 'unreligious' that it takes place, unnamed but really, wherever we are living out our existence."[164] This thinking leads Rahner to approach Christology in a way Torrance did not. Instead of allowing Christ in his uniqueness as God become man to be his sole starting point, Rahner says,

> we are not starting out from the Christological formulations of the New Testament in Paul and John ... we are not assuming the impossibility of going behind such a "late" New Testament Christology to ask about a more original and somewhat more simple experience of faith with the historical Jesus, in his message, his death, and his achieved finality that we describe as his resurrection.[165]

This approach to Christology is precisely what Torrance firmly rejects by insisting that we cannot separate John and Paul from the other New Testament writings with the claim that we can have a relationship with the historical Jesus, which bypasses his uniqueness as truly divine and truly human. He thus insists that "we know Christ by acknowledging that what confronts us is *revelation*, revelation that tells us that here is true man and true God."[166] This revelation is a mystery which we "cannot explain or understand out of our own knowledge" since "he is God, and very God, and yet man and very man: God and man become one person. We know Christ in the mystery of that duality in unity."[167] Therefore, when we know Christ in his uniqueness, that knowledge comes to us from him alone through the power of his Holy Spirit as a miraculous act of God, and not from us or on account

---

[162] Ibid.
[163] Ibid., 37–8.
[164] Rahner, FCF, 132.
[165] Rahner, TI 18:145.
[166] Torrance, *Incarnation*, 3.
[167] Ibid.

of anything we could know from a simple historical experience of Jesus and his message. Torrance says we must be obedient to this mystery

> and seek in every way to let it *declare itself* to us ... we must be faithful to the actual facts, and never allow preconceived notions or theories to cut away some of the facts at the start ... The ultimate fact that confronts us, embedded in history and in the historical witness and proclamation of the New Testament, is the mysterious duality in unity of Jesus Christ, God without reserve, man without reserve, the eternal truth in time, the Word of God made flesh.[168]

All of this thinking undercuts Rahner's attempt to discover what he calls a "questing" or "searching" Christology. Rahner's search for an *a priori* anthropology, which he thinks will result in a proper Christology, engages in exactly the thinking Torrance here claims is impossible. Rahner maintains that his searching Christology (the human search for a savior with or without encountering Jesus) is the basis for understanding Christology and operates without an encounter with the concrete historical Jesus.[169] This approach presumes not only that we can understand the mystery of Christ from our own prior understanding of mystery and reality. It also assumes that we can know something of Christ as savior without a specific encounter with him. Rahner's "transcendental Christology," therefore, "asks about the a priori possibilities in man which make the coming of the message of Christ possible."[170] Torrance, however, tells us that there is no such *a priori* because when we know Christ, we immediately ascribe the possibility of that knowledge to him and only to him. In his words: "He manifests himself and gives himself to us by his own power and agency, by his Holy Spirit, and in the very act of knowing him we ascribe all the possibility of our knowing him to Christ alone, and none of it to ourselves."[171]

Rahner's idea of a supernatural existential allows him to ascribe this possibility directly to us. But in doing this, he obviates the need for Christ at the outset and all along the line to know the truth of revelation and of Christology, including the proper meaning of grace in relation to nature. Many implications follow from this, not the least of which is that he believes "the revealed Word and natural knowledge of God mutually condition each

---

[168] Ibid.
[169] Rahner, FCF, 212.
[170] Ibid., 207.
[171] Torrance, *Incarnation*, 2.

other";[172] that "the *a priori* transcendental subjectivity of the knower on the one hand and the object of knowledge (and of freedom) on the other are related to one another in such a way that they *mutually condition* one another";[173] and that "anthropology and Christology mutually determine each other,"[174] when in fact they do not. Any such ideas would imply that the truth of our knowledge of Christ and of grace comes, at least in part, from us instead of exclusively from Christ. By contrast, Torrance firmly maintains that such views undermine the sovereignty of God's grace and love that meets us in Christ. Here I would just like focus on two key points, namely, the fact that grace cannot be detached from Christ the Giver of grace and the fact that this means grace simply cannot be properly conceptualized as infused grace. Let me return to the reason why Torrance rejected the notion of created grace to explain this matter.

Infused Grace and Created Grace

Torrance states there is a:

> deep and subtle element of Pelagianism in the Roman doctrine of grace, as it emerges in its notion of the Church (to use modern terminology) as the extension of the Incarnation or the prolongation of Redemption, or in its doctrine of the Priesthood as mediating salvation not only from the side of God toward man but from the side of man toward God.[175]

Torrance maintains that from the Reformed perspective, human ministry represents Christ by acting on his authority, but "it does not represent the people, for only Christ can take man's place, and act for man before the Father. In other words, it rejects the notion of created grace or connatural grace, both in its understanding of salvation and in its understanding of the ministry."[176] There is not enough space here to present an entire development of these ideas. It is enough to note where this thinking finally leads.

Torrance claims that in the thirteenth and fourteenth centuries, there was a "medieval synthesis" following the Augustinian tradition using realist Aristotelian terms that was tainted by a nominalistic view "of definable,

---

[172] Rahner, TI 1, 98.
[173] Rahner, TI 11, 87, some emphasis mine.
[174] Rahner, TI 9, 28.
[175] Torrance, *Theology in Reconstruction*, 176.
[176] Ibid.

controllable grace, which we find in Gratian for example, with the realist notion of conferring or causing grace *physice ex opere operato*."[177] This perspective was based on an Augustinian idea of a "sacramental universe" and finally led to the notion that there was "an inherent relation between logical forms and the nature of the truth."[178] In this context, medieval theology developed a view of the relationship between God and creatures in such a way that "even the revelation of God in Christ was interpreted within this system." Unfortunately, this approach "tended to mean that revelation was used to fill out a conception of being established independently on the ground of natural theology."[179] On this basis, when the Church was then regarded as an extension of the incarnation,

> the institutional Church was held to represent in its forms and dogmas the objectification of the truth in its institutional and rational structure ... It was on this ground that the Church itself came to assume supreme authority, for the expression of the mind of the Church in its dogmatic definitions was held to be the expression of the nature of the Truth.[180]

It will be recalled that Torrance opposed this view because it substitutes *logical truth* rather than the *truth of being* in its identity with Christ himself as Lord of the church for the truth itself. The effect of this thinking meant, among other things, that "grace came to be regarded from a more ontological point of view" as "a divine power at work in human being transforming and changing it invisibly and visibly" so that it was understood as "grace actualizing itself within the physical as well as the spiritual, metaphysically heightening and exalting creaturely existence."[181] Grace thus came to be seen as "a divine causation, and there follows from it a divine effect in the creature. It is almost like a supernatural potency that is infused into human beings," which inheres in one's soul, lifting us to a vision of God. That, Torrance says, is the "notion of *created grace*, grace actualizing itself in the creature and elevating it to supernatural existence, *ontological grace* at work in man's very being and raising him to a higher ontological order."[182]

Torrance's main objection here is to the idea of *causality*, which, he says, "appears to import a confusion between Creator and the creature; and to

---

[177] Ibid., 177.
[178] Ibid.
[179] Ibid., 178.
[180] Ibid.
[181] Ibid., 179.
[182] Ibid., 180.

think of grace as deifying man or heightening his being until he attains the level of a supernatural order."[183] But that seems to "do docetic violence to creaturely human nature."[184] Torrance notes that this problem does not just appear in Roman Catholicism but takes the form of theology lapsing into anthropology and subjectivism in Protestant theology with notions of "co-operation and co-redemption." In this context, Torrance conveys his key point by applying the *homoousion* to his view of grace. This application of the *homoousion* eliminates both the medieval "proliferation of *graces*" and "the notion of grace as a detachable quality which could be made to inhere in creaturely being."[185] Torrance asserts, "the doctrine of *created grace* could only be regarded as a species of Arianism."[186] So when he says that in Christ, the Gift (grace) and the Giver are one, he means that the self-communication that meets us in Christ is God himself in the Person of his Son, who is one in being with the Father and the Spirit. That means that grace is nothing other than God himself personally communicating with us.

> The Gift and the Giver are one. Grace is not something that can be detached from God and made to inhere in creaturely being as 'created grace'; nor is it something that can be proliferated in many forms; nor is it something that we can have more or less of, as if grace could be construed in quantitative terms ... Grace is whole and indivisible because it is identical with the personal self-giving of God to us in his Son. It is identical with Jesus Christ.[187]

As noted above, there is no doubt that Rahner and Dych also wanted to speak of grace as God communicating himself personally to us and not as a thing transmitted to us. This intention to speak of grace as God's personal self-communication led Dych to assert that,

> Rahner offers a way to return to the more personal and more immediately religious understanding of grace in Scripture and the Fathers by thinking of grace not just as a created effect of God's efficient causality, but, based on an analogy with the immediate presence of God in the beatific vision,

---

[183] Ibid.
[184] Ibid.
[185] Ibid., 182.
[186] Ibid.
[187] Ibid., 182-3.

as God's actual presence and indwelling through a mode of quasi-formal causality.[188]

Within this perspective, Dych notes that "the supernatural existential asserts that God in his own personal Spirit is present throughout all of history, and that human beings in all of their human encounters are also encountering God."[189] With his notion of the supernatural existential then Rahner uses the notion of "quasi-formal causality" to explain that God has made himself an intrinsic principle of human transcendentality. Thus, while Rahner, like Torrance, wants to say that God communicates himself and not just something to us, the problem appears in his belief that "In a *quasi-formal* causality he really and in the strictest sense of the word bestows *himself*."[190] Rahner uses the word "quasi" to preserve the freedom of God acting causally in this way.[191]

Conceptualized in this way, however, Rahner says God's "self-communication" signifies "that God in his own most proper reality makes himself the inner-most constitutive element of man"[192] so that "God's offer of himself belongs to all men and is a characteristic of man's transcendence and his transcendentality" and "cannot by simple and individual acts of reflection ... be differentiated from those basic structures of human transcendence."[193] For Rahner, then our transcendental knowledge "which is present always and everywhere in the actualization of the human spirit in knowledge and freedom, but present unthematically, is a moment which must be distinguished from verbal and propositional revelation as such."[194] Nonetheless, Rahner claims this still must be understood as God's self-revelation. In his words,

> This transcendental moment in revelation is a modification of our transcendental consciousness produced permanently by God in grace. But such a modification is really an original and permanent element in our consciousness as the basic and original luminosity of our existence. And as an element in our transcendentality which is constituted by God's self-communication, it is already revelation in the proper sense.[195]

[188] Dych, 39.
[189] Ibid.
[190] Karl Rahner, *The Trinity*, trans. Joseph Donceel (New York: Herder and Herder, 1970), 36.
[191] Rahner, TI 1, 330–1.
[192] Rahner, FCF, 116.
[193] Ibid., 129.
[194] Ibid., 149.
[195] Ibid.

The difference between Torrance and Rahner here is enormous because Torrance identifies grace with Christ himself as the *truth of being*, while Rahner thinks "it is only possible to speak of this grace in a meaningful way at all within a transcendental anthropological context."[196] From this, Rahner concludes that "grace is God himself in self-communication, grace is not a 'thing' but—as communicated grace—a conditioning of the spiritual and intellectual subject as such to a direct relationship with God."[197] Thus, grace "can only be understood from the point of view of the subject, with his transcendental nature, experienced as a being-in-reference to the reality of absolute truth and free-ranging, infinite, absolutely valid love. It can only be understood in one's innermost regions as an immediacy before the absolute mystery of God."[198]

How is this different from Torrance's view? It is different in that, at the most critical point in his reflections Rahner turns to the human subject to understand grace, instead of turning to Christ, who is the grace of God acting for us in his unconditional love of us. So Rahner and Dych can then claim that human beings in all their human encounters are encountering God. That conclusion, unfortunately, ends up ascribing grace directly to everyone in their transcendental experiences as the goal of such experiences which can be equated with absolute truth without identifying that truth with Jesus Christ himself, who is the Way, the Truth, and the Life. In this way, grace is detached from the Giver of grace and sought within our depth experiences in a manner similar to the approaches of Tillich, Robinson, and Bultmann, as discussed above.

Grace is Identical with Jesus Christ

The very idea that God's grace, which cannot be separated from Christ the Giver of grace, might be understood as the basic and original luminosity of our existence makes grace indistinguishable from our very existence, as Torrance has already suggested. This conclusion confuses the Creator and the creature by thinking *causally* about grace instead of understanding grace exclusively as God's personal actions of love toward us in his Word and Spirit. The proof of this confusion can be seen in the comments of Stephen Duffy, who writes that "Grace, therefore, is experienced though not as grace, for it is psychologically indistinguishable from the stirrings of human

---

[196] Rahner, TI 9, 36.
[197] Ibid.
[198] Ibid.

transcendentality."[199] Here, the problem of unthematic or nonconceptual knowledge of God rears its ugly head in connection with knowledge of God's grace. One cannot speak of grace in its identity with Christ the Giver of grace without conceptual knowledge of Christ as God himself acting for us here and now through the power of his Holy Spirit. So, the statement that grace can be experienced, "though not as grace," raises the question of what exactly we are then experiencing, if it is not God's coming to us in Christ! Moreover, to claim that grace can or should be understood psychologically rather than theologically with the result that it is "indistinguishable from the stirrings of human transcendentality" clearly implies that creatures in their transcendental experiences cannot be clearly distinguished from God present to them and even indwelling them in his Word and Spirit.

All these difficulties result from the failure to recognize and maintain that grace simply cannot be detached from the Giver of grace without spoiling its proper theological meaning. Let me give one practical example of the problems with Rahner's transcendental method here as it relates to God's self-revelation. Because he conceptualizes grace and revelation by equating them with our transcendental experiences, he does not begin and end his thinking about the resurrection with the crucified and risen Lord himself as Torrance invariably does. So, Rahner claims that,

> If one has a radical hope of attaining a definitive identity and does not believe that one can steal away with one's obligations into the emptiness of non-existence, one has already grasped and accepted the resurrection in its real content ... The absoluteness of the radical hope in which a human being apprehends his or her total existence as destined and empowered to reach definitive form can quite properly be regarded as grace, which permeates this existence always and everywhere. This grace is revelation in the strictest sense ... this certainly is revelation, even if this is not envisaged as coming from "outside."[200]

All of Rahner's presuppositions are here on display. Instead of pointing us directly to the risen Lord, who alone is the object of our faith and hope and is thus himself the enabling condition of our knowledge of eternal life, Rahner directs us to our hope for some sort of "definitive identity." In that

---

[199] Stephen Duffy, "Experience of Grace," *The Cambridge Companion to Karl Rahner*, ed. Declan Marmion and Mary E. Hines (Cambridge: Cambridge University Press, 2005), 48.
[200] Karl Rahner and Karl-Heinz Weger, *Our Christian Faith: Answers for the Future*, trans. Francis McDonagh (New York: Crossroad, 1981), 110–11. Envisioning the resurrection in this abstract fashion led Rahner to make a statement that Torrance never would make, namely, "the knowledge of man's resurrection given with his transcendentally necessary hope is a statement of philosophical anthropology even before any real revelation in the Word" (Rahner, TI 17, 18).

way, he thinks we already grasp the real content of the resurrection. That is simply untrue. As Torrance insists, "the incarnation and resurrection force themselves upon our minds" with the result that "in the life and work of Jesus Christ we are confronted with an ultimate self-revelation of God into the truth of which there is no way of penetrating from what we already know or believe we know, far less of establishing or verifying it on grounds that are outside it."[201] And the truth grasps us by claiming:

> the unreserved fidelity of our minds. It is no blind act of faith that is required, divorced from any recognition of credibility, for the reality of the incarnation or the resurrection is the kind of objectivity which makes itself accessible to our apprehension, creating the condition for its recognition and acceptance, that is, in such a way that belief on our part is the subjective pole of commitment to objective reality, but intelligent commitment to an objectively intelligible reality which is to be grasped only through a repentant rethinking and structural recasting of all our preconceptions.[202]

Torrance here does not just refer to our hope for some vague definitive end, as Rahner did. Torrance here is claiming that the very meaning of Christian

---

[201] Torrance, *Space, Time and Resurrection*, 18.
[202] Ibid., 18–19. Illustrating the fact that if knowledge of God begins with an ill-conceived view of humanity it will lead to a misunderstanding of both God and humanity, Torrance frequently argues that it is precisely the *homoousion* that "does not allow us indiscriminately to read back into God what is human and finite." *Christian Doctrine of God*, 99. Scientific theology he says cuts "away any mythological projection of ideas of our own devising into God" (ibid.). He maintains that while it is not always easy to distinguish objective "states of affairs from subjective states of affairs," since we constantly tend to get in the way because of our "self-centredness," it is still important to do so in all areas of reflection (ibid.). But in theology it is more difficult because "due to our deep-rooted sin and selfishness we are alienated from God in our minds, and need to be reconciled to him. Hence ... a repentant rethinking of what we have already claimed to know and a profound reorganisation of our consciousness are required of us in knowing God, as was made clear by Jesus when calling for disciples he insisted that they must renounce themselves and take up their cross in following him" (ibid., 99–100). Torrance believes it is only by holding together the unity between the economic activity of God in the Spirit and in the Son "that we may be prevented from reading back into God himself the material or creaturely images (e.g. latent in human father-son relations) ... creaturely images naturally latent in the forms of thought and speech employed by divine revelation to us are made to refer transparently or in a diaphanous way to God without being projected into his divine Nature" (ibid., 101). We must therefore exercise "critical discernment of what we may read back from the incarnation into God and what we may not read back into him." Thomas F. Torrance, "The Christian Apprehension of God the Father," *Speaking the Christian God: The Holy Trinity and the Challenge of Feminism*, ed. Alvin F. Kimel, Jr. (Grand Rapids, MI: Eerdmans, 1992), 137. We may not read the kind of sonship we experience on earth back into God because "we cannot project the creaturely relations inherent in human sonship into the Creator. Nor, of course, can we read gender back into God, for gender belongs to creatures only" (ibid.).

hope is determined by the fact that Christ has risen from the dead and is coming again. He says, "*The raising of the Christ* is *the* act of God, whose significance is not to be compared with any event before or after. *It is the primal datum of theology, from which there can be no abstracting*, and the normative presupposition for every valid dogmatic judgment and for the meaningful construction of a Christian theology."[203] For Torrance, "The resurrection cannot be detached from Christ himself, and considered as a phenomenon on its own to be compared and judged in the light of other phenomena."[204] Thus, for Torrance, our hope as Christian hope is shaped by the fact that Jesus, who rose bodily from the dead, now lives eternally as the ascended Lord and promises us a share in that eternal life. The empty tomb points to the fact that he rose bodily from the dead and that he himself, as the incarnate and risen Lord, is the one who enables our hope for eternal life and enables us to live as new creatures in him by sharing in his new humanity through faith in him as the risen, ascended, and coming Lord. Torrance does not refer to the resurrection in some vague way as our hope for something definitive that can be understood apart from the risen Lord himself. It certainly cannot be understood from our radical hope of attaining a definitive identity, as Rahner claimed.[205]

The most important point here is that because Rahner consistently detaches grace from Christ the Giver of grace, he can explain hope from our transcendental experiences of hope instead of exclusively from understanding Christ himself as the risen Lord who alone enables hope for eternal life and enables us to live as part of the new creation through union with Christ. Rahner here equates grace with our radical hope, which he thinks can be explained from philosophical anthropology and then theologically. So naturally enough, he thinks this grace permeates our existence and can also be regarded as God's revelation, which does not have to come from outside us. But the truth is that God's self-revelation and grace cannot be detached from Christ the incarnate, risen, ascended, and coming Lord, and thus must come to us from him and thus from beyond our experiences of hope and in contrast to any logical view of hope grounded in transcendental experience conceived philosophically or theologically. All Rahner's thinking here is confirmed when he claims that self-acceptance is the same as accepting

---

[203] Ibid., 74.
[204] Ibid., 46.
[205] It is no accident that when Rahner speaks of Christ's resurrection he refers to "his achieved finality that we describe as his resurrection" (TI 18, 145). The clear implication is that it is not the risen Lord himself risen bodily from the dead who is the sole object of reflection but some sort of vague "achieved finality" that we choose to describe as resurrection!

Christ. Hence, "Anyone therefore, no matter how remote from any revelation formulated in words, who accepts his existence, that is, his humanity ... says yes to Christ, even when he does not know that he does ... Anyone who accepts his own humanity in full ... has accepted the son of Man ...."[206] The only way this could be true is if one had confused nature and grace utilizing the supernatural existential so that self-acceptance is then equated with acceptance of Christ. The problem here is that, as Torrance claims, one cannot detach atonement from the incarnation and resurrection. If incarnation is not detached from atonement, then it will be seen that it is only by turning *from* ourselves as the sinners we are apart from Christ, and turning toward him as the one in whom our enmity to God is overcome, that we can live as those who are justified by grace alone and thus through union with Christ alone.

Conclusion

Let me conclude by noting how Dych defends Rahner's position as a strictly theological position. He argues once again that Rahner uses his philosophy to explain his theology but that his starting point is a "conviction of faith," that is,

> "a strictly theological proposition". In this instance the faith conviction is rooted in the scriptural assertion of God's universal saving will, and in the belief that if God truly wishes the salvation of all, then it must be a concrete possibility for everyone. One way, although obviously not the only way, of understanding grace as a universal possibility is to understand it as an existential in human life. Philosophy serves theology's task of seeking an understanding of faith in the sense in which Anselm defined theology as *fides quaerens intellectum*, faith seeking understanding.[207]

It is precisely here that Torrance's view of Anselm and Dych's view of Anselm radically differ. Torrance flatly rejects any idea of unthematic and nonobjective or nonconceptual knowledge of God, Christ, revelation, and grace, claiming with Anselm that we cannot have experience of God, belief in God or knowledge of God without concepts: "*fides esse nequit sine conceptione*."[208]

---

[206] TI 4:119.
[207] Dych, 39.
[208] Torrance, *God and Rationality*, 170 and "Truth and Authority," 228.

Thus, for Torrance, knowledge of God comes to us through our knowledge of God the Father, whom we know through union with his incarnate Son in faith. Any other view, Torrance claimed, would end with mythological projection from us as human subjects instead of with objective knowledge of the Trinity grounded in God's economic trinitarian self-revelation. Torrance held this view because he maintained that "our knowing of God is grounded in his knowing of us."[209] That means that "when we speak of God as Father, therefore, we are not using the term 'Father' in a transferred, improper, or inadequate sense; we are using it in its completely proper sense, which is determined by the intrinsic Fatherhood of God himself."[210]

So, when Dych speaks of faith seeking understanding, he claims that if God wills to save all, then salvation must be a concrete possibility for everyone. It is, of course—but the possibility is in the reality of God acting for all people in his incarnate Word and through his Holy Spirit and this cannot be universalized by equating it with something that is supposedly present in each person in the depth of their experiences of self-transcendence. However, with Rahner, Dych holds that "God-talk makes sense and can point to its roots in experience" with the transcendental Thomist view that such God-talk "is always through the world of our objective, historical experience and as an element *within* that experience. God, however, is not encountered as one object among others in that world, but as the deepest dimension of all our encounters."[211] It is exactly here that Dych turns once again to Rahner's view that knowledge of God is not knowledge of an "object which happens to present itself directly or indirectly from outside" because such knowledge has the character of "a transcendental experience."[212] From this he concludes with Rahner's own words that "insofar as this subjective, non-objective luminosity of the subject in its transcendence is always orientated towards the holy mystery, the knowledge of God is always present unthematically and without name, and not just when we begin to speak of it."[213]

Nevertheless, as discussed above, if Torrance is right, and I think he is, then we can only know God as the eternal Father, Son, and Holy Spirit to the extent that we rely exclusively upon the grace of God, which meets us in Christ and through the power of the Holy Spirit. When that occurs, we then know God's name while simultaneously knowing that, apart from grace, which meets us in judgment and forgiveness in Christ, we are at enmity with

---

[209] Torrance, "The Christian Apprehension of God the Father," 137.
[210] Ibid.
[211] Dych, 44.
[212] Ibid. Dych is citing Rahner, FCF, 21.
[213] Ibid.

God and not oriented toward him as some generally known "holy mystery." We also know that while the Christian God is holy and a mystery, that does not mean that we have true knowledge of the Trinity just by referring to God as a holy mystery that can be known from an experience of the nameless. God in Christ is not nameless but has a name, and that is the name into which Christians are baptized.

Consequently, the point of this chapter is to illustrate that there can be genuine union between Catholic and Protestant theologians regarding knowledge of God, revelation, and grace if and to the extent that both sides are willing to begin and end their theologies with Jesus Christ alone and with the justification that comes to humanity in and through him alone. So, instead of claiming that self-acceptance means accepting God, which it does not, one would have to point to Christ himself as the sole possibility and reality of salvation for all humanity and for the whole world. This means that true knowledge of God really does involve knowledge of a definite object, namely, the triune God who makes himself known to us through union with Christ and thus with the Father in faith. Such knowledge does not refer to some nameless reality found in universal human depth experiences but to that particular object which can be experienced and known only as Christ himself is allowed to disclose himself to us through the power of his Holy Spirit. In this way, instead of retreating from the *truth of being*, with the idea of God as the nameless which is identified from a transcendental experience and various depth experiences, we may know the truth of God's being from an encounter with his Word and Spirit and thus know God as the eternal Father, Son, and Holy Spirit.

2

Appreciating How T. F. Torrance's View of Justification by Grace Alone Leads to a Proper Theology of Liberation

Karl Barth famously argued that "there is a way from Christology to anthropology, but there is no way from anthropology to Christology."[1] Barth's student and colleague Thomas F. Torrance would fully agree with Barth's assertion because it implies that a properly Christian theological anthropology begins with Jesus himself as the incarnate Word, in whom we meet God himself. To bypass Jesus is to bypass God in order to speak theologically. That, for Barth and for Torrance, is the height of idolatry because any attempt to speak about our relations with God and our relations with each other which does not begin with God himself will always end in some form of self-justification. However, to begin with God means precisely to acknowledge Jesus himself as the Way, the Truth, and the Life (Jn 14:6).

Torrance frequently cites this important text to connect God's revelation to Moses as "*I am*" with the revelation we encounter in Jesus, noting that this "self-naming" of God was "appropriated by Jesus Christ and identified with his own *I am* proclaimed to us in the Gospel of the saving love and grace of God the Father."[2] Torrance wisely maintained that Jesus' *I am* sayings illustrated that "his own 'I am' is grounded in the indwelling of the Father and the Son in one another, in the eternal Communion which belongs to the inner Life of God as Father, Son and Holy Spirit."[3] That insight was also supported by the important text in Mt. 11:27 and Lk. 10:22, namely, that "All things have been handed over to me by my Father. No one knows the Son except the Father, and no one knows the Father except the Son and anyone to whom the Son wishes to reveal him." That is why Torrance could claim that theological science must find its decisive point in the "ontological relations in

---

[1] Karl Barth, *Church Dogmatics*, 4 vols. in 13 pts., vol. I, *The Doctrine of the Word of God*, pt. 1, ed. G. W. Bromiley and T. F. Torrance, trans. by G. W. Bromiley (hereafter: CD) (Edinburgh: T&T Clark, 1975), 131.

[2] Torrance, *Christian Doctrine of God*, 124.

[3] Ibid.

God" as recognized at the Council of Nicaea when the creed was produced by the Fathers. He says,

> Face to Face with Jesus Christ, they had to do immediately with God, who so unreservedly communicated *himself* to them in Christ that they knew Christ to be the embodiment of God, so that they not only worshipped God through and with Christ but in Christ, worshipping God face to face in Christ who is himself the face of the Father turned toward them.[4]

This, Torrance noted, embodied the "decisive point for theological science" where one moves "from the basic evangelical and doxological level to the theological level of ontological relations in God."[5]

Important implications follow from this. First, if Barth and Torrance are correct, and I think they are, then what we discover in our encounter with Jesus is that we are disclosed to be enemies of grace, that is, those who are at enmity with God. We are the ones who brought Jesus to the cross, and in and through that cross our sins have been forgiven by God himself.[6] That is why Barth said that to engage in theological anthropology,

> We must not, of course, look in any other direction than to Jesus Christ. We must not formulate any other assertions than those of which He is always the true subject. About man as such, about autonomous man, existing otherwise than in Jesus Christ, the only thing we need to know is that he has brought Jesus Christ to the cross and that in this same cross his sins are forgiven; that in his independence he is judged and removed, really removed, i.e., moved and taken up into fellowship with the life of the Son of God.[7]

In view of this, Barth himself insisted that absolutely everything that is now said about God, sin and our relations with God and each other must be said from our "being in Jesus Christ" such that all sound doctrine must follow that rule. Indeed, if that rule is followed, then "the statement that God is knowable to man can and must be made with the strictest possible certainty,

---

[4] Thomas F. Torrance, *The Ground and Grammar of Theology* (Charlottesville, VA: University Press of Virginia, 1980), 159.
[5] Ibid.
[6] Barth, CD II/1, 162. For Torrance "the Truth reveals that we are not in the Truth and delivers us from the vicious circle of our own untruth, reconciling us to the Truth and putting us in the right with it beyond us." Torrance, *Theological Science*, 158.
[7] Ibid.

with an apodictic certainty, with a certainty freed from any dialectic and ambiguity, with all the certainty of the statement 'the Word was made flesh.'"[8] Second, this means that there is no *continuity* to be found in human experience and behavior on the basis of which we are in harmony with God and our neighbors. Whenever that assumption is made, some form of self-justification always is at work and rears its ugly head. And such self-justification simply misses the true meaning of theology and of anthropology as understood christologically. Self-justification always means that we attempt to know God, and ourselves by reflecting on ourselves in some way, perhaps by pursuing our own agenda for various laudable goals, or simply by looking into our own experiences of love or depth to understand God, Christ himself, human freedom, sin, or salvation. For both Barth and Torrance, Christ must be the center from which all else is understood precisely because of who he was and is as the Word made flesh.

What I am claiming then is that whenever it is assumed that we humans possess some sort of innate *continuity* with God, the problem of sin is unrecognized, ignored, or brushed aside, and the proper meaning of salvation and liberation is missed. And the problem (sin) and its solution (salvation by grace alone) are missed just because they are not sought beyond us in Christ alone. Let me explain. T. F. Torrance makes the following claim in his *Theological Science*: "face to face with Christ our humanity is revealed to be diseased and in-turned, and our subjectivities to be rooted in self-will. It is we who require to be adapted to Him, so that we have to renounce ourselves and take up the Cross if we are to follow Him and know the Father through Him."[9] In that way, we sinful human beings are "healed" and "recreated in communion with God," and any distortion in our knowledge of God and relationship with God is overcome precisely through "cognitive union with God in love."[10] Here it is important to stress the "epistemological significance of the Incarnation" because it is precisely in and through the Incarnate Word (Jesus Christ) that "we are summoned to know God strictly in accordance with the way in which He has actually objectified Himself for us in our human existence."[11] And, contrary to Karl Rahner's theory of anonymous Christianity, this cannot occur anonymously because there is no anonymous way to know of Jesus Christ and what he has accomplished for us in his own life, ministry, death, resurrection, ascension and continuing mediation at the right hand of God the Father without

---

[8] Ibid.
[9] Torrance, *Theological Science*, 310.
[10] Ibid.
[11] Ibid.

knowing him conceptually through the Gospel witness. Torrance explains this situation with great insight and with important implications for ethical behavior in his book on Atonement. Following St. Paul, Torrance held that "we are alienated or estranged in our minds, and indeed are hostile in mind to God."[12] He noted that this New Testament view was "deeply resented by the rational culture of the ancient classical world of Greece and Rome" and that our modern world also finds this "very difficult to accept."[13]

This may be something of an understatement in light of the fact that so many contemporary theologians ignore or redefine the problem of sin by claiming it merely refers to imperfections in the human condition. That move unfortunately allows them to marginalize the unconditional grace of God as the sole source of our knowledge of God and of ourselves as forgiven sinners. Nonetheless, Torrance wisely and astutely rejected any such move by sticking closely to the doctrine of justification by grace alone. Thus, he held that relying on God's grace necessarily means not relying *at all* upon ourselves—our religion, our morality, or even our faith. Torrance saw and understood this extremely well as he also noted that "evangelical Christianity" today "does not seem to have thought through sufficiently the transformation of human reason in the light of the Word made flesh in Jesus Christ."[14] Because of this, both within the church and in society, he held that humanity remained "unevangelised." I think he is right. His claim is simple but with profound implications: "the mind of man is alienated at its very root. It is in the human mind that sin is entrenched, and so it is right there, the gospel tells us, that we require to be cleansed by the blood of Christ and to be healed and reconciled to God."[15]

So, the pivotal point here is that because our behavior (ethics) is governed by our minds, Torrance maintained that even though we have free-will, "we are not at all free to escape from our self-will" (which for Torrance means our inveterate attempts to live autonomously instead of in dependence on grace alone). That "self-will" is ingrained within our mind, and it not only controls all our thinking and culture, but it is there that "we have become estranged from the truth and hostile to God." Thus, it is "in the ontological depths of the human mind, that we desperately need to be redeemed and healed."[16] That healing took place for us in the incarnation, since the Son of God assumed our fallen human nature, and bent our wills back to God

---

[12] Thomas F. Torrance, *Atonement: The Person and Work of Christ*, ed. Robert T. Walker (Milton Keynes, UK: Paternoster; Downers Grove, IL: IVP Academic, 2009), 437.
[13] Ibid., 438.
[14] Ibid.
[15] Ibid.
[16] Ibid., 439.

in our place and for us by experiencing God's judgment (opposition to sin) "in order to lay hold upon the very root of our sin and to redeem us from its stranglehold upon us."[17]

Since it is our mind that is sanctified and renewed in Christ, Torrance strongly opposed any Apollinarian view that because our minds are sinful, they had to be replaced by the Word in the incarnation. Instead, for Torrance, the Word assumed our sinful flesh, including our minds and healed us so that through union with him in faith, we may live as part of that new creation. Karl Barth's view is in harmony with Torrance's. For Barth, if we look in any direction but toward Christ himself, we will not see the truth about humanity. As already noted, we will not see our sin and the law against which we have sinned and we will not see the fact that in Christ our sins have been forgiven because in him all human beings in their attempts at "existing otherwise than in Jesus Christ" have been "judged and removed, really removed, i.e., moved and taken up into fellowship with the life of the Son of God."[18] This happens when the Holy Spirit unites us to Christ in faith and thus enables our reconciled fellowship with God in truth.

In knowing God in Jesus Christ, we know that "this does not give us leave to read our own humanity back into God or to confine knowledge of Him within our human subjectivities."[19] This means that when we allow Jesus to be the *first* and *final* Word in theology, we are thinking according to the very movement of grace toward us in the incarnation, with the result that it is through the Holy Spirit that "we are converted from ourselves to thinking from a centre in God and not in ourselves, and to knowing God out of God and not out of ourselves."[20] This is crucial because it means that it is only when the Holy Spirit, who is *homoousios* with the Father and the Son, enables

---

[17] Ibid., 440.
[18] Barth, CD II/1, 162.
[19] Torrance, *Theological Science*, 310.
[20] Torrance, *God and Rationality*, 174. Torrance appealed to the doctrine of election to stress the "unqualified objectivity of God's Love and Grace toward us" so that our faith rests on "the ultimate invariant ground in God himself ... for our salvation in life and death." Thomas F. Torrance, *Christian Theology and Scientific Culture* (Eugene, OR: Wipf and Stock, 1998), 132. This theonomous way of thinking takes place "from a centre in God and not from centre in ourselves" because the doctrine of election excludes any idea that "we may establish contact with God or know or worship him through acting upon him" (ibid.). Torrance rightly insists once again that "the doctrine of election also rejects any projection of human ways of thought, speech or behaviour, or any creaturely representation, into God—that is the way of mythology—but calls instead for a radical discrimination of what is objectively real in God from all our subjective states and creaturely fancies" (ibid.). For Torrance justification means that "it is Christ, and not we ourselves, who puts us in the right and truth of God, so that He becomes the centre of reference in all our thought and action" (*God and Rationality*, 60).

us to know the Father through union with the Son that we have a continuity with God the Creator and Lord of the universe. That continuity does not belong to us innately because we are sinners who cannot escape our self-will which itself is identical with our free-will; however, it becomes ours as that continuity is "continuously given and sustained by the presence of the Spirit."[21] Importantly, since the Holy Spirit is also "the temporal presence of the Jesus Christ who intercedes for us eternally in full truth,"[22] our knowledge of the Holy Spirit and God himself is lost by confusing the Holy Spirit with the human spirit and thus by falling into some form of "subjectivism." Again, Torrance has things just right: "unless we know the Holy Spirit through the objectivity of the *homoousion* of the Son in whom and by whom our minds are directed away from ourselves to the one Fountain and Principle of Godhead, then we inevitably become engrossed with ourselves, confusing the Holy Spirit with our own spirits."[23] When that occurs, knowledge of God, ethics, and anthropology stems from our subjective perceptions, agendas, and experiences instead of from the revelation of God in his Word and Spirit.

This may sound a bit complicated. But Torrance explains this with a clarity and precision that make it impossible to miss the implications of his position. His point is very simple, and it is that Christians need to be childlike in the sense of simply taking up their cross and following Jesus as he originally noted in his book *Theological Science*. But they should not become childish in their faith. What did he mean by this? Torrance says, when the Lord spoke of the Kingdom of God, he never spoke about "maturity and adulthood."[24] Those who seek maturity and adulthood apart from Christ are seeking to ground their humanity in themselves—in their own self-understanding so that they then bring God into the picture only to support their own views of reality. Torrance claims that we live within the Kingdom of God only when, like children, "we are devoid of sophistication and pretentious self-understanding, where we let Christ be everything, and that includes being the mighty Saviour who came to make Himself responsible for us, to shoulder our burdens, and bear away our sins."[25]

True maturity and adulthood, however, should be associated with Dietrich Bonhoeffer's approach who, unlike other Germans, did not yield to authority or to the State and refused to use God as "an 'external prop' for his faith."[26] In

---

[21] Torrance, *Theology in Reconstruction*, 223.
[22] Barth, CD II/1, 158.
[23] Torrance, *Theology in Reconstruction*, 227.
[24] Torrance, *God and Rationality*, 73.
[25] Ibid. Torrance develops this same viewpoint in *The Mediation of Christ* (Colorado Springs: Helmers & Howard, 1992), chapter 4.
[26] Torrance, *God and Rationality*, 73.

him, Torrance said, "German Christianity came to maturity, and adult man emerged upon the scene, free from the shackles of authority and standing on his own feet."[27] However, Torrance also noted that many of his contemporaries in Germany, in the United States, and in Britain were using Bonhoeffer only as "a means of objectifying their own self-understanding and as a symbol on which to project their own image of themselves."[28] They used phrases like "religionless Christianity" and "worldly holiness" to construct systems of thought that were in conflict with Bonhoeffer's theology and Christology. The reason I bring this up here is because Torrance's analysis illustrates the important point that he frequently presented when he discussed the ethical implications of Christian faith. And he did so by explaining morality on the basis of his view of justification by grace alone. Let me briefly explain this.

Torrance believed theology was not childlike but childish if it is only based on "an external authority, be it from the Scriptures or the Church."[29] By way of example he noted how often it is the case that if a minister is taken away from a congregation, then the church members seem to "collapse in their faith" because they were relying on "external props" and thus have not "really grown up in their faith."[30] Then he draws some very interesting and important conclusions. First, he says it is possible to use God himself as a prop in that way to support one's own view of religion. In that way he claims people protect themselves "from the searching judgements of God or from being concluded with all the godly and ungodly in the one solidarity of sin under the divine grace."[31] This is a vital point because it indicates why both Torrance and Barth spoke of revelation as grace being offensive to us. The reason is that even in our goodness we all are in solidarity in sin and that is what the grace of God disclosed in Christ reveals. Second, because of this Torrance then concludes that when we take justification by grace seriously "the ground is completely taken away from [our] feet, and away with it there goes [our] own 'religion' and the 'prop-God' that belongs to it."[32] And his point is that it is this prop-God that Bonhoeffer was rejecting by "radicalizing justification by grace alone over against man's own religious self-justification and self-security."[33]

---

[27] Ibid., 74.
[28] Ibid.
[29] Ibid.
[30] Ibid.
[31] Ibid.
[32] Ibid.
[33] Ibid., 74–5.

Justification by Grace and Moral Concerns

How then does Torrance's thinking play out in relation to morality? Torrance approaches this issue by noting that we cannot answer this question on the ground of natural science because with natural science "we have to think of nature out of nature" without recourse to some *"deus ex machina"* to help us out of difficulties. In other words, you cannot bring God in to explain anything in natural science since such science works only on the level of created nature so that all natural knowledge functions as if God were not given, *"etsi deus non daretur."*[34] This means that it is part of the doctrine of creation not to bring God in to explain the universe and what goes on within it. Indeed, to do this or to bring God in to stem secularization is pointless since doing this amounts to using God "against His will" in ways that can lead only to confusion. This is the case because every such attempt ends by "confounding Him with worldly powers" in a way that only alienates us further from the God of the Bible.[35]

It is this confounding of God with worldly powers that is at the heart of the current attempts by liberation theologians who attempt to understand God from the fight against oppression, no matter what form that fight might take. The God of the Bible, Torrance rightly insists, is "known only through the Cross and weakness of Jesus Christ" in such a way that we know that it is God in him who "conquers the power and space of this world." Hence, the God we must do without is the "'God' who is a prop to [our] self-justification" and not "the God of justification by grace alone."[36] Here Torrance maintains a view that is frequently misunderstood today. He says that if we try to think of God and nature "on one and the same level (or, on two quite separated levels which are merely the obverse of each other, which amounts to the same thing!)," then we fall into naturalism. That unfortunately leads to "a false apologetic that attempts to defend the Christian doctrine of the transcendence of God on the same plane of thought as that in which we engage in merely natural knowledge."[37]

Here Torrance directly links his understanding of cheap and costly grace both to the doctrine of justification and to Christian ethics asking: "Are we to engage in moral decisions without bringing God into them at all, and are we to learn how to behave in this secularized world in a purely secular way, *etsi deus non daretur* [as if God were not given]?" If the answer

---

[34] Ibid., 75.
[35] Ibid.
[36] Ibid., 75–6.
[37] Ibid., 76.

here is yes, then we deny our actual need for God and God's grace and we fall back finally upon ourselves once again. That, he says, would be a total misunderstanding of Bonhoeffer. He wanted to focus on the God of the Bible and not our prop-God so that "the point of departure for *Christian ethics* is not the reality of one's own self or the reality of the world, but the 'reality of God as he reveals Himself in Jesus Christ.'"[38] Importantly, Torrance says that in his *Ethics* Bonhoeffer said we have to "discard the questions 'How can I be good?' 'How can I do good?' and ask the very different question 'What is the will of God?'"[39]

It is with that question that, like Barth, Torrance began his ethics with the basic principle of our justification by grace alone, which means that it is grace alone that "makes a man really free for God and his brothers, for it sets his life on a foundation other than himself where he is sustained by a power other than his own."[40] Here we reach the heart of the matter. *Either* we live the freedom which is ours in Christ, who has loved us and will always love us unconditionally, *or* we rely on external authorities and false props. The right choice here clearly is not to rely on our morality or religion but to live our ethical and religious lives "exclusively from a centre in Jesus Christ."[41] Bonhoeffer would not separate our existence within this world from our existence in Christ because it is in Christ that we see the true meaning of both. Hence, ethics and dogmatics both pivot "upon the fact that in and through the incarnation the Being of God Himself is to be found 'in space and time', for it is by participating in this Christ that we stand at once both in the Reality of God and in the reality of this world."[42]

Cheap and Costly Grace

This, however, means rejecting Neo-Protestant Christianity, Ebionitism (which attempts to ground Christ's uniqueness in human responses to the Gospel instead of in Christ himself) and Docetism (which attempts

---

[38] Ibid.
[39] Ibid.
[40] Ibid.
[41] Ibid.
[42] Ibid., 77–8.

to understand Christology from our ideas about Christ instead of from Christ himself),[43] as well as any dichotomy between idea and reality such as we find in Bultmann. Bonhoeffer's ethics was grounded in Christology and that is how Torrance grounds his ethics as well when he insists that justification is the basis for his view of morality. He argues that justification is the "most easy thing" but "difficult to understand." It is also "the most easy and yet the most difficult to accept." It is easy "because it is so utterly free, and therefore so cheap in the sense that it is quite without price or condition; but it is so difficult because its absolute freeness devalues the moral and religious currency which we have minted at such cost out of our own self-understanding."[44] But Torrance offers another view of cheap grace here as well. He says modern people find it difficult to understand and accept justification by grace alone because they want "'cheap grace', grace which does not set a question mark at [their] way of life" and does not "ask [them] to deny [themselves] and take up the Cross in following Christ." They want a "grace that does not disturb [their] setting in contemporary culture by importing into [their] soul a divine discontent, but one which will let [them] be quite 'secular', grace that merely prolongs [their] already existing religious experience and does not 'spoil' [them] for existence as [people] of the world."[45]

There is yet another meaning that Torrance gives to cheap grace and that relates to the views of those he called the new theologians of his day such as John Robinson with his book *Honest to God*. Robinson spoke of God as the ground of his being by projecting his view of God from his own secular experience mythologically out of himself instead of thinking from a center in God. He, and those who followed him, should have allowed the triune God in his own personal being to define his view, instead of trying to understand God from his own experience. The end result of Robinson's approach, according to Torrance, was that Robinson embraced an inverted deism because the God he presented was powerless to act in relation to us since, in his theology,

---

[43] For a full discussion of Ebionite and Docetic Christology, see Molnar, *Divine Freedom and the Doctrine of the Immanent Trinity*, Chapter Two, "Christology and the Trinity: Some Dogmatic Implications of Barth's Rejection of Ebionite and Docetic Christology," 45-88. This chapter was originally presented as a lecture at the Universities of St. Andrews and Aberdeen in March 1999. After having read that lecture, which was later published in the *International Journal of Systematic Theology* 2 (2000), 151-74 as "Some Dogmatic Implications of Barth's Understanding of Ebionite and Docetic Christology," T. F. Torrance sent me a letter dated January 11, 1999, in which he said that he really appreciated my thoughts on that subject, especially as they related to Rahner. He also mentioned that he used to devote one or two of his lectures in Christology to "the way Barth showed how Ebionite and Docetic christologies imply and pass into one another."
[44] Torrance, *God and Rationality*, 70.
[45] Ibid., 71.

God could not be distinguished from Robinson's own experiences of depth. As noted above, his great mistake was that he was unable "to distinguish God 'out there' rationally as objectively and transcendently other than the depths of his own being, and so he is thrown back upon himself to give content to his notion of God, as what is of ultimate concern *for* him in the depth and significance of his own being."[46] Torrance flatly asserts that this approach to theology is one that is only out for *cheap grace* because it merely uses God for its own ends and satisfaction and says that is precisely what Bonhoeffer rejected as idolatrous projection. Accordingly, Robinson ended up where all the "new" theologians ended, that is, with "the 'God' *they* want, one to suit themselves and modern 'secular' man, rather than the God of *costly grace* who calls for the renewing of our minds in which we are not schematized to the patterns of this world but are transformed in conformity with His own self-revelation in Jesus Christ."[47]

This is an enormously important point because it is obvious that Robinson's approach was in harmony with the approach offered by Paul Tillich, who argued that if you do not like the traditional meaning of the word "God," then you could translate it and speak of the depths of your life or of your ultimate concerns. In doing that he believed you could not be called an atheist. You would only be an atheist if you denied or rejected your own experiences of depth because he believed that the word God means depth and if you know about depth you know about God.[48] This is still a popular methodology today, and it is exactly what Torrance rightly rejects here as an approach that is out for *cheap grace* because it confuses who God is objectively as the eternal Trinity acting for us in the incarnate Word and outpouring of the Holy Spirit with our own subjective experiences of depth.[49]

Importantly then, when Torrance speaks of the God of *costly grace* who meets us in Jesus Christ, he clearly means that Christ himself calls us to renounce ourselves and "take up the cross and follow Him unreservedly all along the road to crucifixion and resurrection."[50] Far from threatening

---

[46] Ibid., 81.
[47] Ibid., 82.
[48] See Tillich, *The Shaking of the Foundations*, 57 and above, Chapter One.
[49] One popular example of this approach can be found in John Haught's book, *What Is God: How to Think about the Divine* (New York: Paulist Press, 1986), where he devotes a chapter (Chapter 1) to explaining that we know God from our experiences of depth. The result is a disaster since he is unwilling and unable to realize that God recognized in Christian faith is the eternal Father, Son, and Holy Spirit so that God simply cannot be known from our experiences of depth at all. Torrance knew that well because his view of God came from his encounter with the grace of God which could never be separated from Christ, the Giver of grace.
[50] Torrance, *God and Rationality*, 82.

those elements of truth that people see as important for the modern world, Torrance insists that the Gospel does not threaten that but threatens our own "self-centeredness," which is the actual threat that the Gospel opposes. Torrance then says that a proper doctrine of creation would affirm "*the liberation of nature* that comes from taking seriously God's creation of the world out of nothing," and a proper doctrine of grace would lead to "*the affirmation of nature* that comes from the doctrine of grace alone" by recognizing the unconditional nature of God's free love by which God maintains his creation in distinction from and dependence upon him. Thus, Torrance concludes: "Cut away that relation to the God of creation and grace and what ensues can only be deism or atheism in some form or other."[51] He claims that the new theology actually smothered the objective truth sought by modern empirical science "with a massive subjectivity in which there is revealed a reactionary flight from scientific objectivity."[52]

It is not insignificant that Torrance maintains that there is an evangelical and an unevangelical way to preach the Gospel. The latter tells people to believe in Jesus Christ *in order* that they may be saved. That, however, throws people back on themselves and their own personal decision or repentance and ends with a mistaken view of conditional salvation. Conditional salvation, however, is no salvation at all since that is the very thing we cannot accomplish and do not need to accomplish, as it has already been accomplished for us by Christ himself. So, the "unevangelical" approach to the Gospel says, "This is what Jesus Christ has done for you, but you will not be saved *unless* you make your own personal decision for Christ as your Saviour. Or: Jesus Christ loved you and gave his life for you on the Cross, but you will be saved only *if* you give your heart to him."[53] The evangelical approach says that salvation is an accomplished reality in the very life, ministry, death, and resurrection of Jesus for all. Therefore, we should accept that new life and live it.

These "unevangelical" views directly conflict with the Gospel of God's unconditional grace. They embody a legalist view of conditional salvation that makes our actual taking up our cross and following Christ impossible by placing the weight of salvation back on us. It should instead point us to the simple fact that Christ has made himself responsible for us. Hence, we do not rely on ourselves at any point at all, but only on him as the one Mediator who loves us unconditionally and thus effectively. Torrance insists that the Gospel is preached evangelically when "full and central place is given to *the vicarious humanity of Jesus* as the all-sufficient human response to the saving love of

---

[51] Ibid.
[52] Ibid.
[53] Torrance, *The Mediation of Christ*, 93.

God which he has freely and unconditionally provided for us."[54] Two key points follow from this. As the man Jesus, God has utterly and freely given himself in his Son by pledging "his very Being as God for your salvation." He has thus "actualised his unconditional love for you in your human nature in such a once for all way, that he cannot go back upon it without undoing the Incarnation and the Cross and thereby denying himself."[55] Christ died for us just because we are sinners and quite unworthy of him, and in that way, he has made us his own even before and apart from our believing in him. That is why Torrance always insists on holding incarnation and atonement together so that he can stress that Jesus' humanity is not merely instrumental in God's hands but he personally acts to save us from sin. Salvation is not just an act of God for us but "also a real human act done in our place and issuing out of our humanity."[56] That is why he insists that we need a view of justification by grace

> which really lets Christ occupy the centre, so that everything is interpreted by reference to who He was and is. After all, it was not the *death* of Jesus that constituted atonement, but Jesus Christ the Son of God offering Himself in sacrifice for us. Everything depends on *who* He was, for the significance of His acts in life and death depends on the nature of His Person.[57]

Importantly, this means that "we must allow the Person of Christ to determine for us the nature of His saving work, rather than the other way round. The detachment of atonement from incarnation is undoubtedly revealed by history to be one of the most harmful mistakes of Evangelical Churches."[58] This means that if we focus on Christ's benefits and not upon Christ himself, we end up with legalism and moralism and miss the whole point of justification. For Torrance, "it is only through union with Christ that we partake of His benefits, justification, sanctification, etc."[59] Hence, Torrance insists that Jesus has bound us to himself by loving us so that "he will never let [us] go, for even if [we] refuse him and damn [ourselves] in hell his love will never cease."[60] Because all of this is in effect for us, we are called to repent and believe in Jesus as Lord and Savior. What he accomplished for

---

[54] Ibid., 94.
[55] Ibid.
[56] Torrance *Incarnation*, 212.
[57] Torrance, *God and Rationality*, 64.
[58] Ibid.
[59] Ibid.
[60] Torrance, *The Mediation of Christ*, 94.

us was both an act of God reconciling us to himself and an act of man living perfectly by grace in our place and as the enabling condition of our living in the freedom for God and neighbor accomplished by him and in him and through him. Torrance says Christ himself believed for us and acted in our place.

Does this mean that Torrance has displaced us in such a way that what we do no longer matters? It could seem that way. But that is not what Torrance says and thinks. What he means is that because Christ's own life of faith and obedience to the Father in our place includes us in our response to God and our own faith, he has already made my decision for God for me. Therefore, his acknowledgment of us before God is "as one who has already responded to God in him, who has already believed in God through him, and whose personal decision is already implicated in Christ's self-offering to the Father, in all of which he has been fully and completely accepted by the Father, so that in Jesus Christ [we] are already accepted by him."[61] Because all of this is true, we are called to renounce ourselves and take up our cross and follow Jesus, the Savior and Lord.

When we live this freedom which is ours in him, then we will not need to look over our shoulders to see whether we have given ourselves sufficiently to him or not in faith. We won't have to wonder about our faith because the strength of our faith does not rest upon our believing but solely upon what Christ has done for us and what he now does for us before the Father. The freedom Torrance has in mind here is this: in Christ "I am completely liberated from all ulterior motives in believing or following Jesus Christ, for on the ground of his vicarious human response for me, I am free for spontaneous joyful response and worship and service as I could not otherwise be."[62] Notice that Torrance has not eliminated our own personal decision of faith or our own spontaneous acts of loving God and neighbor here. Instead, he has grounded them in Christ's active obedience in such a way that it is Christ himself even now as the risen, ascended, and coming Lord who empowers our spontaneous free actions in obedience to God and in loving others. So he claims that in his humanity Jesus Christ "stands for the fact that 'all of grace' does not mean 'nothing of man', but the very reverse, the restoration of full and authentic human being in the spontaneity and freedom of human response to the love of God."[63] This position stands in complete contrast to those who criticize Torrance for presenting Christ in such a way that he does

---

[61] Ibid.
[62] Ibid., 95.
[63] Ibid.

away with our free human actions. His position is exactly opposite such a view.

Torrance, Cheap and Costly Grace, and Legalism

Here I have said enough to be able to explain why those liberation theologians and those who think we can move from anthropology to theology (and Christology) get things wrong both in their theological anthropologies and in their view of Christian ethics. T. F. Torrance once wrote to me telling me that he liked the fact that I was an evangelical Catholic. That was a compliment because any Christian theology that is not properly grounded in the biblical witness will always confuse the Holy Spirit with the human spirit and begin thinking about God and human behavior from a center in human experience rather than from a center in God which God himself has provided in the incarnation and the outpouring of the Holy Spirit at Pentecost. Among contemporary theologians, we have seen that Thomas F. Torrance clearly exemplifies how and why a theology that allows Jesus Christ himself to be the *first* and *final* Word leads both to a proper understanding of God and to a proper understanding of our relations with God. For Torrance, the Nicene faith held prominence in the church, but not for any legalistic reasons. So, while the faith confessed at Nicaea meant genuine knowledge of the truth of the Gospel which was called for by the Gospel itself, it did not mean "laying down decrees … requiring compliance either like apostolic decisions or like imperial edicts."[64] Torrance always opposed a legalistic approach to theology precisely because for him an evangelical approach meant a declaration of the church's saving faith based upon the Scriptural witness and not an imposition of it.

To clarify this point, let us consider more closely Torrance's view of justification, which, as already noted, he explains with the categories of cheap and costly grace. For Torrance, "Grace is not cheap but costly, costly for God and costly for man, but costly because it is unconditionally free: such is the grace by which we are justified in Christ Jesus."[65] For Torrance this means that all people, whether they are good or bad or religious or secular, "come under the total judgment of grace" in which they are completely called into question and "saved by grace alone."[66] That means, however, that our righteousness before God is not grounded in us at all, and especially not in

---

[64] Torrance, *The Trinitarian Faith*, 18.
[65] Torrance, *God and Rationality*, 56.
[66] Ibid.

our religious attempts to reach God without actually relying on Christ, who is the grace of God enabling that possibility in first instance.

Torrance himself preferred to speak of our justification by grace even though Luther correctly referred to our justification by faith in the sense that "It is not faith that justifies us, but Christ in whom we have faith."[67] However, Torrance noted that in both Lutheran and Reformed theology, faith came to be seen as itself a justifying work and that undermined the evangelical meaning of grace and justification. This view made its presence felt in the notion of "*conditional grace*," which became entrenched throughout Protestantism. On the Roman Catholic side, the idea of infused grace was taught. Accordingly, while grace was supernaturally infused *ex opere operato*, we could then cooperate with grace and merit more grace. That idea "obscured the Gospel of free forgiveness of sins granted on the merits of Christ alone."[68] Once it was thought that grace was offered to people on condition of faith, the evangelical message of God's free grace effective in Christ for all was lost and new types of legalism followed. Legalizing follows by making faith into a saving work. This is another problematic view that Torrance opposed with his concepts of cheap and costly grace. Grace is cheap in that it is freely given to all. It is costly because it not only involved Christ's death on the cross but it undercuts even the slightest idea that we could rely on ourselves, that is upon our own faith, hope, or love. It always means taking up one's cross and following Christ.

As already noted, our faith should be grounded in Christ's own active obedience in our place. When it is, then the Gospel is proclaimed as an unconditionally free and effective act of God for us in Christ himself. This is why Torrance maintained that:

> we are yoked together with Jesus in his bearing of our burden and are made to share in the almighty strength and immutability of his vicarious faith and faithfulness on our behalf. Through his incarnational and atoning union with us our faith is implicated in his faith, and through that implication, far from being depersonalised or dehumanised, it is made to issue freely and spontaneously out of our own human life before God.[69]

---

[67] Ibid., 58.
[68] Ibid., 57.
[69] Torrance, *Mediation of Christ*, 84. Notice that here once again Torrance does not see Christ's mediation between us and God the Father as in any way displacing our free human actions. On the contrary, he frees us to spontaneously respond to God in faith.

For Torrance then, "Our faith is altogether grounded in him who is 'the author and finisher of our faith', on whom faith depends from start to finish."[70] Clearly, because Torrance's view of faith is altogether tied up with Christ as the *first* and *final* Word of God he maintained that faith itself "arises in cognitive commitment to the compelling claims of God in Jesus Christ and is linked to the absolute priority of God over all our conceiving and speaking of him."[71] And this means our faith is shaped by the "precise form God's truth has taken in the incarnation of his Word" while it is also open to ever more understanding because it is tied to the "inexhaustible nature of God."[72] This faith, which characterizes the faith of the Nicene Creed, is belief in the eternal Trinity and that means that since Jesus himself is the Way, the Truth, and the Life, belief in any other god is excluded. This, because the only way to the Father was provided by Jesus himself as the incarnate Word in his own personal being and actions. One other key point should be made here. Since faith really is cognitive union with the Word of God incarnate as Jesus Christ, faith cannot be understood "as some form of non-cognitive or non-conceptual relation to God," since in Nicene theology, faith involved "acts of recognition, apprehension and conception, of a very basic intuitive kind, in responsible assent of the mind to truth inherent in God's self-revelation to mankind."[73]

Torrance held that contemporary Protestantism obscured this proper view of faith with a subtle element of "co-redemption." This, of course, is not just a Protestant phenomenon because "co-redemption" is in evidence, as already noted above, whenever one supposes that people cannot be saved "*unless* they make the work of Christ real for themselves by their own personal decision" or that people will be saved "*only if* they repent and believe."[74] What exactly is the problem with these notions? The answer is simple, but with profound implications, as already mentioned above. This thinking makes Christ's unconditional love of us conditional upon what we do. But we are the sinners who can do nothing, even in our goodness, to merit God's love of us that was unconditionally actualized on the cross and disclosed in Christ's resurrection. The idea of conditional salvation in the form of "co-redemption" or any other form therefore throws the weight of salvation back on us sinners who, whether we realize it or not, cannot save

---

[70] Ibid.
[71] Torrance, *The Trinitarian Faith*, 22.
[72] Ibid.
[73] Ibid., 20.
[74] Torrance, *God and Rationality*, 58.

ourselves or anyone else by what we do. That is not good news, as Torrance notes, because if that were true then salvation would be completely lost.

Here Torrance's thinking is consistently christological in just the right sense because his thinking always begins and ends with Christ and never with who we are and what we do. So, he argues that the New Testament's message is that:

> God loves us, that He has given His only Son to be our Saviour, that Christ has died for us when we were yet sinners, and that His work is finished, and *therefore* it calls for repentance and the obedience of faith, but never does it say: This is what God in Christ has done for you and you can be saved on condition that you repent and believe.[75]

This is a pivotal point already noted above and it is missing in much contemporary liberation theology and in Christian ethics. Such theology, as we shall see, tends to begin with peoples' fight against oppression which may take many forms such as the feminist opposition to patriarchalism or the fight of the disenfranchised against those who try to dominate them or the fight against racism. Certainly, women are right to oppose all forms of patriarchalism and Christians should definitely oppose exploitation and domination of some by others and racism as well. However, to assume that theology begins there or with experiences of overcoming these forms of oppression is to embrace what Torrance is calling cheap grace and therefore to stand in opposition to the Gospel of God's unconditional love for humanity. The problem here is that if we begin with what we do and then search for a theology to undergird that activity, we have in fact shifted the weight *from* Christ as the objective source of truth and freedom to ourselves and what we do. The result Torrance astutely notes is that "what becomes finally important is 'my faith', 'my decision', 'my conversion', and not really Christ Himself."[76]

Such thinking, he believed, has led to the idea that we are saved by our "*existential decision*, in which we interpose ourselves, with our faith and our decision, in the place of Christ and His objective decision on our behalf."[77] This happens when our faith is detached from its objective basis in the historical Jesus as the incarnate Word and his actions for us during his ministry and on the cross, and as the risen, ascended, and coming Lord. Such an approach to the Gospel in fact cheapens God's costly grace by equating grace with our own faith, actions, and decisions. What is important

---

[75] Ibid.
[76] Ibid.
[77] Ibid.

then becomes our present *contextual* reaction to the biblical text instead of our obedience to Christ in faith. At this point Torrance explicitly opposes Bultmann's view of the Gospel by insisting that Christ himself has objectively accomplished our justification once and for all through his life of obedience that reached its high point on the cross. By contrast, Bultmann changes this objective meaning into what Christ means subjectively for each of us. Thus, for Bultmann we must cut through that objective act of God on the cross since for him Christ's death is no different than a fatal accident in the street.[78] And what Bultmann discovers is that we don't need that objective historical event of atonement to grasp the meaning of the Gospel. Thus, the meaning of the Gospel is the meaning I get from the Gospel story and apply to myself in my contemporary situation.

Torrance unequivocally rejects this approach not only because it obscures the truth of our justification by grace but because it leads to an incurable form of subjectivism and thus straight to a form of self-justification, which, as I have been arguing, is no justification at all. That is the cheap grace we find in those views which begin with us instead of with faith in Christ. One might say that the ultimate example of how really untheological such an approach is would be Bultmann's claim that if the resurrection was in any sense a historical event, then it was nothing other than the rise of faith on the part of the disciples after Jesus' death. That mistaken view overtly reduces the objective event in the life of Jesus, which is indeed the very revelation of God, into the subjective experiences of faith on the part of those who hear the story of Jesus and his death on the cross. This approach by Bultmann and by many today who might theoretically reject Bultmann's view of the resurrection but still employ his "existential" or "contextual" approach to theology detaches Christian faith from the actual historical events that give it its meaning. Such an approach, Torrance rightly asserts, "imports an astounding egocentricity in which the significance of the *pro me* is shifted entirely from its objective to its subjective pole. And so we see justification by grace being turned into its exact opposite."[79] This problem regularly arises in "contextual" theologies, which invariably are not grounded in Jesus of Nazareth but in the historical context in which he is confessed as the Lord and Savior.

Interestingly, Torrance turns to Barth to stress that we can never take our eyes off "the centrality and uniqueness of Jesus Christ and His objective vicarious work" because if we do, then "the Gospel disappears behind man's existentialized self-understanding, and even the Reality of God Himself is simply reduced to 'what He means for me' in the contingency and necessities

---

[78] Torrance, *Theology in Reconstruction*, 277.
[79] Torrance, *God and Rationality*, 60.

of my own life purpose."[80] He then mentions a book titled *The Elements of Moral Theology* saying that he was astonished that Jesus Christ hardly figured in that work at all. What took his place, Torrance noted, was "the ethical and indeed the casuistical concern." Even more interestingly, Torrance asserted that "what emerged was an ethic that was fundamentally continuous with our ordinary natural existence and was essentially formal."[81] Here we see once again how important it was to Torrance to realize that the kingdom of God made present in Jesus completely overturns any ethical (moralistic) or legalistic approach to the truth of the Gospel.

Love of God and Love of Neighbor

This issue merits some further explanation. One way to do this is to explain exactly why Torrance insisted that we could not love God *by* loving our neighbors. This, for Torrance, is a key example of self-justification. It indicates a failure to live by God's unconditional love which meets us in the incarnation as grace. For Torrance, "To love God through my love to my neighbour is to move toward God. It does not know a movement of God toward man."[82] Since, for Torrance, God's grace cannot be separated from the active mediation of Christ at any time or place because Christ is God's grace for us and in relation to us, it would be a mistake to think of grace as a "transferrable quality infused into and adhering to finite being, raising it to a different gradation where it can grasp God by a connatural proportion of being."[83] This is an extremely important point because many contemporary theologians begin their thinking about Christian ethics with the idea that it is only by loving our neighbors that we can love God. And it is often assumed that it is out of that love of neighbor that we really come to know and love God. Nothing could be further from the truth for two reasons.

First, in ourselves, as we have seen above, we are sinners who are incapable of living by grace. That is why Torrance rightly held that Bultmann's view of ethics was disastrous. This, because "it rejects the objective decision, the actualized election of grace, upon which the whole of the Christian Gospel rests."[84] Though Bultmann's ethics may be considered radical, in reality it is no more than a "prolongation of man's already existing experience and a

---

[80] Ibid.
[81] Ibid.
[82] Torrance, *The Doctrine of Jesus Christ*, 89.
[83] Torrance, *Theology in Reconstruction*, 114.
[84] Torrance, *God and Rationality*, 62.

reduction of it to what his previous knowledge includes" or might "acquire through philosophical analysis."[85] However, in this approach, we humanly remain prisoners of our own "existentialized self-understanding" because that approach firmly disallows Christ acting objectively as our "vicarious Saviour" who *alone* can enable us to escape our self-will, which as such is our free-will. What is implied here is that we do not just sin but that because of the adamic fall, we *are* sinners even in our free-will because sin is the failure to live as God's creatures by acknowledging our total dependence on God.

Sin means that we act as though we could live independently of God by relying on our own goodness in relation to the moral law. Since this really is the problem of sin, it means even in our acts of free-will, we are still "unable to extricate ourselves from the vicious moral circle created by our self-will, in order to be selflessly free for God or for our neighbor in love."[86] Torrance explicitly asserts that since God has interacted with us within history and within our "moral existence," he has "redeemed us from the curse of the law" which kept us in "bondage to ourselves." The result is that, because of Christ freeing us from sin as self-will, we can obey his will "without secondary motives" and we thus become "free from concern for ourselves and our own self-understanding" and also free to "love both God and our neighbour objectively for their own sakes."[87] The key point then is that justification by grace "involves us in a profound moral revolution and sets all our ethical relations on a new basis." That can only happen, Torrance insists, "when Christ occupies the objective centre of human existence and all things are mediated through His grace."[88]

Second, any attempt to come to true knowledge of God or what it means to be truly human which does not begin with the Incarnate Word has already bypassed God in an attempt to justify ourselves. In light of what Christ himself has revealed, it is just this behavior that uses the law to avoid actually relying on God's grace. Think, for example, of two key perspectives from Karl Rahner. First, he says that because "the experience of God and the experience of self are one" and that our self-experience and experience of our neighbor are also one, "these three experiences ultimately constitute a single reality with three aspects mutually conditioning one another."[89] The result is that "man discovers himself or loses himself in his neighbour; that

---

[85] Ibid.
[86] Ibid.
[87] Ibid., 62–3.
[88] Ibid., 63.
[89] Rahner, "Experience of Self and Experience of God," *Theological Investigations*, Vol. 13, *Theology, Anthropology, Christology*, trans. David Bourke (New York: Seabury Press, 1975), 128.

man has already discovered God, even though he may not have any explicit knowledge of it, if only he has truly reached out to his neighbour in an act of unconditional love, and in that neighbour reached out also to his own self."[90] This works for Rahner because he believes that "the personal history of the experience of self is in its total extent the history of the ultimate experience of God itself also."[91]

Notice here that Rahner's view contrasts sharply with Torrance's idea that it is only through conceptual union with Christ and not with some nonconceptual view of God that we seemingly discover by loving our neighbors that we know the true God. For Torrance, grace and our experience of grace in no sense mutually condition each other. That is why, as we have seen, Torrance rejects the idea that we can love God *by* loving our neighbor. Furthermore, in contrast to Torrance, Rahner here places the work of knowing God on us and our love of neighbor instead of recognizing that the enabling condition for true love of neighbor is the love of God revealed and active in Christ alone as described in detail above. Since Christ is God's grace enabling our knowledge of God the Father, it is impossible to claim that knowledge of self and knowledge of God mutually condition each other when grace is not detached from the Giver of grace. Second, Rahner explicitly concludes that "love of God and love of neighbor stand in a relationship of mutual conditioning. Love of neighbor is not only a love that is demanded by the love of God, an achievement flowing from it; *it is also in a certain sense its antecedent condition.*"[92]

It goes without saying that Torrance would flatly reject any such notion of mutual conditioning between us and God because that view obviates the unconditional freedom of God's love in himself and for us. In Torrance's view, such a mutually conditioning view does not know of the incarnation and especially of the fact that incarnation was intrinsically related to atonement in that its purpose was to forgive sin and enable fellowship with God by overcoming our self-will, thus freeing us to love God and on that basis to be free to love our neighbors. Additionally, it is just because Rahner thinks he can know God and the proper meaning of anthropology through loving our neighbors that he grounds theology in us instead of in Christ alone. The result is that his approach offers a perfect example of what goes wrong in

---

[90] Ibid., 128–9.
[91] Ibid., 129.
[92] Karl Rahner, *The Love of Jesus and the Love of Neighbor*, trans. Robert Barr (New York: Crossroad, 1983), 71, emphasis mine. For a detailed development of these ideas, see my "Love of God and Love of Neighbor in the Theology of Karl Rahner and Karl Barth," *Modern Theology* 20 (4) (October 2004), 567–98 and Molnar, *Freedom, Necessity, and the Knowledge of God*, 141–8.

theology when Jesus himself is not allowed to be the *first* and *final* Word in theology. I have documented Rahner's position on this, illustrating that he himself says he cannot begin with Christ alone in considering theological anthropology, because he thinks that is too simple a solution.[93] Instead, he begins by reflecting on our human experiences of self-transcendence which, he assumes, include some sort of nonconceptual knowledge of God as the term of our experiences of self-transcendence.[94] In that way he ignores the real problem of sin as self-will as well as its objective solution in God's electing grace which meets us in the incarnate Word.

It is just because Torrance allows Jesus himself to be the *first* and *final* Word in his theology that he also insists that Christian ethics could not find its criteria in any kind of moral responsibility as dictated by the moral law or by any concept of human goodness. Torrance maintained that "from the point of view of ethics we see that human moral awareness tends to sever its connection with God … to establish itself on an autonomous or semi-autonomous basis."[95] When that happens, people then "relate themselves to God, consciously or subconsciously through duty to their neighbour— that is, they relate themselves to God indirectly through the medium of the universal [the idea of the moral law] … and do not relate themselves to God in particular."[96] This, then, is a form of self-justification.

However, if one considers ethics in a strictly theological perspective and thus within faith, then one will see that this approach amounts to a sinful attempt to seize "the ethical imperative of God, making it an independent authority which is identified with human higher nature, so escaping God and deifying humanity—'you will be like God.'"[97] It is just this sinful human behavior that uses the law of God by relying on the moral law or common law in a way that yields obedience to the law without actually committing oneself to responsible action under God. This, Torrance thinks, is what Jesus set us free from by fulfilling the law for us and justifying us by setting us "free not only from the bondage of external law but from [our] own self-imprisonment in the condemnation of [our] own conscience … he made our judgement of ourselves acquiesce in God's complete judgement."[98] Thus, the "act of grace

---

[93] See Molnar, *Divine Freedom and the Doctrine of the Immanent Trinity*, Chapters Two and Five.
[94] For a full discussion of how Torrance's view of knowledge of God relates to Rahner's nonconceptual understanding of God, see Molnar, *Freedom, Necessity, and the Knowledge of God*, Chapter Four.
[95] Torrance, *Atonement*, 112.
[96] Ibid.
[97] Ibid., 112–13.
[98] Ibid., 116.

in justification which breaks through to us apart from law is spoken of as 'revelation.'"[99] This righteousness as the act of God in Christ, which forgives and justifies us, "could not be inferred logically from the abstract order of law or ethics. From that point of view forgiveness is impossible—it is legally speaking immoral or amoral. And if it is a fact, it is a stupendous miracle."[100]

This is exactly why Torrance spoke of a "'teleological suspension' of ethics. Because it entails this suspension, justification or forgiveness is not something that is demonstrable from any ground in the moral order as such. It only can be acknowledged and believed as a real event that has in the amazing grace of God actually overtaken us."[101] For Torrance, justification by grace means that just because Christ has put us "completely in the right or the truth with God, Christ calls us completely into question."[102] That is the reason why "the way in which he embodied the love of God among men or expounded to them what the Kingdom of God was like so often rebuffed them."[103] He was indeed offensive to them in what he revealed. And what he revealed was "the vast chasm between the heart of man and the Will of God" since this "provoked the bitter hostility of man to God and brought Jesus to the Cross."[104] It is precisely in his suffering that God himself launched his "supreme attack upon man's self-centredness, self-concern, self-security, self-seeking and self-will."[105]

Through all this Jesus remained "the absolute grace of God that will only be grace and nothing but grace" as was disclosed when he said, "Father, forgive them, for they know not what they do."[106] This was God's unconditional love and complete forgiveness by which all are accepted on "the ground of the divine grace."[107] In this way, judgment and grace are connected because we are called into question as those who try to establish ourselves in relation to God by relying somehow on ourselves. But in Christ we are set upon the proper foundation of grace by Christ himself. That is why Torrance maintains that this dialectic of judgment and forgiveness is most evident in our "moral life" because in light of this grace we are all exposed as needy sinners so that we cannot be saved by our works in relation to the moral law or even the Ten Commandments, but only by a faith which totally relies on what Christ

[99] Ibid., 118.
[100] Ibid.
[101] Ibid.
[102] Torrance, *God and Rationality*, 65.
[103] Ibid.
[104] Ibid., 66.
[105] Ibid.
[106] Ibid.
[107] Ibid.

himself has done for us. This is why St. Paul could say that God alone is true while every one of us is a liar (Rom. 3:4).

These are crucial points that separate Torrance's thinking from all those contemporary attempts to reach a proper understanding of the triune God and of human freedom by starting with human acts of fighting oppression or human acts of kindness. Those are important, of course. But the moment it is thought that the truth of our knowledge of God and our knowledge of responsibility as Christians is to be sought in our human acts of opposing oppression or of being kind, then all is lost. Why? Because, as I have been arguing, what is disclosed by the cross of Christ is that, even in our goodness, we are at enmity with God in our self-will and self-reliance and that we need God's grace even to become aware of this in the first place. Moreover, we are completely unable to work our way up to a knowledge of this truth apart from revelation, that is, apart from the reconciliation that has taken place for us in Christ. In this way, Torrance held that "divine revelation conflicts sharply with the structure of our natural reason."[108] This is what rules out the idea espoused by Rahner and many of his followers that natural theology and revealed theology mutually condition each other.[109] Confronted with God in Christ, Torrance thinks that the shape and structure of our minds begin to change. This will involve "a radical repentant rethinking of everything before the face of Jesus Christ" with the result that we would then take up our cross and follow him. He insists that "you cannot separate evangelical theology from that profound experience of the radical changing and transforming of your mind that comes through dying and rising with Christ."[110]

For Torrance, it is specifically in our encounter with Jesus Christ that there takes place a "soteriological suspension of ethics,"[111] which enables us to grasp the fact that our justification is a miraculous action of God who makes us righteous by forgiving our sins. But that means that we cannot understand ethics in a properly Christian sense from within the moral law as it now stands or our justification as a legal transaction because, as already noted, from the point of view of morality and law, "forgiveness is impossible—it is legally speaking immoral or amoral."[112] Thus, forgiveness as justification cannot

---

[108] Torrance, *Atonement*, 443.

[109] Rahner, *Theological Investigations*, Vol. 1, trans. Cornelius Ernst, O. P. (Baltimore: Helicon Press, 1965), 98.

[110] Torrance, *Atonement*, 443.

[111] Torrance, "The Atonement: The Singularity of Christ and the Finality of the Cross: The Atonement and the Moral Order," *Universalism and the Doctrine of Hell: Papers Presented at the Fourth Edinburgh Conference in Christian Dogmatics, 1991*, ed. Nigel M. de S. Cameron (Carlisle, UK: Paternoster Press; Grand Rapids, MI: Baker Book House, 1992), 252.

[112] Torrance, *Atonement*, 118.

be understood "from any ground in the moral order as such" but "only can be acknowledged and believed as a real event that has in the amazing grace of God actually overtaken us. It is a *fait accompli*."[113] The law is not thereby put aside since God's judgment is not put aside. Rather, this means that Christ brought about our regeneration from within his own personal activity from the divine and the human side, and in that way, he embodied "an altogether new way of life for us resulting from our being translated out of the bondage of law into the freedom of the children of God."[114]

Here we see the fruits of Torrance's insistence that we cannot love God *by* loving our neighbor. He claims that God's will is not disclosed to us in terms of abstract ethics or law or even of goodness but only in the free unconditional love of God manifested in Christ himself. That is the love that brings about peace between us and God and thus between us and our neighbors. Torrance claims that as sinners we use the law to "escape from God's judgement, in order to escape from God."[115] This is what he finds so objectionable in Bultmann's thinking. He says Bultmann insisted that Jesus thought out radically and to the end the requirement on us within the relationship between what is and what ought to be. Thus, for him, everything was dependent upon "man's own individual decision." What he left out was the fact that:

> Jesus Christ has to come to lift man out of that predicament in which even when he has done all that it is his duty to do he is still an unprofitable servant, for he can never overtake the ethical "ought". But actually the Gospel is the antithesis of this, for it announces that in Jesus Christ God has already taken a decision about our existence and destiny in which He has set us upon the ground of His pure grace where we are really free for spontaneous ethical decisions toward God and toward men.[116]

Notice once again that, for Torrance, Jesus' vicarious human action as our representative and substitute does not overwhelm or make unimportant our human action because it is the enabling power of that free action. However, this takes salvation completely out of our hands because it is not the moral law or common law or the Ten Commandments which save us. And it is not our obedience to these which saves us either. That is something only God could do, and he did it apart from the law and in fulfilment of its proper meaning. We have seen that Torrance was quite critical of Bultmann's

---

[113] Ibid.
[114] Torrance, "The Atonement: The Singularity of Christ," 253.
[115] Torrance, *Atonement*, 112.
[116] Torrance, *God and Rationality*, 62.

existentializing the Gospel, and for good reason. Here, we may ask exactly what it means to live by grace. Torrance's answer is clear: we are summoned to "live out of God and not out of ourselves, in which everything in religion is justified by reference to Jesus Christ because it can have no justification by reference to itself."[117]

Torrance and Liberation Theology or Theologies of Liberation

Now, let me briefly contrast Torrance's view of faith as knowledge of the truth and justification as God's action in Christ freeing us for spontaneous action in loving God and on that basis loving our neighbors with the views offered by some contemporary theologians who embrace the method of contemporary liberation theology or theologies of liberation. That method, as already mentioned, invariably grounds knowledge of God and of human freedom in the human struggles against oppression and racism and other "isms" that threaten our humanity and the ideology that springs from that struggle. I have already noted the difference between a view of God grounded in our own experiences of depth and the knowledge of God that comes from an encounter with Jesus himself, the crucified and risen Lord. In the former approach, the word "God" is defined from and by us and always leads to some form of idolatry, legalism, and self-justification. That is the approach based on a theology that wittingly or unwittingly is in search of *cheap grace*. A theology grounded in Christ, however, is one in which, as Torrance repeatedly insists, the Gospel calls us to "repent and believe, to take up the cross and follow Christ."[118]

What precisely does that mean in this context? It means that we really must accept Christ as our Lord and Savior specifically and thus conceptually because no one other than Jesus himself could substitute himself for us before God. That has some real meaning. Because he has actually accomplished our reconciliation with God in his own personal life of vicarious obedience for us by virtue of the hypostatic union of his humanity with his being as the Son of God, his action for us is total and not in any sense partial. If we do not accept that fact, then Torrance says, we "empty it of saving significance."[119] Torrance held that it was through the blood of Christ that Jews and Gentiles

---

[117] Ibid., 70.
[118] Torrance, *The Mediation of Christ*, 84.
[119] Ibid.

were united in one body.[120] He also believed that since God the Father, the God of Abraham, Isaac, and Jacob, was personally and actively involved and present in Christ's crucifixion, redeeming us from our lost condition under sin, "the cross was a window into the very heart of God, for in and behind the cross, it was God the Father himself who paid the cost of our salvation."[121] Through Christ's blood then, as he acted in "atoning sacrifice for our sin," Torrance maintains that "the innermost nature of God the Father as holy compassionate love has been revealed to us."[122] Furthermore, Torrance argues that it is the Holy Spirit who pours out this very love into our hearts because the cross and Pentecost belong together. This leads him to offer one of his favorite passages from Calvin, namely, that "God does not love us … because he has reconciled us to himself; it is because he loved us that he has reconciled us to himself."[123]

To clarify his point further, Torrance looks at Jesus' incarnate life and activity in light of the parable of the prodigal son and says his life is "atoning activity from beginning to end." He asserts that Jesus made himself one with us in our "estranged humanity when it was running away into the far country, farther and farther away from the Father, but through his union with it he changed it in himself, reversed its direction and converted it back in obedience and faith and love to God the Father."[124] Jesus, he says, was "baptised 'into repentance' … for as the Lamb of God come to bear our sins he fulfilled that mission not in some merely superficially forensic way, though of course profound forensic elements were involved, but in a way in which he bore our sin and guilt upon his very soul which he made an offering for sin."[125] Torrance goes on to say that Christ's baptism was one of "vicarious repentance for us which he brought to its completion on the Cross where he was stricken and smitten of God for our sakes, by whose stripes we are healed."[126] Hence, Christ "laid hold of us even in the depths of our human soul and mind where we are alienated from God and are at enmity with him, and altered them from within and from below in radical and complete *metanoia*, a repentant restructuring of our carnal mind, as St Paul called it, and a converting of it into a spiritual mind."[127]

---

[120] Ibid., 104–5.
[121] Ibid., 109.
[122] Ibid.
[123] Ibid., 110.
[124] Ibid., 84.
[125] Ibid., 84–5.
[126] Ibid., 85.
[127] Ibid.

Thus, Torrance persuasively argues that we are completely unable to extricate ourselves from the sin which places us at enmity with God because he says "our free-will is our self-will" which, as we have seen, is what puts us at enmity with God and each other to begin with. Once again, he notes that sin "is so ingrained" in our minds that we are incapable of genuinely repenting because to do so would mean we could not rely even on our own repentance before God. In that regard, Christ "laid hold of us even there in our sinful repentance and turned everything round through his holy vicarious repentance, when he bore not just upon his body but upon his human mind and soul the righteous judgments of God and resurrected our human nature in the integrity of his body, mind and soul from the grave."[128] Our regeneration then is completely tied to the fact that Christ repented once for all in our place and that there will be a final transformation when Christ comes again to make all things new. But that means that our conversion, regeneration, or new birth have already occurred in Jesus himself for us. So, conversion means "our sharing in the conversion or regeneration of our humanity brought about by Jesus in and through himself for our sake … we must speak of Jesus Christ as constituting in himself the very substance of our conversion."[129] He is the one and the only one who could take our place before God because he was God himself acting *as* man for us. He is the "substance of our conversion" so that without him all "so-called repentance and conversion are empty." Thus, a truly evangelical view of conversion is one in which we turn completely away from ourselves and toward Christ so that we need to be converted "from our in-turned notions of conversion to one which is grounded and sustained in Christ Jesus himself."[130]

How different this view of conversion is from the view espoused within a liberationist perspective. Elizabeth Johnson persistently argues that exclusively referring to God as Father subordinates women to men. While she notes that God is Spirit and beyond identification with male or female sex, her own thinking is in conflict with this. She claims that "the daily language of preaching, worship, catechesis, and instruction conveys a different message: God is male, or at least more like a man than a woman, or at least more fittingly addressed as male than as female."[131] However, if God is Spirit, then there is no gender at all in God. So, her claim that the language of preaching, worship, catechesis, and instruction which refer to God as Father

---

[128] Ibid.
[129] Ibid., 86.
[130] Ibid.
[131] Elizabeth A. Johnson, *She Who Is: The Mystery of God in Feminist Theological Discourse* (New York: Crossroad, 1992; reissued in 2002 as a tenth anniversary edition and in 2017 as a twenty-fifth anniversary edition), 5.

and Son conveys the message that God is male is clearly mistaken. If one is referring to the Father through the revelation of his Son, then the message is not and could never be that God is male. That message would confuse divine and human being by projecting gender in some way into God who transcends gender!

The actual message is, or should be, that there is an exclusive and unique eternal relation of being between the Father and Son (Mt. 11:27) and that our knowledge of God as Spirit, which itself is enabled by the Holy Spirit who is one in being with the Father and Son, comes *to* us as a revelation through our conceptual union with Jesus himself. It does not come *from* us *at all* but from *God alone*. Because all that Jesus does "in his human life is identical with the act of God himself," we can say that "nothing is done in his human life except what issues out of the love of the Father for the Son and the Son for the Father."[132] The result is that behind his "life in the flesh" we can say that there "stands the closed circle of the intimate and private relation of loving and knowing, of speaking and doing, that exists between the Son and the Father."[133] Torrance himself cites Mt. 11:27 and concludes that,

> the relation between the Father and the Son and the Son and the Father is a closed relation, but entry into it is given through the incarnation of the Son, for in the perfect human life of Jesus the love and truth of God are addressed to man in the concrete form of a historical relationship of man to fellow man, of this man to others.[134]

In his human life, we are directly confronted with God acting as our savior in revelation and reconciliation.

So, Johnson's mistake, and it is not a minor one, is that she thinks knowledge of the triune God comes *from* us. Following the thought of Gordon Kaufman and Sallie McFague, she claims that the symbol God functions, and *we* must make it function to include women since any continued traditional and exclusive reference to God as Father and Son will not function according to her liberationist goal of overcoming male attempts to subordinate women to men. This, of course, is a laudable goal, but the point she misses is that this can be achieved only through faith in Christ who has already liberated us from the sin which leads to patriarchalism in the first place. For Johnson, within her liberationist perspective, it is out of women's fight against oppression that "women are engaged in creative

---

[132] Torrance, *Incarnation*, 127.
[133] Ibid.
[134] Ibid., 128.

'naming toward God,' as Mary Daly so carefully calls it, from the matrix of their own experience."[135] She says, "feminist reflection is ... not alone in its use of human experience as a resource for doing theology. What is distinctive, however, is its specific identification of the lived experience of women ... as an essential element in the theological task."[136] For Johnson then, naming God is grounded in women's emerging identity and not exclusively in the revelation of God as it comes to us through his Word and Spirit. Johnson believes that the conflict that arises over naming God "He" or "She" indicates "that, however subliminally, maleness *is* intended when we say God."[137] This thinking leads her into direct conflict with the God confessed in the Nicene Creed as understood by Barth and Torrance. For Barth,

> we cannot say anything higher or better of the "inwardness of God" [the immanent Trinity] than that God is Father, Son and Holy Spirit, and therefore that He is love in Himself without and before loving us, and without being forced to love us. And we can say this only in the light of the "outwardness" of God to us [the economic Trinity], the occurrence of His revelation.[138]

In a similar vein, Torrance consistently argued that "there is no possibility of stripping God of his Fatherhood or of his Sonship, for there is no God but he who has made himself known to us as the Father and the Son."[139] Arguing on the basis of revelation as that meets us in Jesus Christ, Torrance thus refused to read back into God any kind of supposed knowledge grounded in our experiences of fatherhood or sonship. So, he insists, we must exercise "critical discernment of what we may read back from the incarnation into God and what we may not read back into him."[140] To make his point, Torrance notes that it is precisely "the kind of sonship we know on earth, which is that of a son who is the son and grandson of other sons and who is himself the father of a son and the grandfather of another," that we must not "read back into God."[141] And the reason for this is that "we cannot project the creaturely relations inherent in human sonship into the Creator. Nor, of course, can we

---

[135] Johnson, *She Who Is*, 5.
[136] Ibid., 61.
[137] Elizabeth A. Johnson, *Quest for the Living God: Mapping Frontiers in the Theology of God* (New York: Continuum, 2008), 98.
[138] Barth, CD I/2, 377.
[139] Torrance, "The Christian Apprehension of God the Father," 136.
[140] Ibid., 137.
[141] Ibid.

read gender back into God for gender belongs to creatures only."[142] Moreover, "our knowing God is grounded in his knowing of us, and our understanding of the Fatherhood of God, who is who he is as Father of the Son, is of the one Fatherhood from which all other fatherhood is named."[143] Torrance says this means that when we refer to God as Father, "we are not using the term 'Father' in a transferred, improper, or inadequate sense; we are using it in its completely proper sense, which is determined by the intrinsic Fatherhood of God himself. God alone is truly and ultimately Father—all other fatherhood is a reflection of his."[144] Thus, Torrance insists that "when we hear that 'God *is* Father,' the 'is' is unlike any other 'is,' for it is defined solely by the revealed nature of God ... God is *Father* in an utterly singular and normative way, and it is only on that basis that we may say that the Father of our Lord Jesus Christ is God."[145] This kind of thinking is in harmony with the view of Hilary, who said, "you hear the name *Son*; believe that He is the Son. You hear the name *Father*; fix it in your mind that He is the Father. Why surround these names with doubt and ill will and hostility? ... Father and Son are spoken of; doubt not that the words mean what they say."[146]

Over against the thinking of Elizabeth Johnson, if one is thinking evangelically, on the basis of the Gospel as depicted above, then since we know God is Spirit and that there really is no gender in God, the moment maleness enters the picture, we know that we are not yet or no longer thinking about the God of the Nicene faith. We know that our own images have been read back from us into God in antithesis to what God himself has revealed. Important in Johnson's thinking here is the fact that a key experience of women for her is the experience of conversion. She describes this as women's struggle against sexism which affirms their own human worth. It is foundational, she says, as "a turning around of heart and mind that sets life in a new direction."[147] Accordingly, she thinks this is a "new experience of God" from which new understanding arises from women's experiences of liberation to know "what is fitting for the mystery of God to be and to do."[148] Further, she thinks that in "classical theology," conversion has been defined from the perspective of the

---

[142] Ibid.
[143] Ibid.
[144] Ibid.
[145] Ibid., 138.
[146] St. Hilary of Poitiers, *On the Trinity*, Book III, 22, in *A Select Library of Nicene and Post-Nicene Fathers of the Christian Church Second Series, Vol. IX*, trans. Philip Schaff and Henry Wace (Grand Rapids, MI: Eerdmans), 68.
[147] Johnson, *She Who Is*, 62.
[148] Ibid.

ruling male as "pride or self-assertion" so that such pride must be divested "in order to be filled with divine grace."[149] She thus argues that it is:

> Through women's encounter with the holy mystery of their own selves as blessed comes commensurate language about holy mystery in female metaphor and symbol, gracefully, powerfully, necessarily ... conversion experienced not as giving up oneself but as tapping into the power of oneself simultaneously releases understanding of divine power not as dominating power-over but as the passionate ability to empower oneself and others ... in the ontological naming and affirming of ourselves we are engaged in a dynamic reaching out to the mystery of God.[150]

This approach is so manifestly opposed to any reasonable view of conversion evangelically understood that it offers an unmistakable example of a self-grounded theology that not only ignores the problem of sin but argues for a view of salvation or freedom which is directly opposed to one that is Christ-centered, as depicted above.

First, knowledge of the triune God does not in fact come from knowledge of ourselves, no matter how deep that may be. It comes from the Father through the Son in an encounter with the historical Jesus as attested in Scripture and through the power of the Holy Spirit and thus through faith and by grace alone. And, as noted above, it comes from a conceptual and ontological union with the crucified and risen Lord himself. Therefore, it does not come from "the ontological naming and affirming of ourselves," as Johnson claims. And because our knowledge of God comes from Christ himself, it never really came from the perspective of the ruling male as Johnson thinks, but from God's own self-revelation, his own naming himself to us in his incarnate Son and through the power of the Holy Spirit. Moreover, in her view of "classical theology" she certainly misses Torrance's stress on the unconditional nature of God's forgiving grace by claiming that we must divest ourselves of pride in order to receive grace. We do not have the power to do that because that can only occur through our actual union with Christ who has already accomplished that for us in his vicarious life of perfect obedience. So, Torrance's point is that we do not have to do anything to receive grace because that is freely given in Christ for all. Additionally, "pride or self-assertion" affects men and women and not just ruling males because pride in relation to God refers to our unwillingness to live by grace

---

[149] Ibid., 64.
[150] Ibid., 66–7.

alone. Pride refers to the human attempt to live from our own resources instead of from Christ alone.

Part of the difficulty in Johnson's thought stems from her following Rahner's method in several important ways. So, she argues that "the experience of oneself has a unique importance" as a historical mediation of an encounter with God.[151] This very assertion undercuts Torrance's consistent argument presented above that knowledge of God does not come from our experience of ourselves or any ordinary human experience but from our conceptual union with Christ in faith such that he reveals the love of God the Father to us in that encounter with him. Second, she follows Rahner to argue that since we are "spirit in the world," we humans "are dynamically oriented toward fathomless mystery as the very condition for the possibility of acting in characteristic human ways."[152] However, this also stands in sharp contrast to the knowledge of God that comes to us from the Father, through the incarnate Son, as depicted by Torrance because he insists that we do not know the eternal Father, Son, and Holy Spirit simply by conceptualizing God as "fathomless mystery." For Torrance, that is plainly mythology because such vague knowledge is the result of mythological projection from us back into God since it is not grounded in revelation, that is, in God's knowing us.

Third, language about the Christian God is not simply produced metaphorically and symbolically based on our experiences of who or what we think God is as a fathomless mystery or what Rahner calls holy mystery. Fourth, when compared to the evangelical view of conversion offered by Torrance, one can see with unmistakable clarity the difference between a Christ-centered view of the matter and one that is entirely untouched by such a view. For Johnson, conversion is totally understood based on women's experiences of themselves which are presumed to be inherently in touch with God as holy mystery. Jesus Christ is not even mentioned. For Torrance, conversion is understood as God's amazing grace actualized in Christ himself by his actively converting us back to God the Father through is vicarious life of perfect obedience for our benefit. So, our conversion is not located in any sort of reliance upon what we do or experience, but rather in our participation in the freedom for the triune God achieved through conceptual and ontological union with Christ in faith. In other words, we turn away from ourselves and, thus away from her idea taken from Rahner, that the experience of God is primordially mediated "through the changing history of oneself" so that she thinks God cannot be experienced directly but "as the ultimate depth and radical essence of every personal experience such as

[151] Ibid., 65.
[152] Ibid.

love, fidelity, loneliness and death."[153] For Johnson, that means that it is out of this nonverbal experience of mystery that we know God's mystery. Moreover, following Rahner, she claims that "The personal history of the experience of the self is in its total extent the history of the ultimate experience of God also."[154] Given Torrance's view presented above, one can easily see that this equation of self-experience with knowledge of God entirely misses the fact that true knowledge of God comes from our face to face encounter with Jesus himself as he enables us to know God as our Father. And that occurs in the power of the Holy Spirit as knowledge that comes exclusively from God and through *conceptual* union with Christ.

Furthermore, as we saw above, for Torrance, conversion involves regeneration because we are judged by God's forgiving grace in Christ and so conversion he says is "wholly bound up with Jesus Christ himself" since it is "our new birth, our regeneration, our conversion" which have all already taken place in him for us. The result is that in a properly theological theology that begins and ends with Christ himself, conversion can only refer to "our sharing in the conversion or regeneration of our humanity brought about by Jesus in and through himself for our sake. In a profound and proper sense, therefore, we must speak of Jesus Christ as constituting in himself the very substance of our conversion."[155] So, an evangelical view of conversion is one that sees our "new birth" to knowledge of the true God and of God's purposes for humanity "as a turning away from ourselves to Christ" because it is "conversion from our in-turned notions of conversion to one which is grounded and sustained in Christ Jesus himself."[156] But this means that we may be dynamically oriented to some sort of vague fathomless mystery as we think about ourselves and God in a general way. But, as we are face to face with Christ, we are disclosed as sinners who, in ourselves, are opposed to the true God and offended at his actual disclosure to us in Jesus Christ. We are also disclosed as those who need to repent even of our repentance to know God truly as the triune God who loves in freedom through *conceptual* union with Christ in faith. So, it is not enough to speak, with Johnson, about a supposed "prethematic" experience of God in which we are supposedly grasped "by the holy mystery of God as the very context of our own self-presence" such that "the silent, nonverbal encounter with infinite mystery constitutes the enabling condition of any experience of self at all."[157]

---

[153] Ibid.
[154] Ibid., 66.
[155] Torrance, *The Mediation of Christ*, 85–6.
[156] Ibid., 86.
[157] Johnson, *She Who Is*, 65.

It turns out that the liberationist view of conversion offered by Johnson and many who follow her views is in direct conflict with a properly Christian view of the matter not only because, in her view, Jesus is decidedly absent. It is so also because it is self-grounded with the assumption that we really can know the true God without experiencing the reconciliation of our minds that took place on the cross for us in Christ himself. Thus, her view ignores the real problem of sin and the proper meaning of salvation as liberation from our own self-grounded attempts to know God and fight against the inequality of women and men. The fact is that in Christ we have been liberated from the sin that leads to patriarchalism. And we know about that liberation because it has taken place as an act of God for us in Jesus' own life, ministry, death, and resurrection. Thus, we know that our actual liberation is not and can never be an achievement of ours. It is ours. But it is ours as it is realized for us in him and through our conceptual and ontological union with Christ in faith. To live that freedom is to live by grace alone through faith in Christ. From this it follows that since this approach of liberation theology is self-grounded, it is, as such, a denial of God's grace and it fails to liberate us from captivity to our sinful selves so that it is neither liberating nor theological.

Without experiencing the reconciling grace of God through the Holy Spirit, we will always assume that knowledge of God comes *from* ourselves and the naming of God from ourselves in our struggles for liberation. All of that is fundamentally at odds with the fact that true liberation is the liberation *from* our self-will, which is our free-will. That true liberation is already ours in Christ, but only in Christ and thus it cannot be found by exploring any or all our experiences, no matter how important or deep they may be in themselves. It is liberation from ourselves since in ourselves we are sinners at enmity with God and each other. Importantly, as noted above, when Torrance equates sin with our self-will, what he means is that all our human attempts to live apart from faith in Christ are always attempts to live autonomously and independently of God. That is the impossibility created by sin—God will not let us go, even in our self-will, which places us in conflict with the fact that we are created to be in relationship with God by depending upon him.

Thus, we cannot heal those who sinfully act to subordinate women to men by changing the name of God as Johnson supposes since the power of naming God does not come from us in the first place. And in the second place, we do not have the power to overcome the sin of patriarchalism, no matter how we reconstruct our metaphors and symbols. That power comes exclusively from the power of grace in and through which the reconciliation of the world has already taken place in the history of Jesus Christ for all people. So, there simply can be no true naming of God the Father, Son, and

Holy Spirit by tapping into the power of ourselves as Johnson assumed. That power is always the power of sinners who, in pride and self-will, are unable and unwilling to live by grace alone in its identity with Jesus Christ, who, as the risen, ascended, and advent Lord, still is the only one who can enable knowledge of the Christian God here and now through the power of the Spirit and thus in faith as tied to Jesus himself. It is then a matter of accepting the costly grace of God rather than cheapening it by detaching it from the need to take up our cross and follow Christ alone.

Consider for a moment more how far away Johnson's thinking about the Christian God is from the God of the Nicene Confession. She claims that "seeking the female face of God has profound significance. By relativizing masculine imagery it lassoes the idol off its pedestal, breaking the stranglehold of patriarchal discourse and its deleterious effects. God is *not literally* a father or a king or a lord but something ever so much greater."[158] She goes on to say that male metaphors may also be used. But in both instances her view is distorted theologically because she is reading back those images from us into God. Hence, she then claims that,

> naming toward God with female metaphors releases divine mystery from its age-old patriarchal cage so that God can be truly God— incomprehensible source, sustaining power, and goal of the world, holy Wisdom, indwelling Spirit, the ground of being, the beyond in our midst, the absolute future, being itself, mother, matrix, lover, friend, infinite love, the holy mystery that surrounds and supports the world.[159]

Notice here that every possible concept of God is offered except for the name into which Christians are actually baptized, that is, the name of the Father, the Son, and the Holy Spirit. The reason for this is simple. Her thinking most certainly is not at all grounded in revelation but in the experience of women as she plainly and frequently insists. The final proof of this can be seen with her "pneumatological inflection," which in fact has nothing whatever to do with the Holy Spirit, who is *homoousios* with the Son and can only be known through the Son as the Son unites us to his Father. Instead of claiming with Barth and Torrance that Jesus himself as the incarnate Word gives us true and certain (apodictically certain) knowledge

---

[158] Johnson, *Quest of the Living God*, 99, emphasis mine. It might also be mentioned here that her statement that God is not literally a father is in direct conflict with a properly functioning doctrine of the Trinity which rests upon the fact that God is Father in an utterly unique sense as discussed above in relation to the views of Barth and Torrance.

[159] Ibid.

of God as Father, Son, and Holy Spirit, she claims that Jesus should be understood as a "filter through whom God is made known."[160] From that she reaches the astonishing conclusion that we never have "one straight-as-an-arrow name" for God precisely because she honestly believes we have no literal knowledge of God.[161]

Before finishing this discussion of Johnson's views, it should be noted that Johnson's approach has been naively and foolishly defended in a recent discussion that claims that when I originally held that Johnson's "creative 'naming toward God' ... from the matrix of [women's] experience" amounted to an attempt "to exchange the revelation of God for the experience of women and thus collapse theology into anthropology," then "a grievous closure of thought" took place.[162] Why? Because I supposedly made too hasty an appeal to Barth's early work. This assertion is nonsensical in light of the fact that both the early and later Barth insisted that knowledge of God only comes from God and not at all from us. Even a cursory reading of my book in which those remarks were made would have disclosed that Barth's view of our knowledge of God was structured by his view of justification by faith and by grace in a manner similar to the way Torrance considered such knowledge. That meant that our apodictically certain knowledge of God came only from and through *conceptual* union with Christ through the Spirit, as noted above.[163] This imprudent defense of Johnson claims that while Johnson's early chapters in *She Who Is* "do reckon often with women's experience, later chapters make it clear that what authorizes this focus—or better, what serves as the prior condition of the experiences that Johnson considers—is nothing other than God's activity, routed through (and appropriable to) the unified efforts of the God's three persons: Spirit-Sophia, Christ-Sophia, and Mother-Sophia."[164] Based on this we are told that she actually grounds her perspective in God's revelation.

When one compares the "persons" described here to the actual persons of the Trinity recognized on the basis of the revelation of God attested in the

---

[160] Ibid., 217.

[161] Ibid., 21.

[162] Paul Dafydd Jones, "Liberation Theology and Karl Barth in the Shadow of the Alt-Right," in *Karl Barth and Liberation Theology*, ed. Kaitlyn Dugan and Paul Dafydd Jones (London: T&T Clark, 2023), 225. He was referring to my *Divine Freedom and the Doctrine of the Immanent Trinity: In Dialogue with Karl Barth and Contemporary Theology* (London: T&T Clark, 2002), 10. Unfortunately, he failed to notice or just failed to consider the careful arguments offered in that first chapter demonstrating how Johnson's indebtedness of Gordon Kaufman, Sallie McFague, and Karl Rahner led her to confuse knowledge of ourselves with knowledge of the Holy Trinity.

[163] See Barth, CD II/1, 162 and above.

[164] Jones, "Liberation Theology and Karl Barth in the Shadow of the Alt-Right," 225.

Bible and in the Nicene Creed, one can see how nonsensical this idea actually is. One has only to listen to Barth's definition of revelation to see how wrong these views are. For Barth,

> revelation denotes the Word of God itself in the act of its being spoken in time ... it is the condition which conditions all things without itself being conditioned ... [it] means the unveiling of what is veiled ... Revelation as such is not relative. Revelation in fact does not differ from the person of Jesus Christ nor from the reconciliation accomplished in him. To say revelation is to say "The Word became flesh."[165]

The key here is that Jesus is God himself revealing God to us precisely by reconciling us to the Father since he is the very Word of God (God from God) made flesh in the man Jesus. Johnson arbitrarily substitutes "Christ-Sophia" and "Mother-Sophia" for the Father and Son, thus obliterating any genuine knowledge of the immanent Trinity. Clearly, the three persons presented here have nothing whatever to do with the eternal Father, Son, and Holy Spirit confessed in the Nicene Creed. In fact, this change in the name for God itself, as presented here, demonstrates how far away from actual knowledge of the immanent Trinity Johnson's position actually was and is. Indeed, as noted in my *Divine Freedom*, Roland Frye has shown that thinking of Jesus as Sophia incarnate was not only a Gnostic view but an Arian view that failed to acknowledge Jesus' actual uniqueness. Let me explain this a bit more.[166]

First, as noted above, Johnson deliberately follows Rahner and claims that among possible historical mediations of encounter with God, "the experience of oneself has a unique importance."[167] This assertion, as I have been arguing, is in flat opposition to Barth's insistence that a proper starting point for theology can "neither be an axiom of reason nor a datum of experience. In the measure that a doctrine of God draws on these sources, it betrays the fact that its subject is not really God but a hypostatised reflection of man."[168] Torrance's view of our knowledge of God, as we have seen, is very close to Barth's view just because both theologians allow the doctrine of justification

---

[165] Barth CD I/1, 118–19.
[166] This attempt to name God Sophia is "in line with the Gnostic heresy" (Roland Frye, "Language for God and Feminist Language: Problems and Principles," *Scottish Journal of Theology* 41 (4) (1988), 35) and basically repeats an Arian argument "for the subordination of the Son to the Father by interpreting Jesus Christ as the incarnation not of God but of God's Wisdom" (Ibid., 36). See my discussion of these matters in *Divine Freedom*, Second Edition, 34ff.
[167] Johnson, *She Who Is*, 65.
[168] Barth, CD, II/2, 3.

by grace through faith to shape their understanding of this matter. Thus, Torrance also invariably insists that our knowledge of God comes from God's knowing us in his incarnate Son Jesus Christ as the Holy Spirit actualizes in us the reconciliation accomplished objectively in his life, ministry, death, and resurrection. That takes place through conceptual and ontological union with Christ himself in faith. Second, as noted above, she then embraces Rahner's view of us as spirit in the world in such a way that if we have an experience of radical questioning before a constantly receding horizon, then we supposedly discover that we "are dynamically oriented toward fathomless mystery as the very condition of the possibility of acting in characteristic human ways."[169] From this she concludes that in our personal actions, humans demonstrate "an openness toward infinite mystery" as the basis of their existence. Thus, she thinks we are "dynamically structured toward God."[170] Both Barth and Torrance, however, decisively reject any such thinking because the first thing we discover face to face with Jesus Christ is that we are sinners in need of his reconciling grace *before* we can even begin to understand the mystery of God. Moreover, to claim knowledge of "fathomless mystery" is knowledge of the triune God requires an enormous leap because, while we may be open to such a view of God as "fathomless mystery," we are not in fact open to the true God who meets us in Christ. That is why both Barth and Torrance maintained that we are offended at revelation in its identity with Jesus Christ.

Considering these facts, to suggest that Johnson's approach is grounded in revelation is absurd, given the fact that Jesus Christ in his actual uniqueness is utterly missing from what she says here, following Rahner. Moreover, she does not stop there. She makes two more crucial points that are diametrically in contrast with any proper view of revelation in its identity with Christ the revealer. First, she says God is primordially mediated "through the changing history of oneself" so that God cannot be experienced directly but only "as the ultimate depth and radical essence of every personal experience such as love, fidelity, loneliness, and death."[171] Indeed, as noted above, she claims that it is in these "pre-thematic" experiences that we know God as "holy mystery" and thus, we know God "as the very context of our own self-presence." Moreover, she says, it is this "silent, nonverbal encounter with infinite mystery" that "constitutes the enabling condition of any experience of self at all."[172] Finally, she claims that as our experience of ourselves develops, so also does our experience of God such that these both condition each other. The

---

[169] Johnson, *She Who Is*, 65.
[170] Ibid.
[171] Ibid.
[172] Ibid.

end result is her conclusion that "the personal history of the experience of the self is in its total extent the history of the ultimate experience of God."[173] All of this thinking leads her to marginalize Jesus as God's "envoy" when she says of God "her essence ... might well be called connectedness, for ... she is a breath, an emanation ... The power of relation built into wisdom metaphors comes to unique fruition in the doctrine of Jesus-Sophia, Sophia incarnate. Sophia is present in and with her envoy Jesus."[174] By contrast, Jesus *is* God acting *as* man for us. So, while Sophia might present *in* and *with* Jesus, God himself is hypostatically united with the man Jesus. Her view is hardly based on revelation in its identity with the Word made flesh here and thus she undermines his actual uniqueness and the simple fact that face to face with Jesus we are in reality face to face with the one true God. Consequently, it is wrong to assume that in our self-experience we can find and experience God simply because, face to face with Jesus Christ, we discover that we need to turn *from* ourselves to God in Christ to know and experience God.

It hardly needs to be said that on each of these points both Barth and Torrance would disagree completely because they both claim consistently when knowledge of God occurs for those who encounter Christ, that knowledge does not come *from* us at all, but only from the Father through the Son in the power of the Holy Spirit uniting us to Christ as the source of that knowledge. And it comes through *conceptual* union with God the Father through *conceptual* union with his Son. All of this is lost in Johnson's approach. Even more importantly, the idea that Johnson was basing her views on revelation by claiming knowledge of Spirit-Sophia, Christ-Sophia, and Mother-Sophia as knowledge of the Trinity is beyond ludicrous. The very fact that Johnson thought she could change the name of God from Father, Son, and Spirit in this way demonstrates clearly that her thinking was never grounded within the eternal Trinity in the first place. Jesus was and is the Word of God/the Son of God who became incarnate for us and for our salvation. To substitute Sophia for the eternal Son of the Father and to name God Mother is preposterous if revelation is taken seriously, as Barth and Torrance understood that revelation in its identity with Jesus Christ himself as the incarnate Word.[175] And the main reason why it is preposterous is because it is built on the premise that knowledge of God comes *from* us and not exclusively *to* us from the Father and through an encounter with his incarnate Son. Moreover, it must be stressed once again that this knowledge

---

[173] Ibid., 66.
[174] Ibid., 168–9.
[175] For more on this, see Molnar, *Divine Freedom and the Doctrine of the Immanent Trinity* and *Freedom, Necessity, and the Knowledge of God*.

is always conceptual knowledge and cannot be equated with any sort of pre-conceptual experience of ourselves as Johnson and Rahner suppose.[176]

Several other claims Johnson makes demonstrate beyond doubt that her views are not in fact grounded in revelation. First, as noted above, she repeatedly says we have no literal knowledge of God. If that is in any sense true, then knowledge of God is purely metaphorical, and we can change it at will. For Barth and Torrance, such thinking is the ultimate example of subjectivism and nonscientific theology because it means that we can read back our own metaphors based on experience into God instead of allowing God to transform our knowledge through our sharing in the mind of Christ. Second, she claims that when we speak of God as Father, our analogy develops by negating our experience of paternity at its best and then our claiming that God is infinitely beyond that.[177] But, as noted above, both Barth and Torrance absolutely reject that approach because they claim all true analogies come not from our negating our experiences and then projecting our views onto some generally conceivable infinite mystery. Instead, true analogies come from faithful recognition of God as he has named himself to us in his Word and Spirit. Moreover, Johnson also claims that "God is *like* a Trinity,"[178] when the entire Christian tradition stemming from Nicaea claims that God *is* the Trinity precisely as the eternal Father, Son, and Holy Spirit who loves in freedom. All of these crucial points demonstrate beyond doubt that Johnson's

---

[176] See Molnar, *Freedom, Necessity, and the Knowledge of God*, Chapter Four, for a discussion of Torrance and Rahner on nonconceptual knowledge.

[177] She writes, "analogy ... means that while it [human naming of God] starts from the relationship of paternity experienced at its best in this world, its inner dynamism negates the creaturely mode to assert that God is more unlike than like even the best human fathers" (*She Who Is*, 173). This is exactly opposite the views of Barth and Torrance, who both claim that our analogies for speaking about God are analogies of faith because they begin and end with Jesus Christ himself as the Word of God incarnate and the Old and New Testament witness to him. See my *Divine Freedom*, Second Edition, 39.

[178] Johnson, *She Who Is*, 205. She says, "the symbol of the Trinity is not a blueprint of the inner workings of the godhead ... in no sense is it a literal description of God's being *in se* ... it is a symbol that indirectly points to God's relationality ... our speech about God as three and persons is a human construction that means to say that God is *like* a Trinity, *like* a threefoldness of relation" (*She Who Is*, 204–5). Contrast this substitution of relationality for the eternal Trinity with Barth's remark that "we cannot say anything higher or better of the 'inwardness of God' [the immanent Trinity] than that God is Father, Son and Holy Spirit" (CD I/2, 377). Neither Barth nor Torrance would substitute "relationality" for the eternal relations of the Father, Son, and Holy Spirit confessed in the Nicene Creed. Torrance makes a similar point: "'Trinity' is not just a way for us to think about God, for the one true God IS actually and eternally triune and cannot be conceived properly otherwise ... The doctrine of the Trinity is not something added on to the doctrine of the One God but belongs to the very reality of God. As there is no God except the Father, Son and Holy Spirit, so for us no true conception of God is possible except as Holy Trinity." *Trinitarian Perspectives*, 133.

liberationist perspective was not at all shaped by the revelation of God in Jesus Christ but rather by her agenda which was to argue, as noted above, the symbol God functions, and we must make it function to achieve the social, political, and religious goal of achieving equality between men and women. However, that is precisely the self-justification I have argued against in this chapter in order to affirm that our true liberation which comes from Christ alone as liberation from self-will and sin is the only way that patriarchalism as a sin can be properly seen and overcome. We do not have the power to overcome sin and thus to change people simply by changing the language for God with the idea that God is only *like* a Trinity!

Let me give another example of a liberationist perspective that purports to be grounded in the Holy Spirit but is not properly grounded in the Holy Spirit at all to show the difference Torrance's view makes in this discussion. In his book *Dogmatics after Babel: Beyond the Theologies of Word and Culture*, Rubén Rosario Rodríguez proposes to recognize the presence of the Holy Spirit "in liberating work—especially when such work is located outside the church."[179] In his view, theological analysis is grounded in acts of liberation and humility. He thus advocates a "doctrine of revelation grounded in the ongoing work of the Holy Spirit."[180] But the question is: Can one recognize the Holy Spirit by exploring "liberating work"? From within a proper evangelical theology that allows Christ to be the *first* and *final* Word, the answer to this question is an unequivocal no. Why? Because in a strict doctrine of Christology and of the Trinity, one cannot separate the Spirit from the Word since they are one in being (*homoousios*) in eternity and in the economy. That means that it is impossible to recognize the Holy Spirit simply by exploring liberating works just as it is impossible to know and love God *by* loving our neighbors.

The idea that one can recognize and understand the Holy Spirit by focusing on liberating works is simply another form of self-justification. It begins theology with what we do without recognizing the fact that unless what we do is grounded in the love of God for us actualized in the incarnation and revealed by the risen Lord, then even if that theology is described as faith seeking understanding, it is clearly an untheological theology. Unless faith is enabled by the Holy Spirit uniting us to Christ and thus to the Father, it is not yet or no longer Christian faith. It is an approach that relies on what Torrance called cheap grace, rather than on costly grace, just because it will not recognize that true liberation means taking up our cross and following Christ

---

[179] Rubén Rosario Rodríguez, *Dogmatics after Babel: Beyond the Theologies of Word and Culture* (Louisville, KY: Westminster John Knox Press, 2018), 143.
[180] Ibid.

the Liberator. We need to be liberated from the self-will that refuses to begin and end with Christ himself and not with ourselves. Here, Torrance's view of how we know the Holy Spirit is decisive:

> the doctrine of the Spirit requires the doctrine of the Son. It is only by the Spirit that we know that Jesus is Lord and can assert the *homoousion* of him, but apart from the Son, and the inseparable relation of the Spirit to the Son, the Spirit is unknowable, and the content of the doctrine of the Spirit cannot be articulated.[181]

Importantly, then, for Torrance, "The Spirit does not utter himself but the Word and is known only as he enlightens us to understand the Word."[182] This approach clearly rules out the idea that we can know the Holy Spirit by focusing on any sort of human behavior such as acts of liberation or compassion, however humanly important those acts may be from a purely human perspective.

In light of what I am arguing here, beginning with our liberating works detaches revelation from the incarnate Word as the revealer and makes revelation a general catchword for human acts of liberation. At the outset we see a massive difference of views. While Rosario Rodríguez thinks "no tradition speaks with absolute certainty or universal application,"[183] that very assertion eliminates the possibility of knowing the truth in its identity with Jesus himself who is the Way, the Truth, and the Life. In other words, while it is true that no tradition has control over the truth so that such tradition is in any sense true in itself, it does not mean that one cannot speak with absolute certainty and universal application about the truth. Once that conclusion is drawn, relativism follows. A quick example from Karl Barth will make this point clear. Because he believed there was a way from Christology to anthropology (as did Torrance), as noted above, he held that everything said about anthropology, that is, about our human relations with God, including our sin and God's forgiveness of that sin,

> can only be said from this point, from [our] being in Jesus Christ. If this rule—which is the basic rule of all sound doctrine—is followed, the statement that God is knowable to [us] can and must be made with the strictest possible certainty, with an apodictic certainty, with a

---

[181] Torrance, *Theology in Reconstruction*, 213.
[182] Ibid., 214.
[183] Rosario Rodríguez, *Dogmatics after Babel*, 143.

certainty freed from any dialectic and ambiguity, with all the certainty of the statement "the Word was made flesh."[184]

For Barth this means that we can speak with absolute certainty and universal application as long as we are thinking about humanity from the vantage point of our having been reconciled to God in Christ. Any attempt to speak of humanity in its quest for freedom and its fight against oppression apart from this christological basis will necessarily mean uncertainty because it would accord anthropology a role independent of the truth known christologically. That would imply that we can find truth in ourselves, when what is revealed in and by Jesus Christ is that we are sinners incapable of knowing God and ourselves truly apart from the incarnate Word, that is, apart from God's knowing us. True knowledge of God only occurs when Christ's completed atoning reconciliation is actualized in us with the healing of our minds and hearts through the power of his Holy Spirit.

Torrance makes this same point repeatedly when he speaks of cheap and costly grace, which was discussed above. Thus, he stresses the importance of our justification by grace alone, as we have seen. He also does so when he refers to Jesus himself as the Way, the Truth, and the Life (Jn 14:6). He takes that statement with unqualified seriousness because he firmly and consistently holds that a proper theology must take its stand "on the supreme truth of the Deity of Christ" and thus it must interpret the Gospels "in the light of the epistemic and ontological relation between the historical Jesus Christ, the incarnate Son, and God the Father."[185] For example, Torrance says that it is particularly in the Gospel of John that this evangelical truth is emphasized with clarity. He notes that none of the other gospels stresses Jesus' earthly, historical, and fleshly reality more than the Gospel of John. At the same time the fourth Gospel stresses "the eternal *I am* of the living God," which is "irresistibly evident in Jesus' self-disclosure, above all at those points where he stands forth as the Lord of life and death."[186] In a manner similar to Barth, Torrance concludes that "the central focus of the Gospel upon the Deity of Christ is the door that opens the way to the understanding of God's triune self-revelation as Father, Son and Holy Spirit" and that is why any proper interpretation of the New Testament has to be "at once both

---

[184] Barth, CD II/1, 162.
[185] Torrance, *Christian Doctrine of God*, 48.
[186] Ibid. It is at that point that Torrance cites many supporting texts such as "I and my Father are one" (Jn 10:30); "I am the resurrection and the life ..." (Jn 11:15); "I am the way, the truth and the life; no one comes to the Father but by me ... He who has seen me has seen the Father ... I am in the Father and the Father is in me" (Jn 14:6, 9, 11).

Christological and trinitarian."[187] Torrance's reaction to Bultmann expresses this point quite decisively:

> When Bultmann wishes to reinterpret the objective facts of *kērygma*, e.g. as given in the Apostles' Creed, in terms of an existential decision which we have to make in order to understand, not God or Christ or the world, but ourselves, we are converting the gospel of the New Testament into something quite different, converting christology into anthropology. It is shockingly subjective. It is not Christ that really counts, but my decision in which I find myself.[188]

Additionally, as seen above, Torrance takes seriously the problem of sin and our need to have our minds reconciled to God in Christ *before* we can know God truly and in order for us to love God and neighbor. On this point Barth and Torrance are very close.

Since both theologians think the only way to God is through the incarnate Son and that we are united to the Son conceptually through the Holy Spirit, and therefore in faith, both of them also agree that it is only on the basis of justification by grace alone that we are justified and sanctified. For Torrance, justification cannot be understood as the "beginning of a new self-righteousness" which it would be if our sanctification were thought of as "what we do in response to justification."[189] Such a view of sanctification would have to mean that finally "our salvation depends upon our own personal or existential decision" instead of upon God's grace, namely, upon what Christ has accomplished objectively for us in making us free to live from him alone as the Way, the Truth, and the Life.[190] In this context, Torrance argued that we should not use political theology "as a basic hermeneutic to interpret the Gospel and mission of the Church" because whenever that happens, we are entrapped in "an ecclesiastical will to power" instead of living by grace by taking up our cross and following Christ.[191] It is only because Christ loved us while we were still sinners and forgave our sins that we are truly free to love

---

[187] Ibid., 49.
[188] Torrance, *Incarnation*, 286.
[189] Torrance, *Theology in Reconstruction*, 161.
[190] Ibid., 162–3.
[191] See Thomas F. Torrance, *Theology in Reconciliation: Essays toward Evangelical and Catholic Unity in East and West* (London: Geoffrey Chapman, 1975), 79. Torrance thus maintained that "through sin and self-will the Christian religion, as easily as any other, may be turned into a form of man's cultural self-expression or the means whereby he seeks to give sanction to a socio-political way of life, and even be the means whereby he seeks to justify and sanctify himself before God" (*God and Rationality*, 69).

him and thus to love God and on that basis to fight against oppression by loving our neighbors.

Here, let me briefly contrast the approach of Rosario Rodríguez, who speaks for many to that of Torrance in a bit more detail. As noted, Rosario Rodríguez thinks we can know the Holy Spirit from human works of liberation. With that assumption he methodologically separates the Spirit from the Word and thereby confuses the Holy Spirit with the human spirit. This leads him to several problematic conclusions. He thinks that "to participate in the process of liberation is already, in a certain sense, a salvific work." From this it follows that one can locate revelation "in the work of historical and political liberation."[192] As a result, his key thesis is that since God desires that we all live peacefully together "guided by God's compassionate justice," he can explore biblical views of the Spirit's work in Judaism, Islam, and Christianity before they became "calcified into exclusivist doctrines."[193] On this basis he argues "that the work of the Spirit serves as a theological locus for pluralistic dialogue and cooperation because the sacred Scriptures of all three faiths share an ethical norm grounded in the themes of liberation, justice and compassion."[194] This may sound promising to the uncritical reader. But it is not.

Torrance would certainly oppose this thinking because it clearly replaces Christ himself with an ethical norm. So, instead of grounding his view of the Spirit and of liberation in the Spirit's enabling us to love God spontaneously as he meets us in Jesus Christ here and now based on his forgiving grace, Rosario Rodríguez substitutes an *ethical norm* that he thinks unites the three faiths, and then searches for instances of liberation, justice, and compassion as indications of the actions of the Holy Spirit. This factually undermines the doctrine of justification by grace and separates the Spirit from the Word, thus undoing the unity of the Trinity acting for us in history. The fact that Rosario Rodríguez does this is evident when he asserts that he will begin his theology "with pneumatology *rather than* with christology."[195] As I have been arguing, however, to begin with pneumatology within a properly evangelical theology, one would immediately have to begin with Christology because the Holy Spirit unites us to Christ as our Liberator. To have the Holy Spirit is to recognize and acknowledge that Jesus himself is the Lord who enables our knowledge of God in the first place as he speaks his Word to us here and now.

---

[192] Rosario Rodríguez, 142.
[193] Ibid., 167.
[194] Ibid.
[195] Ibid., 145, emphasis mine.

As such, he is the one who liberates us from any sort of self-reliance to love God and on that basis to love our neighbors.

To claim to be speaking of the Holy Spirit without at once being directed toward Christ the liberator necessarily confuses the Holy Spirit with the human spirit. This would have to mean that sanctification has become a work of ours instead of an accomplished work of Christ for us. That is why Rosario Rodríguez can say that to participate in liberation is in a certain sense already a salvific work. It is not. The key indicator that such confusion has occurred will always be the fact that someone thinks the truth of our knowledge of God and of liberation comes from the *moral law* as it now stands and our obedience to the moral law or from various experiences of compassion or liberation. As seen above, Torrance helpfully maintained that any such approach was bound to fail because it misses the central point that we are not saved and thus not freed from our sin as self-will through faithfulness to the *moral law* or to any abstract *ethical norm*, even if that is constructed from the Bible. That approach is a way of hiding from our true responsibility, which is to hear the Word of God's forgiving grace and thus to love God in Christ for his own sake. On that basis, Christians become free to love their neighbors and to fight against oppression without any ulterior motives for themselves or others since they are impelled to do so by the unconditionally free love of God. That approach is what keeps Christians from falling prey to ideologies in their fight for freedom and against oppression in all its forms. Through the Holy Spirit they are conceptually and ontologically united with Jesus Christ, the risen, ascended, and coming Lord, who alone enables our liberation from sin and empowers us for service of God and neighbors here and now.

While Rosario Rodríguez argues in a general way that "all three faiths share a conception of the Spirit as the *historical* manifestation of God in the world *through* acts of liberation that preserve human dignity,"[196] the truth is that a genuine recognition of the Holy Spirit would require that we look away from our acts of preserving human dignity to Christ himself as the one who justifies and sanctifies sinners. Because Rosario Rodríguez does not do this, he claims that to seek dogmatic certainty "steers us toward theological totalitarianism."[197] Thus, he claims that theological knowledge "is more a matter of personal and communal spiritual formation than of detached scientific observation."[198] Armed with that approach, he claims once again that "God can be known in human history through divinely inspired acts of

---

[196] Ibid., 167.
[197] Ibid., 168.
[198] Ibid.

justice, compassion, and liberation."[199] This is a problematic assertion even if the acts in question were thought to be divinely inspired simply because no such human actions are capable of making God known to us since only God can reveal God. It is crucial to realize here that seeking dogmatic certainty could never steer us toward theological totalitarianism if it *begins* and *ends* with Christ himself.

Torrance captured this perfectly when he noted that we must never "transfer the centre of authority from the objective revelation of God to ourselves" and that it is only when we recognize the "ultimate authority of the Supreme Truth over all other authorities" that there is "freedom for the faithful, for it makes us to know the truth finally out of itself and by its grace alone, and demands of us an obedience that transcends our respect for the authoritative institutions of the Church."[200] Torrance then asserts that it is only when these institutional authorities are subordinated to the "Supreme Truth" of God himself that they avoid being "authoritarian tyrants" and become instruments of the truth itself. Still, the Spirit always directs us away from the institutional teaching of the Church to "the one Truth of God revealed and incarnate in Jesus Christ, in order that it may serve that Truth in such a way that it is allowed to retain its absolute priority over all the Church's teaching."[201]

The problem here is that Rosario Rodríguez believes that it is appropriate to speak about "human struggles for liberation *as* the historical experience of God."[202] He thinks he can describe the Holy Spirit by exploring the spirit latent in various cultural activities. This can be done therefore "*without* adhering to any one confessional or ideological tradition, which in turn facilitates a certain kind of 'body politic' that embodies the emancipatory practices of spirit in the public arena."[203] On this basis Rosario Rodríguez believes that movements such as the Black Lives Matter movement is one of a number of "'confession-less' yet profoundly spiritual movements of liberation" that "have become the new *loci theologici* ('places of theology') for understanding and encountering the work of the Spirit in history."[204] This means that one might uncritically embrace a movement that is more interested in creating chaos and hatred of the police than in caring for the lives of black persons who are frequently threatened by other blacks within their own communities. One

---

[199] Ibid.
[200] Torrance, "Truth and Authority," 240, 242.
[201] Ibid., 242.
[202] Ibid., 169.
[203] Ibid., 170.
[204] Ibid., 172.

might also think that Black Lives Matter "presents itself as an emancipatory spirituality for all black lives."[205] BLM, he says, "invoked Martin Luther King, Jr." while encouraging violent rather than nonviolent actions in the pursuit of liberation from perceived oppression. Of course, Dr. King was irrevocably in favor of nonviolence in the pursuit of racial justice. But Rosario Rodríguez defends the violence of BLM as "recovering the radicalism of King's methods and message for the twenty-first century."[206] This supposedly places them on the same foundation as Martin Luther King, Jr. However, it most certainly does not do so because he never would have advocated the kinds of violence clearly supported by BLM.

While Rosario Rodríguez notes that "white mainstream" resistance to BLM has labeled that group a terrorist group, he thinks that "the tragedy of Michael Brown" has, by the Spirit, been turned "into a sacramental encounter with God."[207] This, in spite of the fact that Michael Brown was not at all innocent but was assaulting a police officer. Notwithstanding this, movements such as BLM become the basis for the theme of Rosario Rodríguez's book: "The argument articulated in these pages is simple: faith ought not be reduced to human emancipation, but faith without the liberating works of the Spirit has lost all 'living connection to the reality of God.'"[208] The problem here is this: Christian faith is Christian only to the extent that the Holy Spirit, who is one in being with the Father and the Son, is the enabling condition of liberation. And liberation in the first instance means liberation from self-will, self-reliance, and thus from sin and enmity toward God and thus freedom to love God and on that basis love our neighbors. So, while it is true that faith and works do go together, one cannot recognize the Holy Spirit by focusing on liberating works simply because it is Christ himself who empowers us to be truly free for others in the first instance. And that freedom comes from him as we rely on him in faith and obedience.

Here we return to the theme of Rosario Rodríguez's book: by focusing on "the work of the Spirit in human history—especially through works of compassion and liberation," he offers,

> a possible strategy for moving past the impasse between *theologies of the Word* that take a fideistic stance on Scripture as God's self-revelation without subjecting their dogmatic claims to external criticism, and the *theologies of culture* that contend that God can only be known

---

[205] Ibid., 173.
[206] Ibid., 170.
[207] Ibid., 174.
[208] Ibid., 175.

through the medium of culture but lack criteria for differentiating revelation from the cultural status quo. The argument has been made that God is encountered in history *in* works of justice, compassion, and liberation, even when the locus of this spiritual work is a body politic not historically associated with any religion whose members describe their emancipatory work without appealing to explicitly theological language.[209]

From this Rosario Rodríguez concludes that "*wherever* the work of establishing justice, extending compassion, and facilitating human liberation occurs, *there* is the true Spirit of God."[210] Since these "emancipatory movements in history" are thought to "embody the divine will for all humankind regardless of confessional or creedal origin," Rosario Rodríguez thinks this supposed work of the Spirit leads to the "notion of history as sacrament" which allows us to speak of "divine agency in human history" so that we also can affirm "the work of the Spirit in the religious and cultural 'other.'"[211] Once again, this approach to understanding the Spirit by focusing on human efforts at liberation instead of the Word of God as we are united to that Word by the Holy Spirit leads to an explicit denial of God's liberating and transformative grace as the basis of and enabling condition of human liberation.

Here is the problem with this analysis: fideism is the view that Christian faith dispenses with human reason. Hence, Rosario Rodríguez claims that faith in God's self-revelation in Scripture, which in the New Testament specifically attests the work of the Spirit as one in being with the Father and Son according to the Nicene faith, is fideistic if it does not subject itself to "external criticism." Unfortunately, however, a faith that subjects itself to criticism external to the Word of God must mean that he thinks there is a criterion for the Spirit, and thus for theological truth and true liberation, that is other than and beyond the very Word of God attested in Scripture. While Rosario Rodríguez is right to want to differentiate revelation from culture, his attempt to find the truth of the Christian faith in human acts of liberation finally is unable to do so. Why? Because he has missed the most important point of Christian theology at the outset. To have the Holy Spirit is to be bound conceptually and ontologically to Jesus Christ himself, who is the incarnate Word who alone liberates us for true knowledge of God and for spontaneous love of neighbor based *solely* on God's loving us in his incarnate Word while we were still sinners. Having the Spirit is based upon God's grace

---

[209] Ibid., 175–6.
[210] Ibid., 176.
[211] Ibid.

which is costly to us, as discussed above, because to live by grace means to take up our cross and follow Christ. To have the Holy Spirit confessed at Nicaea and attested in the Bible means to recognize that Jesus is the Lord (1 Cor. 12:3) and thus to live in union with him by faith.

Identifying works of justice, liberation, and compassion as the locus of the Holy Spirit overtly confuses the Holy Spirit with the human spirit by directing our attention away from Christ the Liberator and toward our own works which permit descriptions of "divine agency" apart from and without knowing God the Father through his Son in the power of the Holy Spirit. Such an approach ignores the problem of sin and the fact that living by faith means living by Christ's forgiving grace and not by our works of justice and liberation. Such thinking inadvertently advances a version of self-justification and modalism by referring to divine action in history apart from the specific actions of God in his Word and Spirit.

A proper theology of liberation does not mean pursuing ideologies that promise liberation but actually enslave their followers by directing them back to themselves and their political and social action as the way toward true liberation. Here I suggest that Torrance has the better view. He insists that Jesus himself *is* the Way, the Truth, and the Life and that no one can come to the Father except through him. He is right. Since Jesus himself is the very Word of God active in history as the incarnate, crucified, risen, and ascended and advent Lord, we cannot know the truth of who God is, who the Spirit is, or what true liberation means apart from him. He liberates us for service of God and neighbor. Without being united to Christ through the Spirit conceptually and ontologically, we will always define truth in a way that grounds knowledge of that truth in us and what we do, instead of in God acting for us within history in his Word and Spirit. That is precisely what Rosario Rodríguez does in the end when he claims that "truth has been defined as an existential appropriation and practical application of the prophetic work of the Spirit to love the neighbor as oneself."[212] Unfortunately, this is just the view of truth that Torrance rightly rejected when he said we cannot love God *by* loving our neighbors, as discussed above. Sadly, having detached the Spirit from the Word methodologically, Rosario Rodríguez offers history itself as a sacrament instead of realizing that one cannot detach the sacraments, Baptism and the Eucharist in particular, from Christ himself, who instituted those sacraments as the way Christians live in and from union with Christ throughout history. Once again, his view of history as a sacrament allows him to direct attention away from Christ and thus away from the Holy Spirit and toward our human actions in history for theological

---

[212] Ibid., 186.

knowledge and proper Christian action. This just misses Torrance's all-important understanding of justification by grace alone and places us in the unfortunate position of having to rely on ourselves to do something we can never accomplish, that is, to live in the freedom which only God can, did and does provide.

Before ending this chapter, I think it would be helpful to briefly consider two other approaches to liberation theology to illustrate the difference it makes when Christ himself really is allowed to be the *first* and *final* Word as the one who alone can and does liberate us for love of God and neighbor. In a recent attempt to construct a theology by means of a dialogue between Marcella-Althaus Reid and Karl Barth, Hanna Reichel categorizes the former approach as a type of constructive theology and the latter as a type of systematic theology. She notes that Althaus-Reid's approach is a "queer-feminist, materialist, decolonial intervention" that is "indebted to and critical of liberation and feminist theologies." According to Reichel, Althaus-Reid's thinking is "marked by sexual storytelling 'from below'" in ways that radically critique "dominant theologies" and is "always in service of liberation—queer and indigenous people's as much as God's own."[213]

Amazingly, Reichel thinks that both Barth and Althaus-Reid are theologically compatible when in truth they are not. To put the matter simply and directly, Reichel never grounds her thinking in the immanent Trinity or in what Barth termed God's primary objectivity. For that reason, her view of God, grace, revelation, and salvation itself is not shaped exclusively by God's self-revelation in Jesus Christ and our participation in Christ through the Holy Spirit. One cannot have supreme loyalty to queer human identity and supreme loyalty to Christ at the same time, as I shall demonstrate. A choice must be made between Barth's view of God, grace, revelation, and salvation and the views of Althaus-Reid. Because Reichel did not make that choice, she failed to make the case that the views of Barth and Althaus-Reid are in fact compatible.

In contrast to Barth's consistently christocentric approach, Reichel upholds "both the doctrinal and the queer approach, as deeply rooted in a theological realism and pursuing decidedly *theo*logical projects, that is, as speaking of (1) the scandalous reality of the wholly other God, (2) the true humanity of the human being, and (3) the relationship between them."[214] The problem with these remarks is simple. Reichel never explains exactly what Barth means when he refers to God as "wholly other" and so she never allows the eternal

---

[213] Hanna Reichel, *After Method: Queer Grace, Conceptual Design, and the Possibility of Theology* (Louisville, KY: Westminster John Knox Press, 2023), 18.
[214] Ibid.

Trinity to shape her view of God from start to finish. She frequently refers to God, but never makes the important statement that Barth made, namely, that:

> We cannot say anything higher or better of the "inwardness of God" [the immanent Trinity] than that God is Father, Son, and Holy Spirit, and therefore that he is love in Himself without and before loving us, and without being forced to love us. And we can say this only in the light of the "outwardness" of God to us [the economic Trinity], the occurrence of His revelation. It is from this that we have to learn what is the real nature of the love of God.[215]

And for Barth that love of God which meets us in Jesus Christ is "the real basis of our love of God" and "determines its character."[216]

Moreover, Barth made an important distinction between God's primary and secondary objectivity in order to make his position clear. He could thus say that "God is known, not simply because he is God in Himself [primary objectivity], but because He reveals Himself as such; not simply because His work is there, but because He is active in His work [secondary objectivity]."[217] However, for Barth, because the grace of God cannot be detached from Christ, the Giver of grace, he also says, "Necessarily, it is all up with the truth of God's work and sign if we cease to adore its grace. For just as certainly as grace is truth, so certainly can truth only be had as grace."[218] For Barth, grace is not identical with any arbitrarily posited experience such as "queer holiness," but God's making himself known to us by setting himself

> as our object and ourselves as knowers of Him. For this will not take place except as His free gift, in the act of His grace—and this in spite of the fact that he is in fact object in Himself and in secondary objectivity in His revelation, in Jesus Christ, in the witness of the Scriptures, in the visibility of the Church [219]

as well as in preaching and the sacraments. For Barth "His primary objectivity [God in himself] and His secondary objectivity [God for us] is objectivity for us, since he Himself makes Himself into object for us and us into knowers of Him."[220]

---

[215] Barth, CD, I/2, 377.
[216] Ibid.
[217] Barth, CD II/1, 23.
[218] Ibid.
[219] Ibid., 22–3.
[220] Ibid.

Reichel's entire approach is thoroughly unscientific from the perspective of Torrance's scientific theology precisely because she honestly believes that beyond the differences between Barth and Althaus-Reid, "there might be significant overlaps in the theology and material *realities* to which they ultimately testify."[221] However, as I have just indicated, the wholly other God who shapes the theology of Karl Barth and the wholly other God presented by Althaus-Reid have nothing in common. For Althaus-Reid "'Queerness is something that belongs to God, and ... people are divinely Queer by grace.'"[222] For Barth God is the eternal Father, Son, and Holy Spirit confessed in the Nicene Creed and is known with apodictic certainty through Christ alone who is the wholly other God present to us as the one he truly is.[223] From this Barth understands faith as our standing on Christ, who is God's grace active for us in history, and it can never mean standing on ourselves.[224] That means one cannot equate grace with our experiences, no matter how they are described.

In contrast to Barth's view just described, for Althaus-Reid, God can be described as her version of the "queer God" constructed from her arbitrary redefinition of God based on queer experience. For Barth, however, to the extent that any theology draws on experience or on reason, as noted above, such theology can never refer to the God of Christian faith, namely, the Trinity.[225] There can be little doubt that when Reichel speaks of "queer holiness" and "queer grace," she has detached grace from the Giver of grace,

---

[221] Reichel, *After Method*, 19.
[222] Ibid., 95.
[223] See Barth II/1, 162 and above.
[224] Thus, Barth insists, "To believe means to believe in Jesus Christ. But this means to keep wholly and utterly to the fact that our temporal existence receives and has and again receives its truth, not from itself, but exclusively from its relationship to what Jesus Christ is and does as our Advocate and Mediator in God Himself ... in faith we abandon ... our standing upon ourselves (including all moral and religious, even Christian standing) ... for the real standing in which we no longer stand on ourselves (on our moral and religious, or even our Christian state) ... but ... on the ground of the truth of God and therefore on the ground of the reconciliation which has taken place in Jesus Christ ... We have to believe: not to believe in ourselves, but in Jesus Christ" (CD II/1, 159). For this reason, Barth insisted that the certainty of our knowledge of God can only be attained if it "does not start from the believing man but from Jesus Christ as the object and foundation of faith" (ibid., 156).
[225] See Barth, CD II/2, 3, where he maintains that the only proper starting point for theology can neither be "an axiom of reason nor a datum of experience. In the measure that a doctrine of God draws on these sources, it betrays the fact that its subject is not really God but a hypostatised reflection of man." There can be no doubt that queer experience is the starting point and criterion for Althaus-Reid's view of God. And Hanna Reichel honestly believes that Althaus-Reid's view of God should be taken seriously in relation to Barth's view. Barth's view, however, is not within a thousand miles of their views.

namely, from Christ himself, and located that in "queer experience," such that she thinks it is acceptable to understand dogmatic theology from within a "queer perspective." Such a perspective might lead to Althaus-Reid's view of Jesus' supposed "bisexuality," to her "kenotic theology of orgies," and to her "indecenting" and "queering" various notions from the Christian tradition.[226] It also leads to a view of truth that is thoroughly antithetical to the view expressed in John's Gospel such that those who believed in Jesus would be his disciples if they remained in his word and that they would thus "know the truth, and the truth" would set them free (Jn 8:31-2). Importantly, this freedom meant freedom from sin so that "if the Son shall set you free, you will be free indeed" (Jn 8:36). Truth in this context cannot be separated from Jesus Christ, who is the Way, the Truth, and the Life (Jn 14:6). By contrast Reichel cites an author claiming that "truth does not assure happiness, or even … the good. Instead, it names only the insistent particularity of the subject … 'tend[ing] toward the real.'"[227] And this truth which she characterizes as "queer negativity" means "negation of all that is seen by society as good and holy."[228]

Yet, the point of Torrance's scientific theology (which is in harmony with Barth's theology, which I have just described) is that proper theology must never domesticate grace with a *cheap* view of grace. That is why he insisted that "it is not faith that justifies us, but Christ in whom we have faith."[229] From within Torrance's theology, the domestication of grace *always* occurs when theology begins from someone's *perspective* and *experience* as the source of true understanding in this matter. Consequently, proper theology for Torrance and Barth will always begin and end its reflections precisely by not using *any* humanly constructed perspective as the lens through which to understand God the Father, through his incarnate Son, Jesus Christ. This, because respecting the doctrine of justification by grace alone means allowing Christ himself, and not our experience of what we think it means to be human, or even our view of the real, understood apart from faith in Christ, to define our theology.

Reichel claims that "Queer grace results in a twofold commitment to the reality of God and the reality of real human beings."[230] Yet, if Barth is right in claiming that we can only have apodictically certain knowledge of God when that knowledge occurs from within *our new being in Jesus himself*, the crucified, risen, and advent Lord, then we cannot know the meaning of sin, the law, holiness, or grace at all by pursuing theology from a "queer"

---

[226] Ibid., 41.
[227] Ibid., 95.
[228] Ibid., 94.
[229] Torrance, *God and Rationality*, 58.
[230] Reichel, 21.

perspective or a liberationist perspective, or a feminist perspective, and certainly not from a patriarchal perspective either. Of course, we all have our perspectives and can never dispense with them. However, the point of the doctrine of justification by grace alone is that we must never allow our perspective or anyone else's perspective to become the starting point or norm for our theological analysis. Why?

Because a proper scientific theology must always begin and end from a *center in God* and not from a *center in ourselves*. All of these approaches just mentioned obviously begin from a center in ourselves, and end with a self-justifying theology in spite of Reichel's claim that she wants to avoid self-justification. Instead of turning consistently to Christ himself as the revelation of God in history, Reichel turns, with Althaus-Reid, to "sexual stories" as a "primary site for its practice."[231] She thus can claim that "God's incarnational insistence queers God to the point of no return, and, more importantly, queers any binary division—not only the boundary between heaven and earth, divine and human, but also the clear-cut distinction of sin and grace, virtue and vice, salvation and existence."[232] From this perspective, she erroneously claims that "faith, love, and hope … are essentially grace, God's gifts to the world, they are … actually existent incarnations of grace that offer us concrete sites where something of God and God's hope for this world can be glimpsed and experienced."[233] Thus, she says, "faith, love, and hope in the world are epistemologically salient: they constitute ways of being introduced to God. God allows Godself to be found in faith, love, and hope."[234]

Nonetheless, from within Torrance's view of grace, as well as Barth's view of grace, which cannot be detached for a moment from the Giver of grace, namely, Christ himself, one simply cannot claim that faith, love, and hope are "epistemologically salient" because these are not the way we are introduced to the God who meets us face to face with Christ. For Torrance, it is not our faith that justifies us but the object of faith, namely, Christ himself. For Barth, faith cannot be grounded in our experience of faith because it means standing on Christ alone. Therefore, we must say that any attempt to invest these experiences with the ability to disclose the triune God to us in the manner suggested by Reichel misses the simple fact that such disclosure can only come from God himself in his Word and Spirit actively disclosing himself to us through our encounter with Christ and in the power of his

---

[231] Ibid., 123.

[232] Ibid., 125. Amazingly, we are told that "Queerness is something that belongs to God, and that people are divinely Queer by grace" and that is what allows us to find God in such experiences (ibid., 112).

[233] Ibid.

[234] Ibid.

resurrection and of the Holy Spirit. That means we are always pointed *away* from our experiences of faith, love, and hope to Christ as the one who enables knowledge of God and salvation.

That is why Barth, for instance, insists that,

> in Holy Scripture the love of God to us speaks the language ... of His election, guidance, help and salvation—and it is in this language that it has to be heard and understood. But all the expressions of this factual language meet in the name of Jesus Christ ... It is in the fact that God intercedes for man, that he takes upon Himself the sin and guilt and death of man, that laden with it all He stands surety for him.[235]

It is at this point that Barth sums up our knowledge of God's love by citing Jn 3:16, namely, that "God so loved the world, that he gave his only begotten Son, that whoever believeth on him should not perish, but have everlasting life."[236] Hence, "this self-sacrifice of God in His Son is in fact the love of God to us" because this is the one in whom God has reconciled the world to himself by bearing away our sin and death so that we speak of the love of God "only by pointing to this fact" which "is the work and gift of the Holy Spirit" when it speaks to us.[237] Torrance's view is the same, because for him, any attempt to describe God's love apart from the love of God revealed when we are face to face with Christ would have to mean that we have described "cheap grace" rather than God's "costly grace," as described above.

Simply appealing to experiences of faith, love, and hope as Reichel does, without allowing the object of faith, hope, and love, namely Christ himself in his uniqueness as the incarnate Son, to determine the truth of what is said is to offer an understanding of grace from a secularized and even un-Christian view of human being. From the vantage of Barth and Torrance, this approach is clearly an example of self-justification precisely because, by definition, its epistemology is grounded in peoples' experiences of faith, love, and hope as generally understood, instead of exclusively in the object of faith, hope, and love. That object in fact is the love of God revealed and active in Christ himself as this meets us in judgment and forgiveness. Torrance's view of this matter was also close to Barth's view and can be illustrated easily once again by noting that we only know God truly in faith, hope, and love when we actually turn away from our own experiences of faith, love, and hope toward Christ in whom alone we may know God the Father in truth as this is enabled

---

[235] Barth, CD I/2, 378.
[236] Ibid.
[237] Ibid.

by the Holy Spirit. Unless that specific conversion occurs, we have not even begun to speak of God's actual grace and unconditional love of us.[238]

[238] Instead of referring to our conversion as a turning from ourselves toward Christ, in whom we are in fact reconciled to God through his vicarious actions for us on the cross, Reichel speaks of epistemic conversion to "an Other" to an encounter with "the real possibility of a different world" (Reichel, *After Method*, 68). Whatever else this is, it is not Christian conversion as Torrance so ably presented it and as that was described above. And it is certainly not Barth's either since for him faith, hope, and love are all shaped by the fact that "in Jesus Christ man is directed by God to awakening and life in the freedom for which He has made him free" (CD IV/1, 102). But that means that faith is our obedience to Christ just as our love of God is our obedience to him. For Barth the work of conversion to God "was done for all" in Christ's life of perfect obedience to the Father (CD IV/1, 148). Barth describes our love to God and to our neighbors as "a pure act of obedience" because it is exercised without any ulterior motive as an act of freedom. And Christian hope is the final form of our justification and sanctification because it is "the moment of the promise to man in Jesus Christ, and therefore Christian hope, and therefore the calling of man side by side with his justification and sanctification" (CD, IV/1, 108). Hope is thus determined by Jesus Christ, its object, and thus Christian hope "derives from Jesus Christ" and it does so as someone "hears and understands the pledge which God has given in Him, making it his own, letting his life be shaped by this promise and opened up for the future ... Jesus Christ is also the content of the divine pledge, the One in whom the Christian is summoned to hope" (CD IV/1, 116). As the "eternally living man who as such is the future of the world and of every man, and the hope of the Christian," Jesus Christ pointed to himself as the hope of the disciples in the forty days after his resurrection (CD IV/1, 117). By contrast Reichel says, "Hope as a theological category is not so much the belief that things will get better, might get better, or can get better once we do the right thing. The hope we have invoked has pointed to the fact that what we see and understand may not be all there is to reality, while also feeling acutely that what is 'is not enough'" (*After Method*, 114). That is why she thinks "queer and theological analysis overlap" because they identify whatever it is that remains "'outside' any symbolic order" and outside any "political project of inclusion or epistemic pursuit of understanding" and as such constitutes its "boundary as much as its condition, its revelation as well as what demands our commitment in faith and love" (ibid.). Notice what is completely missing in this analysis. It is the fact that truth, reality, freedom, and genuine hope are all grounded in Jesus Christ himself as the one who alone reveals God the Father to us through the power of the Holy Spirit and as the one who promises us not only knowledge of the truth, but eternal life. This abstract thinking leads Reichel to the utterly confused conclusion that "This is where queer and theological analysis overlap, calling this outside 'queerness' or 'God,' respectively. Queer theology is a realistic theology that starts where these two analyses are read together" (ibid., 114–15). The only problem, and it is a major problem, is that what is presented here is no theology at all because one cannot know the God of the Nicene faith, the eternal Father, Son, and Holy Spirit, by calling something that supposedly lies outside one's symbolic viewpoint God or in Althaus-Reid's view the "queer God." In this respect queer theology is not even remotely realistic because it is grounded in queer ideology and based on human experience instead of what is revealed by God himself in his Word and Spirit. That is why she feels free to employ what she calls a "cruising method," which she thinks resonates "with the order of grace" because it operates outside the law and it "refuses the need for absolute disciplinary coherence" (174–5). She says, "cruising allows us to envision ways of *using* method that recognize their penultimate, transitory, and yes, instrumental status while fiercely committed to an ethic of consent and care" (176). From this she concludes that we can appreciate grace which she says is "encountered without staking one's salvation on it" (ibid.). This whole line of reasoning is a blatant marginalization of the salvation by grace alone advocated by Barth and Torrance because our salvation is actually found in Jesus Christ and in him alone.

Instead of consistently directing us to Christ alone as our savior, helper, and friend, Reichel directs us to experiences of faith, love, and hope claiming that "they can become sites not just for discerning God's presence and God's work, but also for guiding the human response and correspondence to such grace."[239] Astoundingly, grace is here equated with general experiences of faith, love, and hope precisely in such a way that the truth of God himself is effectively detached from God as he actually meets us in his Word and Spirit and calls us away from all such self-reliance to take up our cross and follow Christ alone. Thus, Reichel can claim that love of God and love of neighbor "are inextricably intertwined to the point of being co-constitutive, and their ethical intertwinement is preceded by their ontological one."[240] I will not get into all the details that Reichel offers in her attempted dialogue between Barth and Althaus-Reid here because my sole point in mentioning her approach here is to illustrate once again that any view of love of God and neighbor that is conceptualized as "co-constitutive" is a view that has fundamentally ignored or misunderstood the evangelical view of justification by grace alone as presented by Torrance and Barth.

We have seen above that Torrance would have nothing to do with any view of grace as "co-constitutive."[241] Barth held a similar view stressing that "when we try to describe to ourselves the love of God, we can only express and proclaim the name of Jesus Christ. That is what it means to speak concretely of the love of God."[242] Here, Barth once again stresses the freedom of God's love by insisting that,

> God has no need to love us, and we have no claim upon His love. God is love, before He loves us and apart from it. Like everything else that He is, He is love as the triune God in Himself. Even without us and without the world and without the reconciliation of the world, He would not experience any lack of love in Himself.[243]

---

[239] Reichel, *After Method*, 125.

[240] Ibid., 117. It will be recalled that Torrance's rejection of the idea that we can love God by loving our neighbors, which was discussed above, was seen by him as another form of self-justification. See also my "Love of God and Love of Neighbor in the Theology of Karl Rahner and Karl Barth," *Modern Theology* 20 (4) (October 2004), 567–98, for why it is impossible to claim that love of God and neighbor mutually condition each other in this way when God's grace is taken seriously as his unconditional love of us which is the actual basis of our love of God and neighbor.

[241] See my discussion of the proper relationship between love of God and love of neighbor above, 70ff.

[242] Barth, CD I/2, 379.

[243] Ibid.

It is because God's love is free love that we cannot simply equate the love of the triune God with an understanding of God based on our experiences of faith, hope, and love detached from Christ and the Holy Spirit. Above all this means that one cannot redefine grace, revelation, and knowledge of God in the manner suggested by Reichel. She claims that,

> rearticulating grace as divine faithfulness, kenosis, and revelation, with Barth and Althaus-Reid leads to "queer virtues" of stubborn excessiveness, messy solidarity, and indecent honesty. As craters and signposts of queer holiness, they are reflections and glimmers of divine grace in a world that to some extent remains surprised by their presence. These queer "virtues" might be traced in many areas of human existence; the one that concerns me here are their epistemological versions.[244]

Reichel writes "the Queer Theologian in me scoffs at this desire [to use the triptych of faith, love and hope as a blueprint of grace], and insists that nothing protects such 'virtues' from becoming romanticized into pure and clean characteristics ascribed to a speculative deity" and into "idealized versions of Christian life (and epistemology)."[245] She says they need to do justice to the "determinate character of God."[246] However, here she has not said one word about the God who is the object of reflection presented by Barth and Torrance. And that is the case because Jesus Christ himself is completely absent from this part of her presentation. Apparently, that is why she can finally conclude that "a notion like 'revelation' can never ground or explain theological insight; rather, it is the concept designed to name the fact that it happens, inexplicably, and for us accidentally."[247]

This view stands in stark contrast to Barth's statement that revelation means "The Word became flesh" because it is in Christ himself that God reveals himself to us as the one who loves us. Hence, "It is by God's revelation that we know God as the One who is absolutely perfect and self-sufficient … He does not need another … God reveals Himself to us in Jesus Christ as the One who does not owe us Himself, but has bestowed Himself upon us."[248] Reichel's view also contrasts with Torrance's view that if we cut the bond between Jesus, the incarnate Son, and the Father, then "there would be no identity between God and the content of his revelation" and therefore

---

[244] Reichel, *After Method*, 125.
[245] Ibid., 125–6.
[246] Ibid., 126.
[247] Ibid., 252.
[248] Barth, CD II/1, 206.

we would have no access to God the Father through the Son and Spirit. That would mean that "we would be left completely in the dark about God. God would be for us no more than an absolute blank, of which we can neither think nor speak."[249] That is why he insisted that the content of God's revelation is God himself in his actions in the incarnate Son such that "In Jesus Christ the Giver of grace and the Gift of grace are one and the same, for in him and through him it is none other than God himself who is savingly and creatively at work for us and our salvation."[250] This particular revelation is indeed the ground of our understanding of God, revelation, grace, sin, and salvation. Sadly, Reichel confuses anthropology with Christology along with so many others such as Rahner himself with his mutually conditioning view of the two. She claims that "the substance of epistemology is anthropology, but the substance of anthropology is soteriology, harmartiology, eschatology and at the end of the day Christology."[251] This remark moves exactly in the opposite direction from the view of Barth, who insisted that there is a way from Christology to anthropology, but no way from anthropology to Christology. This is a view that, as seen above, Torrance also held.

So, she concludes by saying that we can do justice to the "determinate character of God" where "the concrete shapes of the real lives of real people ... taking as seriously the reality of grace to be found in both ... they become messy, excessive, indecent—in short: queer."[252] Hence, her "material reality check ... is one that understands theology as a material practice of conceptual design as informed by faithfulness to sites of failure, excess, and marginality; kenotic solidarity with the messiness of real life ... and indecently honest appraisal of its own conditions of production."[253] Regrettably, none of this has a thing to do with "grace" as Barth and Torrance understand the meaning of that word because Reichel has completely detached grace from Christ, the Giver of grace, and equated that with "messy" experience and "queer" experience.

Before ending this chapter, it would be useful to briefly consider one other widely recognized approach to liberation offered by James Cone in his landmark book *A Black Theology of Liberation*.[254] We have already seen that for Torrance:

---

[249] Torrance, *The Trinitarian Faith*, 133.
[250] Ibid., 138.
[251] Reichel, 252.
[252] Ibid., 126.
[253] Ibid.
[254] Many today think this book has been superseded to a certain extent by Cone's *The Cross and the Lynching Tree* first published in 2011 and *God of the Oppressed* first published in 2012. But my intention here is simply to explore his position in this work which is not entirely abandoned in these later works.

a proper christology ... must be faithful to the whole fact of the mystery of Christ. It can never start from one aspect of that mystery such as the historical or the eschatological, or the transcendental—but from the dual fact, the whole mystery of true God and true man. That fact calls into radical question the basic assumption (of both idealism and liberalism) that no fact in the time series can have absolute and decisive significance

because in Christ "we are confronted by the eternal in union with time."[255] Clearly, Torrance consistently allows Jesus Christ himself in his uniqueness as the incarnate Word to be the *first* and the *final* Word in his approach. On the surface it may seem that in his book *A Black Theology of Liberation*, James Cone offers a similar view when he says, "Christian theology begins and ends with Jesus Christ. He is the point of departure for everything to be said about God, humankind, and the world."[256] He asks, "What is the essence of Christianity?" and answers that this "can be given in the two words: Jesus Christ."[257] From these remarks it might seem that Cone is allowing his thought about God, Christ, and liberation itself to be determined by who Jesus was and is in his own time and now as the risen, ascended, and coming Lord.

But things immediately take a wrong turn because he is only interested in Christ as a "symbol" that we use in the Tillichian sense to understand our religious condition today. So, he writes on the very same page: "Because Jesus Christ is the focal point for everything that is said about the Christian gospel, it is necessary to investigate the meaning of his person and work *in light of the black perspective*."[258] Here, his thinking clearly does not begin with what Torrance called the mystery of Jesus himself who could not be understood in light of anyone's prior perspective or knowledge because of his utter uniqueness as God become man. Naturally, as noted above, we cannot and do not need to get rid of our perspectives when we engage in theology, but it is a fact that the moment our perspective becomes the lens through which we interpret Jesus in his uniqueness, we are substituting ourselves and our viewpoints for the Holy Spirit, who alone can enable our knowledge of Christ and his will for us here and now. The fact that this can happen and does happen was understood well by both Torrance and Barth when they insisted that revelation, in its identity with Jesus Christ, is offensive to us. That is why we think we need to interpret him from our own perspectives in accordance

---

[255] Torrance, *Incarnation*, 7–8.
[256] James H. Cone, *A Black Theology of Liberation Fiftieth Anniversary Edition* (New York: Maryknoll Orbis Books, 2020), 116.
[257] Ibid.
[258] Ibid., emphasis mine.

with our own agenda. Doing this means failure once again to recognize the decisive nature of our justification by grace alone.

For Cone, it is the "black perspective" which becomes the criterion for understanding Jesus, thus displacing Jesus himself as the risen, ascended, and advent Lord from the picture. This is in harmony with his distorted and bizarre concept of truth. He writes, "In the struggle for truth in a revolutionary age, there can be no principles of truth, no absolutes, not even God."[259] With those odd remarks, Cone abandons any possibility for serious Christology or any theology at all. He says his characterization of black theology is "analogous to Paul Tillich's analysis of the 'existential thinker.'"[260] Tillich goes on to quote from Feuerbach saying that "Only what is an object of passion—really is."[261] That is another strange remark as that perspective undermines the fact that reality simply is what it is whether it is an object of anyone's passion or not. From this Cone makes a number of disturbingly disastrous remarks.

He says in relation to "black theology" that,

> truth for the black thinker arises from a passionate encounter with black reality. Though that truth may be described religiously, as God, it is not the God of white religion but the God of black existence. *There is no way to speak of this objectively; truth is not objective.* It is subjective, a personal experience of the ultimate in the midst of degradation. Passion is the only appropriate response to this truth.[262]

It is amazing that Cone proceeds to use the word "truth" at all since he gave up the question of truth methodologically at the outset by claiming that "truth is not objective."[263] The really disturbing feature of this subjectivism which could never lead to any truth in theology is the fact that Cone equates the reality considered by black theologians to be "black reality" which he immediately and consistently opposes to "white reality." The problem with that approach is not only its racist overtones by defining reality solely in terms of race but the false assumption that objective reality could be different for different people.

To put this in the theological terms I am espousing in this book: Jesus is the Way, the Truth, and the Life (Jn 14:6) and he died for the sins *of all people*. Not so for Cone. He claims that "whites … are rendered incapable

---

[259] Ibid., 19.
[260] Ibid., 20.
[261] Ibid.
[262] Ibid., 20–1, emphasis mine.
[263] Ibid., 21.

of making valid judgments on the character of sin."²⁶⁴ That is an unfortunate remark because any such valid judgments could only be made based on Christ's forgiving grace, which is unconditionally there for all people. Cone even claims that "To be black is to be committed to destroying everything this country [the USA] loves and adores."²⁶⁵ He claims, "when white theology attempts to speak to blacks about Jesus Christ, the gospel is presented in the light of the social, political, and economic interest of the white majority."²⁶⁶ Yet, if that were in any sense true, then such theology would have already lost the mystery of Christ according to what Torrance said above. There really is no such thing as "white theology," and if any theology is presented in light of the social, political, and economic interests of any group, it has already lost its objective grounding in Christ himself; it has failed to live by grace alone.

Instead of allowing Christ alone to dictate the truth of his theology, Cone says, "The black experience is a source of black theology because theology seeks to relate biblical revelation to the situation of blacks in America."²⁶⁷ However, if Jesus Christ is the point of departure for everything said in theology, as Cone initially claimed, then this statement is already more than a little questionable. The whole of his book on black liberation theology therefore is profoundly untheological because he simply uses the "symbol" Jesus as a symbol of black oppression at the hands of whites. The entire book then is an argument for the destruction of everything "white" in favor of "blackness," which is equated with oppression. He claims that "white society … uses Christianity as an instrument of oppression" by presenting images of "a white Jesus that are completely alien to the liberation of the black community."²⁶⁸ Whether or not he is right or wrong about "white society" misusing Christianity, the point here is that, for Cone, it is liberation in and of the black community that actually is his norm for assessing who Jesus was and is for the faith of the community. To that extent, he has already denied the mystery of Christ and cannot allow him to be his sole criterion of truth and freedom, as he initially seemed to propose.

What is the proof of this? He asserts, "If Jesus is white and not black, he is an oppressor, and we must kill him."²⁶⁹ However, Jesus really was neither white nor black. And Cone's attempt to identify his uniqueness by appealing to race misses completely the mystery of Jesus Christ as identified by Torrance.

---

[264] Ibid., 113.
[265] Ibid., 21.
[266] Ibid., 24.
[267] Ibid., 26.
[268] Ibid., 117.
[269] Ibid.

As an aside, it is worth pointing out that Torrance claimed that "Separated from Israel gentiles have to do only with some unrevealed God who is not God, and are in fact 'without hope and without God … in the world'. As our Lord himself said to the woman of Samaria 'You worship what you do not know, we worship what we know, for salvation is of the Jews.'"[270] Torrance claims that in both East and West, "we have steadily gentilised our image of Jesus. We have tended to abstract Jesus from his setting in the context of Israel and its vicarious mission in regard to divine revelation."[271] He thinks we cannot detach the patterns of our thought from "their embodiment in Israel as they" were "presented in the Old Testament Scriptures, or even in the New Testament, and then schematise them to our own culture, a western culture, a black culture, an oriental culture, as the case may be."[272] To do so or to interpret Jesus "within the conditioning of our European culture" would mean to lose him for who he was and is by,

> plastering upon the fact of Jesus a mask of different gentile features which prevents us from seeing him and understanding him as he really is, as a Jew—and certainly prevents our brethren the Jews from recognising in this stylised Christ which we equate with "the historical Jesus" the Messiah whom they are still expecting. The time has surely come for us to enlist the aid of the Jews in helping us to interpret Jesus as he is actually presented to us in the Jewish Scriptures.[273]

His point is that we cannot project cultural images from ourselves onto Jesus if we are to understand him as he was and is.

Now back to Cone. His purpose is to equate "the historical Jesus and the oppressed, showing that the equation of the contemporary Christ with black power arises out of a serious encounter with the biblical revelation."[274] Thus, we are told Jesus is "the Black Messiah" because he is the kingdom "whose relationship to God and human beings is defined by his words and work."[275] That assertion, however, is extremely problematic because Jesus' uniqueness as the incarnate Word is not defined by his words and work. It is exactly the other way around: his words and works are relevant because he is God from God, true God from true God. As such, he has come into history from

---

[270] Torrance, *The Mediation of Christ*, 105–6.
[271] Ibid., 19.
[272] Ibid.
[273] Ibid., 19–20.
[274] Ibid., 120.
[275] Ibid., 120 and 122.

outside to reconcile both Jews and Gentiles to God. This is not the case for Cone. He says, "Jesus is the Oppressed one whose work is that of liberating humanity from inhumanity ... This and this alone is the meaning of his *finality*."[276] From this he concludes, with Bultmann, that our task today is to interpret the Jesus of history "by the theological significance of the death-resurrection event."[277] That remark may sound good to the untrained ear, but it is a disaster because it is not the risen Lord himself who determines truth here but us employing the "death-resurrection event" to interpret who Jesus was and is today. So, Cone concludes from this that "*God is present in all dimensions of human liberation*"[278] with the result that he thinks we can find God and Christ wherever humans work for liberation.

That, however, is a huge mistake, as I have been arguing throughout this chapter, because such a view essentially offers us a Pelagian view of grace and an espousal of self-justification in the form of our human working for liberation. Indeed, for Cone, that work should not take the form of Martin Luther King's advocacy of nonviolence. He advocates violence or whatever it takes to overcome "whiteness"! But here we come to the real problem with Cone's book. On the one hand, he says quite rightly that we cannot just project our images onto Christ. But on the other hand, that is exactly what he does. He does this because he says we know who Jesus was "through a critical, historical evaluation of the New Testament Jesus."[279]

From what Torrance said above, it is easy to see that this approach unequivocally ignores the *whole fact* of Christ by assuming we can know him through a critical and historical evaluation of the New Testament. According to Torrance, we can only know him as the Lord in faith as the Holy Spirit enables that knowledge here and now. To just approach him through history puts the norm for Christology in our hands instead of in Christ's hands. There is a price that is paid for this when, with Cone, or anyone else, we do not actually rely on Christ himself to know the true meaning of liberation and the true meaning of theology.

Cone argues that "the soteriological value of Jesus' person must finally determine our Christology."[280] However, it is the other way around—it is his person as the incarnate Son that determines the fact that he is the Savior. Cone's false theology stems, as it did with Bultmann and John Robinson, from his complete reduction of the immanent Trinity to the economic Trinity

---

[276] Ibid., 124.
[277] Ibid.
[278] Ibid.
[279] Ibid., 126.
[280] Ibid.

when he analyzes the views of Gordon Kaufman. He says, "Kaufmann's [sic] view also suggests that there is knowledge of God as God is *in se*."[281] Cone, however, argues that "Theologically this seems impossible. We can know God only in relationship to the human race, or more particularly in God's liberating activity in behalf of oppressed humanity."[282] Torrance had already rejected this thinking by rejecting a similar remark by Bultmann in his *Jesus Christ and Mythology* and by rejecting the view of John Robinson as well.[283] The problem here is that Cone's view reduces God to what God does in history and it is no longer grounded in the eternal being of God as Father, Son, and Holy Spirit. So, he can claim, with Tillich, that God is the infinite and then claim to find God directly in historical events of liberation without first knowing our justification by faith and by grace as this has taken place objectively in Christ for all people.

Hence, he claims that "Only those who live in an oppressed condition can know what their love-response ought to be to their oppressors."[284] We are then told that whites can "think only in white thought-patterns, even in reference to God."[285] That is certainly a puzzling remark because he is claiming that white people think of Jesus as white and then project that image into God. But if he had even thought for a moment about God, the eternal Trinity (the immanent Trinity), as the ground of our knowledge of God, he would have realized that God is Spirit and cannot be defined at all by culture, race, or any other human condition. This projection into God is the mythology that was rejected when Arianism was rejected in the fourth century.

In any case he argues that "Black theology will accept only a love of God which participates in the destruction of the white oppressor."[286] We are told that "To be God, God must protect both the freedom and the structure of human behavior."[287] But theologians who actually recognize God's freedom in himself realize that this thinking reduces God to his relations with us and loses God's actual freedom *in se* and *ad extra*. To be God, God does not have to do anything for us. That he does so is an expression of his free grace. As Barth never tired of insisting,

---

[281] Ibid., 74.
[282] Ibid., 74–5.
[283] See above, Chapter One, at n.74, where Torrance directly rejects this viewpoint of Bultmann.
[284] Cone, 76.
[285] Ibid.
[286] Ibid.
[287] Ibid., 77.

God has no need to love us, and we have no claim upon His love. God is love, before He loves us and apart from it. Like everything else that He is, He is love as the triune God in himself. Even without us and without the world and without the reconciliation of the world, He would not experience any lack of love in Himself.[288]

That's not the end of it. Again, while Cone paid lip-service to the fact that Christ is the only point of departure for Christian theology, he then claimed that to understand God's love in a racist society, he was "Using blackness as the point of departure" so that "black theology believes that God's love of humankind is revealed in God's willingness to become black. God's love is incomprehensible apart from blackness."[289] Again, that is a puzzling statement in light of Jn 3:16, which refers to all who would believe in Christ. Cone then says, "God is black because God loves us; and God loves us because we are black."[290] However, that is another puzzling remark from the vantage of salvation by grace through faith because God does not love any of us because he finds us lovable or because of anything we are or might be. He loved us in Christ, according to St. Paul, while we were still sinners with an unconditional love that was not based on anyone's race or personal condition.

Furthermore, instead of claiming that God was made known uniquely in the Person and Work of Christ, Cone claims that "Believing that the biblical God is made known through the liberation of the oppressed, the black theology analysis of God begins with an emphasis on God's blackness."[291] Here's the problem: Cone is clearly preoccupied with race as the key to understanding God, Christ, and salvation. But the real key, according to his own stated view of Christianity, was supposed to be Christ himself. However, he cannot allow that to be so because for him Christ is only a "symbol" we use to speak about overcoming racism and other forms of oppression. That is the central problem I am highlighting by indicating that Christ, the incarnate Word, must be both the *first* and the *final* Word in theology, because he himself is God acting as man for us, irrespective of our race and who we are or who we think we are.

Cone's problem is that for him, as for Tillich, God is a symbol we use to create our own freedom.[292] He can thus say, "God is not 'above' or 'beyond'

---

[288] Barth, CD I/2, 379.
[289] Cone, 78.
[290] Ibid.
[291] Ibid., 78–9.
[292] Ibid. 80–1.

the world. Rather transcendence refers to human purpose as defined by the infinite in the struggle for liberation."[293] Indeed, according to Cone, "the nature of God is to be found in the concept of liberation."[294] Notice how truly untheological this position is. Transcendence for Christians refers to the eternal existence of God as Father, Son, and Holy Spirit, who loves in freedom (the immanent Trinity), and thus, the nature of God is not found in the concept of liberation or any other concept for that matter, because the nature of God can only be known through an encounter with God himself as he meets us in his Word and Spirit in the economy (economic Trinity). The triune God confessed in the Nicene Creed existed before creation and could well have always existed in perfect freedom and love without creation if he so chose. So, God *is* indeed above and beyond the world. But he is in the world in his incarnate Word and through the power of his Holy Spirit and the power of the risen and ascended Lord himself. This God, however, is not identical with the infinite as we conceive that, because the infinite so conceived cannot exist without the finite. And one can certainly speak of the infinite, as Cone does and as Tillich did, without acknowledging God as the eternal Father, Son, and Holy Spirit. This triune God who became incarnate certainly came into history as our liberator, but the crucial point is that in Jesus himself he effected our justification and sanctification precisely by liberating all people from sin as self-will. That is because "if the Son sets you free, you will be free indeed" (Jn 8:36).

Instead of pointing us to Christ as the point of contact for our relations with the eternal God, Cone says of blacks that "We are *free*, free to defy the oppressor's laws of human behavior, because we have encountered the concreteness of the divine in our liberation, which has revealed to us the transcendence of our cause beyond all human definitions."[295] Once again that statement may sound nice to the untrained ear. But it is a problematic remark from a truly theological point of view because Cone has clearly substituted human liberation, abstractly understood, for God's unique act of liberation from sin which took place in Christ's vicarious humanity for all people. This once again is a Pelagian theology because he thinks blacks are free, and as they fight against oppression, they encounter revelation in that experience. That is untrue because blacks and whites are in fact sinners who are not truly free for God at all in themselves, and thus in what they do humanly in their struggles for liberation. They may become free only as they hear and obey the Word of God in Jesus Christ and obey him alone; that is,

---

[293] Ibid., 82.
[294] Ibid., 67.
[295] Ibid., 82.

only as the Son sets them free from sin which is identical with their free-will which is their self-will.

Let me return to the point I am making here once more. Cone is right to say that all Christian theology must start with Jesus Christ himself. But he does not do that because he invariably starts his theology with what we do to fight against oppression. So, he says, "It is the oppressed community in the situation of liberation that determines the meaning and scope of Jesus."[296] Nothing could be further from the truth. It is Jesus—the incarnate Word who lived a life of perfect obedience to the Father for us and who died for our sins and rose from the dead—who alone, even now, determines the meaning and scope of who he was and is. Cone claims, "We know who he is when our own lives are placed in a situation of oppression, and we thus have to make a decision for or against our condition."[297] We must reject this thinking also because it ascribes knowledge of Christ to us as we find ourselves in a situation of oppression and then make a decision for or against that condition. Everything in this analysis is grounded in us and what we do when it should be grounded in the fact that in Christ we are saved by grace alone, which simply cannot be detached from his saving actions for us there and then, and here and now. He is the one who liberates us from the oppression of sin which is our self-will, and which is what leads to the oppression of others in the first place. Consequently, we only know who Jesus really is when we are empowered to do so by the risen Lord himself and through the power of his Holy Spirit just as Torrance consistently claimed. And when that occurs, we know for sure that it is our decision for or against him that really is our decision for or against God himself because face to face with Christ we are in fact face to face with God who frees us from sin to love him and on that basis to love our neighbors and to fight against oppression.[298] Hence, we do not know Christ by deciding for or against our condition. That is just another version of self-justification.

---

[296] Ibid., 126.

[297] Ibid.

[298] Torrance says, "I myself like to think of the doctrine of the Trinity as the *ultimate ground* of theological knowledge of God, for it is there that we find our knowledge of God reposing upon the final Reality of God himself, grounded in the ultimate relations intrinsic to God's own Being, which govern and control all true knowledge of him from beginning to end" (Torrance, *The Ground and Grammar of Theology*, 158–9). He says this was the great concern at the Council of Nicaea when the "Fathers, so to speak, on their knees" expressed this doctrine with "a profound doxological orientation ... Face to face with Jesus Christ, they had to do immediately with God, who so unreservedly communicated *himself* to them in Christ that they knew Christ to be the embodiment of God, so that they not only worshipped God through and with Christ but in Christ, worshipping God face to face in Christ who is himself the face of the Father turned toward them" (ibid., 159).

Once again, as with Bultmann and probably also Pannenberg, whom Cone cites, he says, "to say no to oppression and yes to liberation is to encounter the existential significance of the Resurrected One. He is the liberator *par excellence* whose very presence makes persons sell all that they have and follow him."[299] This remark might also sound good, except for two things. First, we can easily say no to oppression and yes to liberation without even the slightest knowledge of the risen Lord. Second, these comments by Cone are followed immediately by the following remarks: "The black community is an oppressed community because of its blackness; hence the christological importance of Jesus must be found in his blackness."[300] Thus, "If he is not black as we are, then the resurrection has little significance for our times. Indeed, if he cannot be what we are, we cannot be who he is."[301] On the one hand, Cone has projected "blackness" onto the historical Jesus, who was neither black nor white. Such projection suggests that he is not allowing what Torrance called the whole fact of Jesus in his mysterious duality in unity to determine what is of christological significance. On the other hand, he claims that if Jesus cannot be "what we are, we cannot be who he is."[302] That assertion misses the whole point of Jesus' uniqueness.

We can never be who he is because only he, of all humans who ever existed, is truly God and truly human and thus the one and only mediator of God's free reconciling love to us and for us all, irrespective of our culture or race. Contrary to the New Testament witness, Cone claims that "Any statement about Jesus today that fails to consider blackness as the *decisive* factor about his person is a denial of the New Testament message."[303] Once again, Cone has missed the most important message of the New Testament which is that the decisive factor about Jesus' person is the fact that this man is God himself acting for us and liberating us from our self-will and from all our attempts to overcome oppression (including all forms of racism) by relying upon ourselves instead of upon Christ's forgiving grace and the freedom for God and others that comes from him alone.

Finally, Cone claims that "The black Jesus is also an important theological symbol for an analysis of Christ's presence today because we must make decisions about where he is at work in the world." Hence, "to speak of the presence of Christ today means focusing on the forces of liberation in

---

[299] Ibid.
[300] Ibid.
[301] Ibid., 126–7.
[302] Ibid., 127.
[303] Ibid.

the black community."³⁰⁴ All of this is mistaken for one simple reason. Jesus is not a symbol. Thus, we cannot find his presence by focusing on forces of liberation because those forces, apart from Christ who is the grace of God active in history, are little more than our efforts to justify and sanctify ourselves by fighting against oppression. If those actions depicted by Cone were truly acts of obedience to Christ, then Cone would have had to admit that the only way to speak of Christ's presence today is to point away from the community toward Christ himself as the only saving power and the only one who thus can truly liberate us from racism as from all that oppresses us in our human condition.

Instead of doing that, he pits whites against blacks and blacks against whites. That can never lead to a reconciled community working together in obedience to the Word heard and believed. Cone claims that "The definition of Christ as black means that he represents the complete opposite of the values of white culture. He is the center of a black Copernican revolution."³⁰⁵ Thus, for Cone, "The blackness of Christ clarifies the definition of him as the *Incarnate* One. In him God becomes oppressed humanity and thus reveals that the achievement of full humanity is consistent with divine being."³⁰⁶ For Cone, this means that "Blackness is a manifestation of the being of God in that it reveals that neither divinity nor humanity resides in white definitions but in liberation from captivity."³⁰⁷

Here we must ask: Were the definitions of Christ's uniqueness presented at the Council of Chalcedon "white definitions"? How can anyone claim that "blackness" or "whiteness" is a manifestation of God when God is truly manifest only in his Word and Spirit? Moreover, since it is a fact that there is neither gender nor race in God because God is Spirit and must be worshipped in Spirit and truth (Jn 4:34), even the slightest idea that we can have a "white God" or a "black God" represents an illegitimate reading back into God a logical necessity based on one's political, social, or cultural agenda. It is true that, in Christ, God has liberated us from captivity. But it is the captivity of sin as self-will that he has liberated us from. This is the key point that is not recognized at all in Cone's presentation because he equates goodness with one race and evil with another. But, according to the Gospel, we are all sinners, and all forgiven through the blood of Christ.

Cone does refer to Jesus as "the son of God, son of Man, messiah, lord, son of David" but then says these are "first-century titles" and "To cling to them

---

³⁰⁴ Ibid.
³⁰⁵ Ibid., 128.
³⁰⁶ Ibid.
³⁰⁷ Ibid.

without asking, 'What appropriate symbol do these titles refer to today?' is to miss the significance of them altogether."[308] It is just here that Cone demonstrates once again that he has completely misunderstood the simple fact that those "titles" were not just symbolic attempts by the community to speak of Jesus' significance for faith. The truth of those titles was grounded in the fact that Jesus really is the Lord who alone can reveal God to us. He alone can justify and sanctify sinners and overcome oppression because he alone is God acting as man not just for blacks or for whites or for any other specific race but for all people.

Amazingly, Cone could even claim that "To be a disciple of the black Christ is to become black with him. Looting, burning, or the destruction of white property are not *primary* concerns. Such matters can only be decided by the oppressed themselves who are seeking to develop their images of the black Christ."[309] These are truly astonishing remarks when one considers the fact that God really was in Christ reconciling the world to himself. If it is the decision of a community to loot, burn, and destroy white property based on their images of the black Christ, should that not be enough of a warning that the true reconciliation of all humanity can never be achieved by what we do based on the development of our own images of Christ? That is not within our power, of course, because Jesus Christ himself really is the Lord who humiliated himself for us on the cross in order to overcome the sin and self-will that pits blacks against whites and whites against blacks in the first place. Cone mistakenly places the power of God in our sinful hands, and that can only lead to more and more conflict between blacks and whites. But if Jesus is recognized as the Reconciler and Redeemer of all, then one could never argue that some people would be justified in destroying the property of others depending upon how they decide to employ their images of Christ!

Conclusion

In this lengthy chapter, I argued for a liberation theology that is truly liberating when it begins and ends by recognizing that Jesus Christ himself as the incarnate Word of the Father is the one and only Liberator. To recognize and acknowledge that truth is to live our justification and sanctification by grace alone in and through Christ as our reconciler and redeemer. He thus came to us as our Savior, Helper, and Friend in order to liberate us from the sin and self-will displayed in our efforts to live autonomously in relation to

---

[308] Ibid., 129.
[309] Ibid., 130.

God, wherein we rely on ourselves and then try to reconstruct who God is and what grace is by detaching true freedom from Christ as the giver of grace and freedom. Christ came to empower us to find our actual freedom, which is freedom from the sin as self-will that leads to oppression in its many forms, including racism and sexism. However, that freedom is ours and can only be found in and from Christ himself in his vicarious humanity as the Spirit unites us to him as the risen and ascended Lord in faith. Thus, my argument is and has been that we cannot understand the true meaning of sin, salvation, or liberation in the Christian sense by starting theology with peoples' battles against oppression and for liberation. When that happens, we are prone to create more conflict among ourselves by advancing our own political, social, and religious agendas pitted against each other as "oppressor" versus "oppressed." That is why I have argued that such a starting point always leads directly to self-justification, in which people use Jesus as a means toward a particular social, religious, or political goal. Starting with the freedom of grace in its identity with Jesus the incarnate Word and reconciler allows all people as well as all races, cultures, and political or religious affiliations to live the freedom which was and is unconditionally given in Christ himself. On that basis, we would then fight against every form of oppression as God himself empowers us to do so since he has freed us to do so by unconditionally loving us in Christ while we were still sinners.

3

A Fine Point in Christology: Discovering Why It Is Important Not to Read the Missions of the Economic Trinity Back into the Immanent Trinity

It is a truism that Christology has a profound bearing on the doctrine of the Trinity. That is the case for obvious reasons; if Jesus is the incarnate Son of the Father, then what he reveals of God shapes our understanding of God as Father, Son, and Holy Spirit. That is the simple part. Matters become more complex the deeper we probe into the meaning of these remarks for us and for our understanding of God. In this chapter, I will explore and critically analyze Bruce L. McCormack's thesis that the Council of Chalcedon (451), which set the parameters for christological accuracy, needs repair and what that repair might imply for a proper Christology and theology of the Trinity. I have chosen to set McCormack's position in relation to the views of two of the twentieth century's greatest theologians, Thomas F. Torrance and Karl Barth. With the help of what they say I will demonstrate that they achieve McCormack's goal of recognizing and maintaining Jesus' full humanity and full deity precisely on the basis of the Chalcedonian teaching.

Thus, I will illustrate that the idea that Chalcedon needed to be repaired in the manner suggested by McCormack is misguided because it not only conflicts with the teaching of Chalcedon but ends up collapsing the immanent into the economic Trinity. The importance of relying on Barth and Torrance lies in the fact that the concerns they articulate, and would articulate, are broadly representative of the historic ecumenical consensus stemming from Nicaea and Chalcedon. They are an appropriate choice to use because they are close to McCormack's Reformed background without being narrowly Reformed or idiosyncratic. Their thinking illustrates that McCormack is a deviant voice even within his most immediate tradition as well as within the broader conciliar traditions. Whether from a broader or a narrower perspective, they speak for all those who would contend that no "repair" of Chalcedon is necessary, and that the proposed remedy is worse than the supposed flaw. This is "new Eutychianism," with all the problems of the old one plus some new ones that have never been heard of before. Let me begin by concisely stating McCormack's position and the reason for his position.

McCormack notes that his book on Christology is the first of a trilogy that would include one on the "person" of Christ, another on "the triune God of electing grace," and another on the "'work' of Christ."[1] He stresses that his view of the person of Christ is already shaped by Christ's work because he says it is the "narrated *history* of Jesus of Nazareth that will be basic" to his concept of God.[2] He thus appropriately maintains that "the doctrine of God should be grounded Christologically—which is why the Christology must come first."[3] In order to understand God properly then, he asks, "what are the ontological conditions in God of the possibility that Jesus of Nazareth should rightly have been worshipped as God?"[4] In this work, he wishes to provide an alternative to views grounded either "in cosmology (as with the ancient church) or anthropology (as with a good bit of 'modern' theology)."[5] Further, he wishes to adhere to what he calls "Barth's 'rule,'" which is that "'statements about the divine modes of being antecedently in themselves cannot be different in content from those that are to be made about their reality in revelation.'"[6] According to McCormack, this means that statements about the immanent Trinity must be rooted in the economy and that implies that there

---

[1] Bruce Lindley McCormack, *The Humility of the Eternal Son: Reformed Kenoticism and the Repair of Chalcedon* (Cambridge: Cambridge University Press, 2021), 1.
[2] Ibid.
[3] Ibid., 2.
[4] Ibid.
[5] Ibid.
[6] Ibid., citing Barth CD I/1, 479. What Barth means here is what Torrance means when he says, "What God is toward us in his saving condescension to be with us in Jesus Christ, he is in himself, and what he is in his real presence with us and in us as the Holy Spirit, he is in himself." Torrance, *Christian Doctrine of God*, 92; also ibid., 8, 108–9, 172, and 198–9. However, Torrance makes an important additional set of assertions, namely, that "This is not to say that God is constituted in his Being or in the personal nature of his Being through the relations of his love toward us, any more than he is constituted in his Being through relation to the universe which in his ungrudging love he has created out of nothing" (ibid., 4). That is because "God freely wills not to be without us and wills to be with us as those whom he has eternally chosen to coexist with himself … It is the sheer gratuitous grace of God … for he does not need relation to us to be what he is as the living acting God" (ibid.). Torrance notes that it was Origen who mistakenly held that "God's relation to the created universe is necessary to his own Being" and that this thinking was "comprehensively destroyed by Athanasius" (ibid.). On this point Torrance and McCormack differ because McCormack thinks creation is in some sense necessary to God as when he says that because God's "eternal life-act" is one of "self-knowing and self-willing" which is also "'person-forming' both as it looks inward (toward the processions) and outward toward that which will be created" and concludes that "*necessarily* to will himself as self-giving, self-donating, self-emptying love contains in itself a relation to another. And since that which is other than the Maker of heaven and earth can only be 'finite,' the love of God for himself as self-giving love *necessitates*

can be "no metaphysical 'gap'" which "would make the immanent Trinity to be somehow 'more' than what is given to be known in the economy."[7] So, he advocates a "quasi-transcendental method that asks, for example, what must God be in God's Self if it is true that Jesus is Lord?" or "what are the ontological conditions in God of the possibility that Jesus of Nazareth should rightly be worshipped as God?"[8] His method then is to pursue what he says is "a dialectical movement in thought 'from below to above' and only then, and on that basis, 'from above to below.'"[9]

---

[7] the existence of the finite," Bruce L. McCormack, "The Passion of God Himself: Barth on Jesus's Cry of Dereliction," *Reading the Gospels with Karl Barth*, ed. Daniel L. Migliore (Grand Rapids, MI: Eerdmans, 2017), 171. The problem here is that McCormack makes no distinction between the love of God within the eternal Trinity as Father, Son, and Holy Spirit and the otherness of the finite which God freely brought into being in an act of will by creating the world. In line with this approach, McCormack also ascribes God's love for us directly to the Father's generation of the Son as when he maintains that Barth's talk of the Father's command and the Son's obedience "as an event in pretemporal eternity must be understood as simply a way of describing the eternal generation of the Son" so that in his view "what we have before us is the eternal generation of the Son, but *an eternal generation of the Son that has embedded in it the self-humiliation that is his incarnation in time*" (McCormack, *The Humility of the Eternal Son*, 116, emphasis mine). It is that last claim that the Son's self-humiliation in grace for us is already embedded in his generation from the Father that flatly confuses the immanent and economic Trinity. And that is what Torrance and Barth consistently opposed in order to recognize and maintain the freedom of God's grace and the sovereignty of the triune God.

[7] Ibid. This view certainly contrasts with the views of Barth and Torrance, as we shall see, because Torrance holds that the immanent Trinity has priority over the economic Trinity and Barth insisted that the immanent Trinity simply refers to God's eternal being and act which is what it is and would have suffered no lack even if he never decided to create and become incarnate.

[8] Ibid.

[9] Ibid. Interestingly, when Torrance begins his Christology he refuses to begin "from below" or "from above" because, like Barth, he held that those starting points always end with what they both termed "Ebionite" or "Docetic" christologies, namely, christologies which espoused either a purely human Jesus who was thought of as unique or a divine being thought to be incarnate in Jesus based on an idea of divinity gained elsewhere than from Jesus himself. See Torrance, *The Trinitarian Faith*, 60 and 112–13. See also Molnar, *Divine Freedom*, Second Edition, Chapter Three, "Christology, Resurrection, Election and the Trinity: The Place of the *Logos Asarkos* in Contemporary Theology" and Paul D. Molnar, *Thomas F. Torrance: Theologian of the Trinity* (Farnham Surrey, England: Ashgate, 2009), Chapter Four, for more on this. Torrance insisted that we must begin Christology by acknowledging the mystery of Jesus Christ as "true man and true God" which is the actual "object which we seek to know theologically" (Torrance, *Incarnation*, 3). For Torrance, "the ultimate fact which confronts us, embedded in history and in the historical witness and proclamation of the New Testament, is the mysterious duality in unity of Jesus Christ, God without reserve, man without reserve, the eternal truth in time, the Word of God made flesh" (ibid.). Because this is a *mystery* which we cannot resolve or understand except through God's own act of revelation, Torrance insisted that "we do not seek to understand the Person and work of Jesus Christ by approaching him either from below or from above, but from below and from above at the same time ... we apprehend both together" (*Christian Doctrine of God*, 114).

In order to pursue his theology from below, the first point he emphasizes is that he believes the idea of "divine impassibility" is a "pagan one in its origins" and that unfortunately this idea has made a comeback "with a vengeance" today.[10] He strongly opposes this because this view, in his understanding, makes it impossible to assert, with the Bible, that "God suffered in Christ."[11] He thus argues that if Christology is the "testing ground" for this concept, then this concept must be rejected. And that is the reason why he thinks Chalcedon needs to be repaired. In his view, the "'orthodox' Christology in the fifth century stood very much under the control of a doctrine of God whose most basic commitments (simplicity and impassibility) were already firmly in place" since the second century.[12] Because of that he then insists that one can no longer appeal to "the orthodox Christological dogma to defend impassibility, since impassibility was necessary to its construction in the first place."[13]

Let us be clear: McCormack is claiming that a proper testing of the concept of impassibility cannot be achieved based on the christological dogma espoused at Chalcedon. He asks, "should a God-concept that had its origins in the regnant philosophy of the time (i.e. 'Middle Platonism') be allowed to *continue* its unquestioned control of even the reformation of 'orthodox' Christological doctrine?"[14] His basic thesis then is that "divine impassibility has no clear warrant in any biblical text or set of texts."[15] In his view, the only way "divine impassibility" could be espoused is in relation to God conceptualized as "'pure being', 'being-itself', or 'the Absolute.'"[16] He opposes that as a way of supporting the view that "God does not change" because the idea that God does not change is located not in some transcendent realm of the Absolute but "here in the *personal* realm of God's relation to Israel (i.e. the realm of life and love). 'Immutability' here does not mean (as it does in metaphysical reflection) that *what* God is, he always is without diminishment or enhancement. It means instead that God always remains unchangeably *who* he is as the God of the covenant of grace."[17] Instead of the word "immutability" McCormack notes that Barth used the word "constancy," which McCormack claims is not only a "relational term" but a term that belongs "to the sphere of 'psychology'—that is, to that which

[10] McCormack, *The Humility of the Eternal Son*, 3.
[11] Ibid.
[12] Ibid.
[13] Ibid.
[14] Ibid., 3–4.
[15] Ibid., 4.
[16] Ibid.
[17] Ibid.

pertains to a *person*, and to a concept of 'being' elaborated under the control of an understanding of this person as revealed in Jesus Christ."[18]

Having said all of this, McCormack goes on to state that he is in search of a Logos or Word of God who can be acted upon by the human experiences of Jesus' own life. He says the answer to this question was "universally negative" in the early church because their view of the Logos was shaped by the simplicity and impassibility thought to be inherent in "the members of the Godhead."[19] On the one hand, then, he wishes to oppose impassibility because it always offers us a view of God who cannot be "acted upon ... even when God is 'present' in bodily form to those he encountered."[20] This, because God was thought to be "'changeless' in an absolute sense" since "absolute changelessness—and, indeed, timelessness—are necessary consequences of this more basic definition of 'impassibility'". On the other hand, if we abandon impassibility, McCormack says we can then say that God is acted upon, although not every such view, such as the one found in process theology will work, because that is not compatible with the biblical view of the matter. So, his fundamental question is this: "what must God *be* if it is the case that God really is acted upon *in Jesus Christ*? To give a satisfactory answer to this question will require a new Christology—and a new theological ontology."[21] That new ontology will then let us affirm the view that Jesus' human history somehow "constitutes" his being as the second Person of the Trinity, as we shall see in detail below. Needless to say, it is that idea that both Torrance and Barth consistently opposed by opposing what they termed Ebionite and Docetic Christology.

In any event, McCormack's ultimate goal in this and his other volumes "is to construct a personal ontology of the triune God that takes as its starting point the act of God's self-revelation in Jesus Christ; a Christologically based ontology."[22] His new Christology will advance two claims: (1) "the eternal Son has an *essential* relation to the personal life of Jesus" and (2) "the nature of that relation is best understood in terms of 'ontological receptivity.'"[23] From this it follows that the *kenosis* referred to in Phil. 2:7 will limit what can be said about "God's 'being' as God to what belongs to the sphere of personal life. The result will be what my sometime collaborator Alexandra Pârvan has called a 'psychological ontology'; an ontology that breaks from the confines

---

[18] Ibid.
[19] Ibid., 5–6.
[20] Ibid., 6.
[21] Ibid.
[22] Ibid.
[23] Ibid., 7.

of concepts like 'being itself,' the 'Absolute,' the 'Unconditioned,' the utterly simple 'One,' in order to restrict its attention to divine life and love."[24] McCormack notes that while he was wrong to claim that Barth was "'anti-metaphysical' or even 'post-metaphysical,'" because Barth actually was "doing 'ontology,'" that is, "metaphysical reflection," he wants to stress that Barth's ontology "reached no higher than God's life and love."[25] Before proceeding, I should also note that McCormack's rejection of simplicity and impassibility goes hand in hand with his rejection of two other crucial christological categories, namely, *enhypostasis* and *anhypostasis*. We will consider these in due course. It should be stated here, however, that McCormack's view of God's "life and love," which begins from below, is not the same as Barth's view because Barth invariably and decisively claimed that,

> God's love for us is an overwhelming, overflowing, free love. It speaks to us of the miracle of this love. We cannot say anything higher or better of the "inwardness of God" than that God is Father, Son, and Holy Spirit, and therefore that He is love in Himself *without and before loving us, and without being forced to love us*. And we can say this only in the light of the "outwardness" of God to us, the occurrence of His revelation. It is from this that we have to learn what is the real nature of the love of God for us.[26]

In any case, McCormack begins his new Christology by claiming that "*Humility And Obedience Are Proper To The Eternal Son.*"[27] He attributes this position to Barth noting Barth's remark that "in the condescension in which he gives himself to us in Jesus Christ, he exists and speaks and acts as the One he was from all eternity and will be to all eternity"[28] because for Barth it is just as natural "for God ... to be lowly as to be high, to be near as it is to be far, to be little as it is to be great, to be abroad as to be at home ... he is amongst us in humility ... God for us."[29] He recognizes that Barth is here referring to the immanent Trinity when he then says we have to affirm "the offensive fact that there is in God himself an above and a below, a *prius* and a *posterius*, a superiority and a subordination."[30] McCormack interprets this

---

[24] Ibid.
[25] Ibid., 7–8.
[26] Barth, CD I/2, 377, emphasis mine. Here Barth wisely rejected Ritschl's understanding of God's love from below!
[27] McCormack, 9.
[28] Ibid., 10, quoting Barth's CD IV/1, 193.
[29] Ibid.
[30] Ibid., quoting Barth, CD IV/1, 200–1.

to mean that Barth "is reading the lived relation of the Son to the Father characteristic of the Son's mission in time back into the eternal processions."[31] Hence, if Jesus' human humility and obedience are indeed grounded in

> God's being as God ... then Barth has come very close to saying *not only* that there is in God an eternal humility and obedience that is rooted in the eternal generation of the Son, but also that this eternal humility and obedience has been concretely realized in time in, through, and *as* the obedient existence of Jesus; that the relation of the two is best described as one of an identity-constituting "anticipation" (in the procession of the eternal Son) and the fulfilment of that anticipation (in the incarnate life of the human Jesus in time), that these are not really two acts at all but one and the same act performed ... by two agents (one divine and one human). What I have in mind is a conception that preserves the logic (if not the categories) of Chalcedon's differentiation of God and the human—but does so in the form of a new, previously unheard of and untested, application.[32]

McCormack's innovative claim then (his unheard of and untested application) is that what happens in Christ begins as divine and ends as human, while it is "one and the same action performed by two agents."[33]

McCormack's position then rests on the idea that "where the missions are read back into the trinitarian processions (as the self-constituting life-act of God), the 'determination' of the eternal Son for receptivity would rightly be seen as *proper to him*, as belonging to the triune God in what Barth referred to as his second 'mode of being.'"[34] Importantly, he mentions that "Barth himself did not get this far" and thus left us with some unanswered questions.[35] He believes his view of "ontological receptivity," which we will consider in detail below, will answer those questions.

[31] Ibid.
[32] Ibid., 10–11.
[33] Ibid., 11.
[34] Ibid., 12.
[35] Ibid. I will argue that Barth did not get that far for definite reasons, the most important of which is that he never reduced the immanent to the economic Trinity and he never intended to confuse the missions with the processions. Barth would have been better off if, with Torrance, he just followed Calvin and held that "the subordination of Christ to the Father in his incarnate and saving economy cannot be read back into the eternal personal relations and distinctions subsisting in the Holy Trinity. The mediatorial office of Christ does not detract in any way from his divine Majesty." Torrance, *Trinitarian Perspectives*, 67. Thus, with Calvin, Torrance insisted that "the *principium* of the Father does not import an ontological priority, or some *prius aut posterius* in God, but has to do only with a 'form of order' (*ratio ordinis*) or 'arrangement' (*disposition*) of inner trinitarian relations governed by the Father/Son relationship, which in the nature of the case is irreversible, together with the relationship of the Father and the Son to the Spirit who is the Spirit of the Father and the Spirit of the Son" (ibid., 66).

Let me just present the implications of reading the missions back into the processions in the manner suggested by McCormack. He himself notes that if obedience and humility are "proper to the eternal Son," then "the ramifications for how the Christian God is understood are many and they are indeed profound. If the Son is eternally humble and obedient unto death, then a relation to this world in Jesus Christ is proper to the being of God."[36] Here then is the monumentally important issue to be discussed in this chapter. Is the relation of the world to God the result of God's free grace, or it is proper to the being of God? If it is the former, then one cannot simply read the missions back into the processions without reducing the immanent to the economic Trinity. If it is the latter, then one is espousing a view of God's relations with us that makes creation necessary for God. There is no doubt that Barth and Torrance rejected the latter view even though Barth did mistakenly read elements of the economy back into the immanent Trinity.[37] However, Barth also consistently maintained the freedom of God in himself

---

[36] Ibid. 22.

[37] For a detailed discussion of this matter and how Barth's view relates to Torrance's more accurate view, see Paul D. Molnar "The Obedience of the Son in the Theology of Karl Barth and of Thomas F. Torrance," *Scottish Journal of Theology* 67 (1) (February 2014), 50–69 and *Faith, Freedom and the Spirit*, Chapter Seven, "The Obedience of the Son in the Theology of Karl Barth and of Thomas F. Torrance," 313–54. In this piece I explained that Barth was right to argue that God can be one and also "above and below, superior and subordinate" in the incarnation and the mission of the Son of God obeying God the Father for us. But I posed the question as to why he thought he had to ascribe superiority and subordination to God's inner life to say this. I believe this was unnecessary, and in fact it has led McCormack to some extent toward his mistaken view that the missions are an intrinsic part of the processions within the immanent Trinity. Barth's view presented in CD IV/1 which ascribed superiority and subordination to the eternal Son seemed odd even in light of his earlier rejection of this notion when he said that "If revelation is to be taken seriously as God's presence, if there is to be a valid belief in revelation, then *in no sense can Christ and the Spirit be subordinate hypostases*" (CD I/1, 353, emphasis mine). With Barth, Torrance believes that what God is toward us he is in himself, as noted above. But Torrance never needed to ground that assertion in a superiority and subordination within the immanent Trinity. And he never claimed that there was a *prius* and a *posterius* in God's inner being. He followed Calvin and argued that "The *principium* of the Father does not import an ontological priority, or some *prius aut posterius* in God, but has to do only with a 'form of order' … of inner trinitarian relations governed by the Father/Son relationship, which in the nature of the case is irreversible." Torrance, *Trinitarian Perspectives*, 66. He noted that for Calvin "the subordination of Christ to the Father in his incarnate and saving economy cannot be read back into the eternal personal relations and distinctions subsisting in the Holy Trinity. The mediatorial office of Christ does not detract in any way from his divine Majesty," ibid., 66–7. Against this proper view, McCormack explicitly claims that "the Son is in some sense subordinate to the Father– not just in time but in himself" (McCormack and McCormack, *The Humility of the Eternal Son*, 288). See also *Trinitarian Perspectives*, "The Doctrine of the Holy Trinity in Gregory Nazianzen and John Calvin," 21–49, esp. 28–36 and "Calvin's Doctrine of the Trinity," 71. See also, ibid., 113–20 and 133. Torrance noted that for Calvin "'the Father is the fountain of Deity with respect, not to Being, but to order,'" ibid., 71.

and so he never held the view of McCormack, namely, that God's actions *ad extra* are actions in which God *constitutes* himself as the triune God. Barth insisted on distinguishing "the Son of God in Himself and for me" saying that "On the distinction between the 'in Himself' and 'for me' depends the acknowledgement of the freedom and unindebtedness of God's grace, i.e., the very thing that really makes it grace."[38] Thus, when Barth referred to Christ's true and eternal deity, he never described his deity as "divine-human relation"[39] but as the antecedent existence of the eternal Son who did not need incarnation to be who he was and is as the begotten Son of the Father. Acknowledging this deity meant the rejection of "an untheologically speculative understanding of the 'for us'" since that would deny grace as God's free grace.[40]

One brief example here will do. Above it was noted that for McCormack "'Immutability' here does not mean (as it does in metaphysical reflection) that *what* God is, he always is without diminishment or enhancement. It means instead that God always remains unchangeably *who* he is as the God of the covenant of grace." This led to the idea that "life and love" define who God is and to the view that this could be understood in a psychological ontology. This leads finally to the notion that understanding God out of his "*lived* relation to the world in Christ" means that we cannot conceive of eternity and time in a strictly oppositional way, but we must think of "God's eternity as God's irreducible otherness *in* God's relation to time."[41] Notice what has happened here. The eternal existence of the immanent Trinity is no longer conceptualized as God existing as the eternal Father, Son, and Holy Spirit without needing creation (the view of Barth and of Torrance); God is now conceptualized only as other *in relation* to creation. While God certainly is other in relation to creation, he is that other as the eternal Trinity who is who he is and would be who he is with or without creation. That was a constant theme in Barth's theology since he insisted on the freedom of God (the freedom of grace). So, as noted above, he claimed that there is nothing higher or better in God than that God is eternally Father, Son, and Holy Spirit who is that God without needing to be with us because his choice to be with us is a free choice of his grace and mercy.

What I will argue in this chapter is that McCormack's repair of Chalcedon turns out to be a view that ends up reversing the roles of creator and creature with his claim that Jesus' humanity constitutes the being of the second person

---

[38] Barth, CD I/1, 420.
[39] We shall see below that this is McCormack's view of the second person of the Trinity.
[40] Barth, CD I/1, 420.
[41] McCormack, *The Humility of the Eternal Son*, 23.

of the Trinity. Not only that, but he is led to redefine the second person of the Trinity as generated from the Father as what he calls divine-human relation. This is in clear contrast to the actual view expressed at Nicaea and beyond, namely, that it is the eternal Son or Word alone who is generated from the Father as God from God and as begotten and not made. That is why Calvin, for instance, held that "the Sonship of the Son" is "just as ultimate and eternal as the Fatherhood of the Father."[42] Further, he is led to claim that God the Father generated the Son for the external purpose of incarnation, suffering, humiliation, and death when in fact that would again make God dependent on history. Moreover, this had to happen for McCormack because what makes the Son to be the eternal Son in McCormack's view is his metaphysical concept of "ontological receptivity" such that "ontological receptivity" becomes the subject, while God personally acting for us in his incarnate Word and in the outpouring of the Holy Spirit becomes the predicate. Finally, he is led by his Christology from below to equate the Logos *incarnandus* with the Logos *asarkos*, thereby obliterating the distinction between the immanent and economic Trinity once again. In this chapter, I will illustrate how these mistakes follow from his rejection of divine simplicity and impassibility together with his rejection of the important concepts of *enhypostasis* and *anhypostasis*. In the end, McCormack's Christology from below finally denies Christ's actual uniqueness as the eternal Son of the Father and then flatly collapses the immanent into the economic Trinity—two conclusions Barth and Torrance wanted to avoid at all costs throughout their careers.

We may begin our analysis and critique by noting that McCormack's assertion that Karl Barth was mistaken to embrace the patristic ideas of *enhypostasis* and *anhypostasis* is an astonishing claim since for Barth the doctrine upheld with these two ideas is "a doctrine unanimously sponsored by early theology in its entirety."[43] Thus Barth claimed that in the incarnation, in virtue of the Word's becoming man, the Word assumed human nature in Christ. That meant that his human nature was *anhypostatic* in that it had no independent existence but had existence only in the Word since it was *enhypostatic*. These are crucial terms because what they affirm is that Jesus' humanity "does not possess" its subsistence "in and for itself, *in abstracto*."[44] Therefore, "apart from the divine mode of being whose existence it acquires it has none of its own; i.e., apart from its concrete existence in God in the event of the *unio*, it has no existence of its own, it is ἀνυπόστατος."[45] For

---

[42] Calvin cited in Torrance, *Trinitarian Perspectives*, 71.
[43] Barth, CD I/2, 163.
[44] Ibid.
[45] Ibid.

Barth, "*Enhypostasis* asserts the positive." By virtue of the ἐγένετο, that is, the becoming incarnate of the Word (the Word's assumption of human nature), "human nature acquires existence (subsistence) in the existence of God, meaning in the mode of being (*hypostasis*, 'person') of the Word."[46] So Barth held that the purpose of this doctrine "was to guard against the idea of a double existence of Christ as Logos and as Man, an idea inevitably bound to lead either to Docetism or to Ebionitism."[47] Importantly, Barth insists that what the Word made his own by giving it existence was "not a man, but man's nature, man's being, and so not a second existence but a second possibility of existence, to wit, that of a man."[48]

Barth was well aware of the fact that the Lutherans and Reformed disagreed about how to understand these categories because the former tended to see the relation of natures in the incarnate Word as reciprocally related, while the Reformed held that since the Logos continues to be the subject of the event, the relation was one-sided. Still, they both held to the importance of the hypostatic union. Nonetheless, Barth goes on to note that this doctrine of the *enhypostasis* and *anhypostasis* "has occasionally been combated by the primitive argument, that if the human nature of Christ is without personality of its own, it is all up with the true humanity of Christ and the Docetism of early Christology holds the field."[49] Barth says this is a primitive argument because it is claimed that modern people ascribe personality to "true human being," while the *anhypostasis* does not do this because *anhypostasis* was translated into Latin as "*impersonalitas*." However, Barth claimed that this term is misunderstood from this modern perspective because those who held to the *anhypostasis* were not denying personality to Jesus' human nature. Early church theologians called this *individualitas* and "never taught that Christ's human nature lacked this but rather that this qualification actually belonged to true human being."[50] *Personalitas* in reality referred to what we think of as existence or being. What they wanted to affirm was that "Christ's flesh in itself has no existence, and this was asserted in the interests of their positive position that Christ's flesh has its existence through the Word and in the Word, who is God Himself acting as Revealer and Reconciler."[51]

---

[46] Ibid.
[47] Ibid. For more on Barth's rejection of Ebionite and Docetic Christology, see Molnar, *Divine Freedom*, Second Edition, Chapter Two "Christology and the Trinity: Some Dogmatic Implications of Barth's Rejection of Ebionite and Docetic Christology," 45–88.
[48] Ibid.
[49] Ibid., 164.
[50] Ibid.
[51] Ibid.

In this chapter, as noted above, I will show why I think both Barth and Torrance were right to embrace versions of divine simplicity and impassibility based not only on the biblical witness but on the teaching of Chalcedon. It is my view that the teaching of Chalcedon was not grounded in a philosophy of being but in the revelation of God given in the Old and New Testaments. One key New Testament text was Mt. 11:27, and it was that text that led Athanasius to insist that "it would be more godly and true to signify God from the Son and call him Father, than to name God from his works alone and call him Unoriginate."[52] I will develop my thesis first by comparing Karl Barth's view to Bruce McCormack's view. According to McCormack, Barth's Christology verged on Apollinarianism just because he accepted these two categories throughout his theology in traditional form.[53] I will also rely on Thomas F. Torrance's careful presentation of exactly what is at stake in recognizing what these terms imply. Neither Barth nor Torrance was even remotely Apollinarian in their christologies, and both gave full import to the true humanity of the incarnate Son based on the two natures, one Person Christology of Chalcedon. So, what I hope to show is that the goal of maintaining the full humanity of Jesus Christ, the incarnate Word which all three theologians share, was achieved by Barth and Torrance precisely by grounding his humanity in his being as the Word. Thus, the whole argument by McCormack that Chalcedon needs repair is based on the false assumption that for Jesus to have a properly functioning humanity, that humanity must be understood to be constitutive of the second person of the Trinity. Such a view undermines not only Christology but also the doctrine of the Trinity, as we shall see.

In his recent work, Bruce McCormack argues for the "repair" of Chalcedon because he believes the bishops at that Council mistakenly grounded Jesus' humanity in the Logos *asarkos* who became the Logos *incarnatus* at the incarnation. In his view, unless Jesus' human history in some sense constitutes the eternal being of the Son, a proper view of his human individuality will never be acknowledged and presented. The error of the bishops at Chalcedon, according to McCormack, was that the majority of them "followed Cyril in making the preexistent Logos as such to be the 'person of the union.'"[54] That, he thinks, led to an aporia with regard to the Chalcedonian definition which identified the person with the preexistent Logos. That aporia simply is this: "Jesus of Nazareth contributes

---

[52] Athanasius, cited in Torrance, *Christian Doctrine of God*, 117 and *The Trinitarian Faith*, 49.
[53] McCormack, *The Humility of the Eternal Son*, 118. See also, ibid., 120.
[54] Ibid., 31.

nothing to the constitution of the 'person.' He has no constitutive role to play in the composition of the 'person' in which two natures are said to 'subsist.'"[55] McCormack's entire argument hinges on the fact that for him Jesus must have a constitutive relation to the Logos; if he is only added to the Logos, then his human history would have no ontological significance for the Logos and that would always lead to an instrumentalist view of his humanity, which both Barth and Torrance rejected. In any case, without that "ontological significance," McCormack insists that "it is necessary to deny to Jesus any spontaneous, self-activating agency."[56] McCormack follows Sergius Bulgakov, who, he says, "made the astute observation that the *anhypostasia* of the human 'nature' of Christ constituted (historically) a rehabilitation of Apollinaris, however unintentional."[57] From this it follows for McCormack that "despite the vestigial presence of a rehabilitated Apollinarianism in his thinking, Barth did try valiantly to overcome the ancient conflict between those who laid all of their weight on the unity of the 'person' and those who were primarily interested in the duality of the 'natures'—even if his efforts could not be crowned with success."[58]

It is worth observing here that those theologians who McCormack claims come closest to his own position all mistakenly think that for Jesus' humanity to be fully affirmed one must hold the view that his humanity had to be constitutive of the second person of the Trinity. Unless that is so, he believes, the Logos becomes the basis of all Jesus' human actions and thereby replaces his full humanity as in Apollinarianism. However, this is exactly the view that Barth early on identified as "primitive" because it fails to notice that even in the early church the affirmation that Jesus' full and true humanity had its basis in his being as the incarnate Word never actually undermined his true humanity but was the basis *of* that positive affirmation. As such his was a full and complete human nature in every respect except that, unlike the rest of us, he never sinned.

According to McCormack, human properties cannot be "predicated of a Logos understood to be simple and impassible."[59] This means that McCormack also rejects the whole notion of impassibility as well. In his view there is "a fairly direct line of connection joining Origen, Apollinaris,

---

[55] Ibid.
[56] Ibid.
[57] Ibid., 119.
[58] Ibid., 120.
[59] Ibid., 31.

and Cyril. All three wanted to understand the Christological subject as the preexistent Logos."⁶⁰ In McCormack's opinion,

> Cyril's identification of the "person of the union" with a preexistent Logos understood to be simple and impassible would not allow for a real relation of Jesus of Nazareth to the Logos ... that created an insuperable problem. If the Christological subject (the one *hypostasis*) is the Word, then there is *only one* subject to whom the properties of the human "nature" can be assigned. But the prior commitment to simplicity and impassibility would not allow that to happen.⁶¹

This is why McCormack claims that "any repair of Chalcedon would have to begin with the surrender of simplicity and impassibility."⁶² There is, however, a serious problem in the way McCormack has here understood the incarnate Word. He speaks of a "real relation of Jesus of Nazareth to the Logos."

But one might ask how can Jesus be *related* to the Logos if he *is* the Logos acting *as* man for us? This is a crucial question because the very attempt to speak of the human Jesus in *relation* to the Logos methodologically separates the human Jesus from who he was and is as the incarnate Son or Word of the Father. In other words, in McCormack's approach, the fact that for Chalcedon there was only one person with two natures cannot allow for the fact that the eternal Word who was and is impassible could really experience suffering and death and other human "properties." Yet, as we shall see, in Torrance's reading of Cyril's Christology, just because the Word who became incarnate for us and for our salvation was not lessened or changed in any way in his impassible divine being by becoming incarnate for us, he could be our savior precisely by experiencing suffering and death even *as* God for us.

For Torrance, since the Word became man without ceasing to be God, he was both impassible and passible as the one who acted as our Reconciler both from the divine and human side. Consequently, he could and did experience suffering and death both as the divine Word and as man. Torrance's view here is in direct conflict with McCormack's misguided assertion that the Chalcedonian definition "can never succeed because a *real* relation of Jesus to the 'person of the union' can never be allowed so long as one remains committed to the idea of impassibility."⁶³ The problem here is that the man Jesus is not just related to the Logos; his humanity is what it is as fully

---

⁶⁰ Ibid., 52.
⁶¹ Ibid., 57–8.
⁶² Ibid., 58.
⁶³ Ibid., 64.

and completely human in every respect, except that, unlike us he never sinned, precisely as it *is* the humanity *of* the Logos. All his personal human actions are grounded in the Word. But they are not for that reason less than spontaneously human.

Torrance carefully maintained that in the incarnation, the Word did not undermine Christ's true and fully human nature by overriding it in some way but it is the Word who enabled Jesus' full and complete human existence. That is why he rightly held that when we do not try to impose "a pattern upon theological knowledge but rather to discern the pattern inhering in its material content" by letting it reveal itself to us, "we are directed to Jesus Christ, to the Incarnation, to the hypostatic union, the unique togetherness of God and man in Christ which is normative for every other relationship between man and God."[64] For Torrance the hypostatic union is not some "ideological truth" that can function "as the masterful idea of a system of thought."[65] The reason for this is that the notion of the hypostatic union "does not have its truth in itself"[66] but only in Jesus Christ, who is truly God and truly human. This union is not "some static relation" but the actual union of "God and man in the one Person of the Son running throughout all His historical life from His birth to His resurrection."[67] This is the center from which "we consider the doctrine of the Trinity, of the Father and of the Holy Spirit as well as of the Son, and therefore of creation as well as of redemption."[68]

Importantly, Torrance argues further that we can only understand the hypostatic union properly as "the expression of the act of divine Grace and the irreversible relation between God's Grace and man."[69] God's election of grace is actualized for all in the movement of love actualized in Christ's own perfect obedience to God for us and in his own living by grace for us. So, Torrance refers to the logic of Grace and the logic of Christ to explain *anhypostasia* and *enhypostasia*. The former refers to "the unconditional priority of Grace, that everything in theological knowledge derives from God's Grace, while all truths and their relations within our thinking must reflect the movement of Grace."[70] The latter refers to the fact that "God's Grace acts only as Grace. God does not override us but makes us free" by

---

[64] Torrance, *Theological Science*, 216.
[65] Ibid., 217.
[66] Ibid.
[67] Ibid., 216.
[68] Ibid.
[69] Ibid., 217.
[70] Ibid.

enabling us to share in his life and love. That is how he "sets us on our feet as persons in personal relation with him, affirming and recreating our humanity in communion with Him."[71]

Importantly, however, because Torrance allows Jesus himself to shape his view of divine and human relations, his view that in Christ, God does not "override us but makes us free" is itself founded on the fact that the human Jesus acting as the Word of God to and for us did not override the human Jesus in any way but rather enabled him to act in his own characteristic human way of obedience. Thus, the union of God and humanity that was actualized in Christ's life for us was "an essential part of Christ's reconciliation."[72] This, because "the *mystery* of Christ is the hypostatic union of true God and true man in one person; and as that union is enacted in atonement and in resurrection it issues in the community of the reconciled, the community of the resurrection."[73] For Torrance, "in the incarnation, the mystery of the union of God and man, of the oneness of God and man in Christ, is inserted and enacted in our midst" both in the teaching of Jesus and "in the revelation of the Father through the Son to the disciples, giving them communion or participation in God's knowledge of himself."[74] Here, Torrance refers to Mt. 11:27 and to Jn 13–17 to say that our true knowledge of God comes to us as an act of the Father through the Son which we can only have by relying upon Christ himself through the Spirit and in faith. He makes an often-repeated remark, namely, that "What God is in Jesus Christ in relation to man, he is antecedently and eternally in himself" to insist that the hypostatic union refers to a oneness between God and us grounded in God himself, that is, "in the eternal communion of Father, Son and Holy Spirit within the holy Trinity."[75] Importantly, it must be observed here, Torrance did not begin his Christology from below as McCormack did because Torrance held that we had to begin with the mystery of the union of humanity and divinity in the incarnate Word and thus one could not begin from above or from below but only with the actual union of natures in Christ. And Torrance repeatedly asserts with Athanasius, Epiphanius, Gregory Nazianzen, and others that his view of God's being is not shaped by metaphysics or any philosophy but

---

[71] Ibid., 217–18.
[72] Torrance, *Incarnation*, 173.
[73] Ibid., 174.
[74] Ibid., 172.
[75] Ibid., 175.

only by God's self-revelation attested in the Old Testament and in the New Testament, especially God's revelation of himself as "I am."[76]

Moreover, unlike McCormack, Torrance does not read our human relations back into the Trinity to affirm this union of divine and human action and being which is ours in Christ. Instead, he asserts that the incarnate Son who was born of the virgin Mary "is the eternally begotten Son of the Father" since he "spoke of himself as Son of the Father in a relation of exclusiveness and closed circularity, 'no one knows the Son except the Father, and no one knows the Father except the Son.'"[77] This allows Torrance to maintain that "the act of atonement was a trinitarian act, historical to be sure, but it rested

---

[76] Among many possible references, see Torrance, *Incarnation*, 64 and 73. "'I am the truth,' Jesus said and that applies not only to his bringing the truth of God to mankind but to his whole human life as truth done into the flesh, as truth enacted in the midst of our untruth, as truth fulfilled from within man and from the side of man truth issuing out of human life in obedient response to the truth of God" (ibid., 64). See also Torrance, *Christian Doctrine of God*, 118–35. That is why he insists that "Moses is taught that while God reveals his Name, he does not thereby resign his transcendence or glory, but makes himself known nevertheless in the utter freedom of his grace, within the covenant fellowship he has established with his people" (ibid., 122). Thus, "while the Being of God is not to be understood as constituted by his relation to others, that free outward flowing of his Being in gratuitous love toward and for others reveals to us something of the inmost nature of God's Being" (ibid., 123). Importantly, Torrance then connects God's self-naming in Israel to Jesus' appropriation of that name as attested in the New Testament. Thus, "the full significance of this 'I am' on the lips of Jesus ('I am the Light of the word', 'I am the bread of life', 'I am the Resurrection and the life', 'I am the Vine', 'I am the Way, the Truth and the Life', 'I am with you', etc.) becomes disclosed in what Jesus said to his disciples, 'I am in the Father and the Father is in me', for he thereby showed them that his own 'I am' is grounded in the indwelling of the Father and the Son in one another in the eternal Communion which belongs to the inner Life of God as Father, Son and Holy Spirit" (ibid., 124). Because the three Persons of the Trinity are co-equal in dignity, majesty, and in Being as the one who loves in himself and for us, Torrance notes that Athanasius constantly emphasized that the God's Being is "simple, uncompounded and undivided … in sharp opposition to the Arian separation of the Son from the Father, and the semi-Arian separation of the Spirit from the Godhead" (ibid., 130). God is thus personal since "For God *to be*, is to be for himself in himself, that is, for the three Divine Persons which God is to be *for one another* in the onto-personal relations of the Holy Trinity" as one who loves (ibid., 131). Torrance makes a clear distinction between God's internal love within the immanent Trinity and his free and gracious love of us saying that while God freely wills to be in fellowship with us, his eternal love within the immanent Trinity "is not to be regarded as constituted or determined in any way by God's relation to others, any more than God himself is" (ibid., 132). Still, his outward movement toward us in love in his free grace "reveals the innermost nature of God's being, as at once transcendent and immanent: God in the highest and God with us" (ibid.). Hence, "the eternal ground in God from which there flows his communion-seeking love and grace toward us, is the Communion which the Father, Son and Holy Spirit have among themselves, and, let it be repeated, really are" (ibid.).

[77] Torrance, *Incarnation*, 175. He is here referring once again to Mt. 11:27. He also mentions Jesus' prayer noted in Jn 17: "now, Father, glorify me in thy own presence with the glory which I had with thee before the world was made," ibid.

ultimately on relations within the holy Trinity."[78] Listen to how carefully Torrance states and maintains Jesus' eternal Sonship in his unique and eternal relation with the Father. He says, "If Jesus Christ is the Son of God for us, he must be Son of God for God. As the incarnate Son, his sonship reaches back to eternal sonship in the Godhead. If he is Son of God on earth, he is Son of God antecedently and eternally in himself."[79] Unless that is recognized and understood to be true, "the revelation we are given in Christ would not have eternal validity or ultimate reality."[80] Torrance notes that is why John's Gospel begins with the "eternity of the Word in God, for it is from the eternal God that the Word proceeded, and all that follows in the Gospel—all that Jesus said and was in his dependence as the incarnate Son upon the Father—goes back to and is grounded in that eternal relation of Word to God within God."[81] Thus, "all that Jesus did has reality and validity just because it rests upon that eternal relation of the Son with the Father … he is antecedently and eternally in himself as the eternal Son of the Father" so that in Jesus' ministry of reconciliation and forgiveness, we encounter an "eternal event" because all his human actions have their "ground in the action of the eternal God."[82]

Considering the Person of the Son or Word and the Hypostatic Union

Here Torrance makes a crucial distinction, namely, that the Person of Jesus is eternal and not his humanity. This is a crucial distinction because without it, one is forced to deny both Jesus' true divinity and his true humanity. So, Torrance says that the fact that what God is toward us in Christ he is in himself *cannot* mean that "the humanity of Jesus is eternal, that it was eternally pre-existent. It does mean that his person is eternal, that his person is not human, but divine."[83] Has Torrance here advocated a version of Nestorianism? No. Because he goes on to assert that this "also means that the humanity of Jesus was assumed into oneness with the eternal Son and shares eternally in the glory of the only begotten Son of God which he had

---

[78] Ibid., 176.
[79] Ibid.
[80] Ibid.
[81] Ibid.
[82] Ibid.
[83] Ibid., 177.

before the world was created."[84] This is the case because "the doctrine of the hypostatic union asserts a union of two natures in one person. It does not assert the pre-existence and in that sense the eternity of the human nature, for the human nature of Jesus was a creature of God, and in Jesus himself the human nature had no independent *hypostasis* prior to the incarnation."[85] Importantly, then, "the humanity of Jesus … was given *hypostasis*, reality, real personal being, in the eternal Word, in the eternal Son, in the eternal *hypostasis* of God the Son."[86] From this Torrance draws two significant conclusions. First, "in the incarnation something altogether *new* happened, even for God, for God the Son was not always man but he now became man … without ceasing to be God."[87] Second, "the relation of the incarnate Son to the Father did not arise within time. The life of Christ on earth was the obverse of a heavenly deed, and the result of an eternal decision, an eternal *prothesis* which God had purposed in himself from all eternity."[88] However, for Torrance, "election means … the eternal beginning of all the ways and works of God in Jesus Christ."[89]

Reflecting on the uniqueness of Jesus Christ, Barth was led to wonder about what he called one of the hardest problems in Christology. That problem concerned the question of whether Jesus is the revealer in his humanity as such. His answer was no, because the revealing power of Jesus came from his being the Word.[90] Here is how he put it: "Can the incarnation of the Word according to the biblical witnesses mean that the existence of the man Jesus of Nazareth was as it were in itself, in its own power and continuity, the revealing Word of God? Is the *humanitas Christi* as such the revelation?"[91] Further, Barth asked: "Does the divine sonship of Jesus Christ mean that God's revealing has now been transmitted as it were to the existence of the man Jesus of Nazareth, that this has thus become identical with it?"[92] To these questions he replied that whenever this view was held then it became impossible to avoid "the possibility of having God disclose Himself through man, allowing man to set himself on the same platform as God, to grasp Him there and thus to become His master."[93]

---

[84] Ibid.
[85] Ibid.
[86] Ibid.
[87] Ibid.
[88] Ibid.
[89] Ibid., 178.
[90] See Barth, CD I/1, 323ff.
[91] Ibid., 323. See also Molnar, *Divine Freedom*, Second Edition, 111ff.
[92] Ibid.
[93] Ibid.

Here, Barth directly rejected the approach of mysticism, pietism, and the Enlightenment which suggested that Jesus was "the teacher of wisdom and friend of man" or "the quintessence of enhanced humanity in Schleiermacher" or "the embodiment of the idea of religion in Hegel" or "a religious personality" as found in Carlyle.[94] Each of these conceptions represents an attempt to understand God's presence in Christ from "certain conceptions deriving from humanity."[95] Barth here insisted that,

> even Christ's humanity stands under the caveat of God's holiness, i.e., that the power and continuity in which the man Jesus of Nazareth was in fact the revealed Word ... consisted here too in the power and continuity of the divine action in this form and not in the continuity of this form as such ... the Godhead was not so immanent in Christ's humanity that it does not also remain transcendent to it, that its immanence ceases to be an event in the Old Testament sense, always a new thing, something that God actually brings into being in specific circumstances.[96]

Therefore, as noted briefly above, one vital point in this chapter is that both Barth and Torrance could and did hold that in the incarnate Word, as Torrance so clearly stated, "There is certainly a sense in which we must think of God as impassible (ἀπαθής), for he is not subject to the passions that characterise human and creaturely existence, but that is not to say that he is not afflicted in all the afflictions of his people or that he is untouched by their sufferings."[97] In making that remark, he was answering the key question McCormack raises, namely, "What does the suffering of Christ really mean for what he was and is in his own *Person* as the one Mediator between God and man?"[98] Following Athanasius, Torrance went on to maintain that "we cannot think of the sufferings of Christ as external to the Person of the Logos.

---

[94] Ibid.
[95] Ibid.
[96] Ibid.
[97] Torrance, *The Trinitarian Faith*, 185-7. See also *Christian Doctrine of God*, 221 and 246-54. While Torrance flatly rejects the "Greek or Stoic" view of impassibility (*The Trinitarian Faith*, 185 and *Christian Doctrine of God*, 251), he also held, following the theology of Cyril of Alexandria and Athanasius, that because God retains his transcendence "over all space and time" even as he suffers for us *as* God in Christ such that "what Christ felt, did and suffered in himself in his body and soul for our forgiveness was felt, done, and suffered by God in his innermost Being for our sake" (ibid., 249). However, since he did not cease being God even in suffering and dying for us, he overcame suffering and death for us precisely because he brought his impassibility to bear upon that suffering and death. Torrance insists once again this can only be understood soteriologically and not logically (ibid., 250).
[98] Ibid., 184.

It is the very same Person who suffered and who saved us, not just man but the Lord as man; both his divine and his human acts are acts of one and the same Person."[99] From this it follows that,

> we may say of God in Christ that he both suffered and did not suffer, for through the eternal tranquility of his divine impassibility he took upon himself our passibility and redeemed it. In the nature of the case this is not something about which a logical account can be given, for logically impassibility and passibility exclude one another. Rather is it to be understood dynamically and soteriologically on the ground of what has actually taken place in the vicarious life and passion of God's incarnate Son. Nor can God be thought of as 'impassible' in the Greek or Stoic sense, but on the contrary as God who in his measureless love and compassion has stooped to take upon himself our passion, our hurt and suffering, and to exhaust it in his divine impassibility (τὸ παθητὸν ἐν ἀπαθείᾳ) in such a way that he masters and transmutes it within the embrace of his own immutable peace and serenity.[100]

In these statements Torrance accomplishes exactly what McCormack claims cannot be accomplished if we hold to the traditional view of impassibility while thinking in a strictly theological manner. Additionally, Torrance can and did maintain that Jesus' human actions are all actions of the Word in union with the Holy Spirit. Thus, it is perfectly possible and

---

[99] Ibid., 185.
[100] Ibid., 185–6. Torrance very clearly opposes a static view of the hypostatic union also because such a view follows the idea that in Christ, God assumed "a neutral and perfect humanity" instead of our actual fallen humanity in order to "heal and sanctify it, not only through the act of assumption, but through a life of perfect obedience and a death in sacrifice," thus completing our reconciliation with God from the divine and human side (*Incarnation*, 201). For Torrance, it was imperative that incarnation and atonement be held together by recognizing that in the one Person of Christ the mediator there were united the two natures, divine and human (ibid., 199). Unless his atoning work as the incarnate Son is given its proper place in Chalcedonian Christology, Torrance held that his humanity would be absorbed into his deity as in monophysitism (ibid.). Torrance insisted that we cannot understand human nature from some idea of human nature in general but only from Christ's human nature which was and is in hypostatic union with God so that "it is the human nature of Christ alone that is the norm and criterion of all true human nature" (ibid., 202). Further, he insisted that we cannot understand the divine nature from some "general concept of divine nature, which somehow we have already formed in our minds" because "if Christ is the Son of God become man, then it is the divine nature of Christ which must be our only norm and criterion for the understanding of divine nature" (ibid.). Because of these two problematic tendencies Torrance thinks that while Chalcedonian Christology intends to move toward dyophysitism, there is always the temptation to a counterbalancing of this "by a new monophysitism" (ibid.).

indeed only possible to maintain the full humanity and spontaneity of all Jesus' human actions as the incarnate Son from within the traditional Chalcedonian view that his humanity exists precisely as it is grounded in his divinity as the eternal Son or Word of the Father. Indeed, following Irenaeus and Athanasius, Torrance insightfully maintained that "the Holy Spirit is mediated to us by and through the humanity of Christ who sanctified himself in the Spirit that we might be sanctified in him."[101] This sanctification "did not take place for the promotion of the Word himself, but for our sanctification, that we might share in his anointing … 'for when the Lord, as man, was washed in Jordan, it was we who by him were made recipients of him.'"[102]

Torrance says the giving and receiving of the Holy Spirit "actualised within the life of the incarnate Son of God *for our sakes* is atonement operating within the ontological depths of human being … the indwelling of the Spirit mediated to us through Christ is the effective counterpart in us of his self-offering to the Father through the eternal Spirit."[103] It will be noticed here that Torrance never separates the Spirit from the incarnate Word with the claim frequently espoused by McCormack that the only action of the Word was the act of becoming incarnate; all other actions of Christ are *only* actions of the *human Jesus* guided by the Spirit.[104] McCormack here follows John Owen, who held that the Holy Spirit "is the immediate operator of all divine acts of the Son himself, even on His human nature."[105] His only correction of this would be that he "would not even make the assumption itself a direct work of the Son" because for him "all the Son's work is indirect, mediated by the Spirit who is at work in His human nature."[106] By contrast, Torrance insists correctly that "Christ is fully man, but while man, he himself in the whole course of his life is also God. Christ is God, true God as well as true man. The significance of his deity lies in the fact that it is God himself who acts in Jesus Christ, in his teaching and reconciliation."[107] Torrance concludes that "the actions of Christ are not in time only, not just temporary or temporal actions, but the eternal action of God, eternally real in the Godhead."[108] For Torrance the doctrine of atonement itself:

---

[101] Torrance, *The Trinitarian Faith*, 189.
[102] Ibid., 190, Torrance quoting Athanasius.
[103] Ibid.
[104] McCormack, *The Humility of the Eternal Son*, 250–1 and 257–8.
[105] Bruce McCormack, "The Lord and Giver of Life: A 'Barthian' Defence of the *Filioque*," *Rethinking Trinitarian Theology: Disputed Questions and Contemporary Issues in Trinitarian Theology*, ed. Robert Wozniak and Giulio Maspero (London: T&T Clark, 2012), 251.
[106] Ibid.
[107] Torrance, *Incarnation*, 187.
[108] Ibid.

presupposes the doctrine of the hypostatic union of two natures in one person, for the whole work of reconciliation depends upon the fact that *one person acts both from the side of God, and from the side of man*, both in his divine acts and in his human acts, and that these acts are really and truly identical in the person of the mediator.[109]

Moreover, Torrance insists that Jesus' full humanity is crucial as it not only "signifies the objective actuality of God's coming and presence" to us in space and time but his humanity "guarantees to us that we have *God* among us" so that "if that humanity were in any sense unreal, God would be unreal for us in him."[110] Without Christ's full humanity the actuality of the atonement as an act of God himself in our "actual human nature" would be lost with a "docetic view." That would mean "that God only appears to act within our human existence."[111] Atonement is real because "the mediator acts fully from the side of man as man, as well as from the side of God as God ... if Jesus Christ is really and truly man, then his death for sin is an act of God himself in human nature, and not just an external act upon human nature."[112] Hence, "what Jesus does in forgiveness is not just the work of man, but the work of God, and is therefore of final and ultimate validity."[113] Here, however, Torrance warns that it is a form of the "monophysite heresy" which would deny his true humanity if we were to speak of Jesus by speaking of "divine humanity" because that phrase would obscure the actual fact that while Christ is fully human throughout his life, he is "also God. Christ is God, true God as well as true man. The significance of his deity lies in the fact that it is God himself who acts in Jesus Christ, in his teaching and reconciliation."[114]

To accomplish his "repair" of Chalcedon, McCormack reads the missions back into the processions, a move we have just seen Torrance wisely refused to make, and claims that the purpose of the Son's generation from the Father was not only the incarnation but the whole life of humility, suffering, and death he would undergo for us. The very existence of the Son, even in eternity, therefore, means that the second person of the Trinity "is eternally generated as divine-human relation, which accounts for the inseparability of natures

---

[109] Ibid., 184.
[110] Ibid., 185.
[111] Ibid., 186.
[112] Ibid.
[113] Ibid., 187.
[114] Ibid.

in the incarnated Christ."[115] He thinks that if that is said in anticipation of future incarnation, it is an acceptable "repair" of Chalcedon. However, in light of what was said above, it is totally unacceptable because that very idea obliterates both Jesus' true eternal Sonship so clearly stated and presented by both Barth and Torrance, and his actual historical being which came to exist when he was conceived of the Virgin Mary. In reality, it is the Son or Word who is begotten of the Father before all worlds and not the human Jesus. His humanity came into existence at a particular point in time and thus it was not generated by the Father in eternity, not even by anticipation. The failure here is the failure to properly distinguish the immanent and the economic Trinity.

Amazingly, McCormack thinks he is not collapsing the immanent into the economic Trinity with his approach. But that is exactly what he does. He follows the thinking of Sergius Bulgakov and says, "the great achievement" of his (Bulgakov's) view "was to have made the 'hypostasis' of the Logos to be eternally 'compound'—consisting in both divinity and humanity."[116] By doing this McCormack says *anhypostasia* would no longer threaten "the integrity and freedom of the human Jesus."[117] He then says, "Christ has a human hypostasis—precisely in the eternal Logos."[118] However, this is not the proper meaning of the hypostatic union according to Barth and Torrance simply because neither of them read the missions back into the eternal Trinity with the idea that an external purpose (incarnation, suffering, and death) was the purpose of God's giving himself his triune being. The reason for this is that God simply is the Holy Trinity from eternity to eternity, and the beginning of his ways *ad extra* means that the Logos *asarkos* cannot be reduced to the Logos *incarnandus* who will become *incarnatus*. For Torrance, following Athanasius, the incarnation was a new act of God, new for God and for us. But McCormack mistakenly thinks that any such view opens a gap between the immanent and the economic Trinity.

According to McCormack, as noted above, when Barth envisioned an eternal obedience and humility, and thus a super and subordination, a *prius* and *posterius*, in the eternal Trinity, he read the economy "'up' into the intertrinitarian relation of Father and Son."[119] So, in his understanding of *kenosis*, Barth held that humility was "proper to God in the most inward depth of his

---

[115] Alexandra Pârvan and Bruce L. McCormack, "Immutability, (Im)Passibility, and Suffering: Steps towards a 'Psychological' Ontology of God," *Neue Zeitschrift für Systematische Theologie und Religionsphilosophie* 59 (1) (March, 2017), 1–25, 25.
[116] McCormack, 141.
[117] Ibid.
[118] Ibid.
[119] McCormack, *The Humility of the Eternal Son*, 114.

Godhead."[120] Accordingly, Barth did not stop there, because he added that Jesus' human obedience was itself an act of obedience that was not "alien to God."[121] So, the great mystery is that God is understood to be able to obey God. How does this make sense? According to McCormack the only way it could make sense is "*if* the humility and obedience of the eternal Son simply *is* the humility and obedience of the human Jesus in time; if, that is to say, the first is 'realized' (made concretely real) in the second."[122] And he says this because in his view "it could have no reality as a disposition in and an act performed by an eternal Son 'as such,' as a disposition and act complete in itself to which Jesus' disposition and act could only 'correspond'; not on Barth's model of the Trinity at any rate."[123]

When compared to the thinking of Torrance, one can easily see all the difficulties involved in McCormack's attempted repair of Chalcedon that are on display here. First, he claims that the eternal obedience of the Son is "realized" or "made concretely real" in the incarnation. That is a disastrous assertion because if the Son is eternally begotten of the Father as God from God, true God from true God, then his eternal being and being begotten do not need an external action in history to be realized. Barth himself was extremely clear on this point.[124] God is fully realized as the eternal Father, Son, and Holy Spirit and does not need any relations with us to be God in himself. Barth put this with great clarity:

> We cannot say anything higher or better of the "inwardness of God" than that God is Father, Son and Holy Spirit, and therefore that He is love in Himself without and before loving us, and without being forced to love us. And we can say this only in the light of the "outwardness" of God to us, the occurrence of His revelation.[125]

The key insight here is that God is God "before loving us, and without being forced to love us." Moreover, for Barth "The eternal generation of the Son by the Father tells us first and supremely that God is not at all lonely even without the world and us."[126] Above we saw that for Torrance, it was the Son or Word who was eternally begotten of the Father and not the human Jesus. That is why Torrance and Barth espoused the categories of *enhypostasis* and

---

[120] Ibid.
[121] Ibid., 115.
[122] Ibid.
[123] Ibid.
[124] See Barth, CD IV/1, 52 and IV/2, 113 and below.
[125] Barth, CD I/2, 377.
[126] Ibid., CD 1/1, 139.

anhypostasis and thus refused to reduce the immanent to the economic Trinity with any claim that Jesus' human existence constituted his person as the second person of the Trinity. Second, the properties that Barth did indeed read back into the immanent Trinity were not meant to be understood as human properties as McCormack states this. He meant to say that in eternity, obedience, and subordination were eternal divine actions within the Trinity on the basis of which God could humble himself for us in the incarnation. What Barth did not realize was that in saying that, he opened the door precisely to the misunderstanding embedded in McCormack's logical presentation of this matter—that is, that Barth made the missions part of the eternal processions.

He never intended to do that because that would obliterate the freedom of God's grace. As noted above, Torrance was better able to assert and maintain the freedom of grace by insisting that the logic of grace was irreversibly related to what occurred in the history of Jesus in his revealing and atoning activities for us. And the logic of grace together with the logic of Christ meant for Torrance that one could not read obedience and subordination back into the Trinity as preconditions for God's actions in the economy.[127] However, the fact that Barth did not wish to deny God's freedom here resides in the fact that he never revised and never would have revised his important remark that,

> in the intertrinitarian life of God the eternal generation of the Son or Logos is, of course, the expression of God's love, of his will not to be alone. But it does not follow from this that God could not be God without speaking to us. We undoubtedly understand God's love for man, or in the first instance any reality distinct from Himself, only when we understand it as free and unmerited love not resting on any need. God would be no less God if He had created no world and no man.[128]

In any case, McCormack proceeds to explain exactly what he thinks Barth had in mind when he spoke of the Father's "command" and the Son's "obedience." Thus, he says, "Clearly, Barth wanted to say that humility and obedience are proper to God—and proper to him in his second mode of being as 'Son.' So talk of the Father's 'command' and the Son's 'obedience' as an event in pretemporal eternity must be understood as simply a way of describing the eternal generation of the Son."[129] Here, then, according to

---

[127] See n. 37 above.
[128] Barth, CD I/1, 139.
[129] McCormack, *The Humility of the Eternal Son*, 116.

McCormack, we have "an eternal generation of the Son that has embedded in it the self-humiliation that is his incarnation in time."[130] So when Barth speaks of the above and below and the *prius* and *posterius* of the eternal Father and Son, he was referring to the ontological ground of "divine self-humiliation in time." And he thought none of this impaired "the coequality of Father and Son."[131] From this McCormack concludes that for Barth "There is no such thing as an eternal Son *as such* (i.e. a Son without relation to the humanity to be assumed)."[132] Now this assertion directly contradicts Barth's own explicit statement that:

> The second "person" of the Godhead in Himself and as such is not God the Reconciler. In himself and as such He is not revealed to us. In Himself and as such He is not *Deus pro nobis*, either ontologically or epistemologically. He is the content of a necessary and important concept in trinitarian doctrine when we have to understand the revelation and dealings of God in the light of their free basis in the inner being and essence of God.[133]

Has Barth completely rejected the Son *as such*? I think the answer is no because he goes on to say that since here, he was concerned

> with the revelation and dealings of God, and particularly with the atonement, with the person and work of the Mediator, it is pointless, as it is impermissible, to return to the inner being and essence of God and especially to the second person of the Trinity as such, *in such a way that we ascribe to this person another form than that which God Himself has given in willing to reveal Himself and to act outwards*.[134]

Here, Barth is not denying the reality of the second person of the Trinity as such; he is insisting that because the form of revelation *is* the human history of the incarnate Son acting outward, we cannot go behind this Jesus of Nazareth to know the eternal Son. Here it is important to note several key statements of Barth that undercut McCormack's "repair" of Chalcedon.

---

[130] Ibid.
[131] Ibid.
[132] Ibid.
[133] Barth, CD IV/1, 52.
[134] Ibid., emphasis mine.

Barth says that since God became man,

> we have to recognise and respect His eternal will and purpose and resolve—His free and gracious will which He did not owe it either to Himself or to the world to have, by which he did not need to come to the decision to which He has in fact come, behind which, in these circumstances, we cannot go, behind which we do not have to reckon with any Son of God in Himself, with any λόγος ἄσαρκος ... we must not imagine ... a 'Logos in itself' which does not have this content and form.[135]

Any such view would be a creation of our own idea of God. Barth insists that, in light of the fact that God freely became incarnate for us, we must not and indeed we cannot return "to a pre-temporal being of the Word of God which is not His incarnate being." This is the case because we cannot set ourselves "on the throne of God and there to construct the content and form of His will and Word which He Himself has not chosen, although He might perhaps have chosen it."[136] Here it is clear that Barth fully admits that God has the form of the Son as such, but that he is not revealed to us directly in that form but in the form of the incarnate Son. He is there "at the beginning of all things" because he is the basis and purpose of God's covenant; thus "He and He alone is the content of the eternal will of God which precedes the whole being of man and of the world. He is, therefore, the concrete reality and actuality of the promise and command of God, the fulfilment of both, very God and very man, in one person amongst us, as a fellow-man."[137]

Returning to McCormack's claim that there is no Son *as such*, we are told that "Barth needed something more, which he failed to see."[138] He needed to explain the identity of "the Son with the humble Jesus who obeys."[139] And he needed to do that in a way that would not introduce "essential change" into God. He could do that only by understanding "the eternal generation of the Son as *necessarily* ordered to the history of Jesus (by virtue of a necessity of the nature proper to the eternal Son)."[140] Consequently, "'Identity' on this showing would mean that the eternal humility and obedience of the Son *is* the earthly and historical humility and obedience of Jesus; the *same act* viewed from the two angles of its origin in pretemporal eternity and is realization in time."[141] From Torrance's perspective as presented above, this

---

[135] Ibid.
[136] Ibid.
[137] Barth, IV/1, 53.
[138] McCormack, *The Humility of the Eternal Son*, 116.
[139] Ibid.
[140] Ibid., 117.
[141] Ibid.

is exactly wrong because all Barth needed to say was that the eternal Father, Son, and Holy Spirit did not change in doing something completely new, that is, in creating and then reconciling the world to himself in the incarnate Son and through the power of the Holy Spirit. He became incarnate in his Son without ceasing to be the eternal God in that act for us. That's all he needed to say. And that is exactly what Torrance was so clearly able to affirm with the categories of *enhypostasis* and *anhypostasis* in accordance with the teaching of Chalcedon that in the incarnation Jesus was one person, two natures. McCormack has changed the meaning of person by reading a logical necessity back into the Trinity and claiming that the second person of the Trinity was generated as divine-human relation and that the Son was generated for an external purpose. Both of these ideas were rightly and firmly rejected by Torrance and also by Barth because they both wanted to assert the freedom and priority of God's grace.

McCormack claims that Barth's treatment of the hypostatic union in CD IV/2 made this issue of "identity" worse. He needed to "posit an ontological ground of this communication [of humility and obedience] in an eternal humility and obedience in the Logos. But that is not a step that the theologians who devised the terminology could take. And Barth too found it difficult to take this step with as much clarity as was needed."[142] There are two obstacles, namely, "a fulsome appropriation of the *genus tapeinoticum*" and the idea that the Logos was the subject of all Jesus' human actions. According to McCormack, Barth failed to solve both problems. He recognized the first. But he demonstrated no awareness of the second. And it is the second that was more important. Barth's problem supposedly was that he affirmed the *enhypostasis* and *anhypostasis* "in its traditional form."[143]

Here is where McCormack's attempted "repair" of Chalcedon goes completely off the rails because he clearly does not want to affirm with Barth that "The human 'subsists' not in itself (as an independent existent) but 'directly in and with the one God in the mode of existence of the eternal Son and Logos.'"[144] McCormack claims the problem with this assertion is that "it demands that the Logos be understood as the 'acting subject' of all that is done by the God-human."[145] Since it is the Logos here who "'hypostasizes' the human 'nature' by giving it reality in his own hypostasis," that is what makes him the "Christological 'subject.'" However, according to McCormack, this makes any affirmation of the "*genus tapeinoticum* (whether cautious

---

[142] Ibid.
[143] Ibid., 118.
[144] Ibid., referring to Barth, CD IV/2, 49.
[145] Ibid.

or fulsome) … impossible."¹⁴⁶ With this position, the Logos could only "act through and upon the human Jesus; Jesus cannot be conceived as an agent whose actions and whose experiences at the hands of others could ever have any ontological significance for the Logos (or his divine 'nature')."¹⁴⁷ In a revealing footnote, McCormack presents what he thinks is the right view by appealing to Sergius Bulgakov. He says Bulgakov "made the astute observation that the *anhypostasia* of the human 'nature' of Christ constituted (historically) a rehabilitation of Apollinaris, however unintentional."¹⁴⁸ Why is this the case? Because this view means that "'the human hypostasis in Christ is replaced by the Logos' with the result that 'the human essence is in a certain sense incomplete in him.'"¹⁴⁹ This, however, is the very mistake that Barth identified and rejected in CD I/2, as noted above. Barth and the early church theologians he relied on never used the *anhypostasis* to assert that the Logos replaced Christ's human nature or to suggest or imply that Jesus' human nature was incomplete in any way. They were merely asserting that because his human nature only exists and existed as that which was assumed by the Logos in the incarnation, therefore, his human nature had no independent existence apart from the Word. Any such view (of an independent human existence apart from the Word) would be inherently Nestorian. As seen above, that is exactly how Torrance understood this matter as well.

McCormack claims that Barth never saw this problem and so his theology "vacillated between the Chalcedonian and post-Chalcedonian definitions of the Christological 'person.'"¹⁵⁰ In McCormack's estimation, Barth needed to offer "a one-way communication from the human to the divine" in order to give us a "worthy alternative to Cyril's unified Christological subject."¹⁵¹ That means he would have to stop referring to the Logos "as the 'acting subject'" by "surrendering the *anhypostasia* in its traditional form" and thus allow the human Jesus "in the power of the Holy Spirit" to act as "the performative agent of all that is done by the God-human in his divine-human unity."¹⁵² As noted above, McCormack concludes that there is a "vestigial presence of a rehabilitated Apollinarianism" in Barth's thinking because he refused to allow for the idea that Jesus' human history is what constituted him as the eternal Son of the Father! However, the problem here is that Barth's thinking

[146] Ibid.
[147] Ibid., 118–19.
[148] Ibid., 119.
[149] Ibid.
[150] Ibid.
[151] Ibid.
[152] Ibid.

was not Apollinarian at all because he simply refused to put aside the *mystery* of the hypostatic union when thinking of this matter. So, he insisted with the tradition that in the incarnate Son the Logos was the acting subject but that because there was a real union of natures in that person by virtue of the incarnation, he also acted in characteristically human ways in the power of the Holy Spirit, who is *homoousios* with the Word. One key example of this was at his baptism. He was acting humanly in the Spirit receiving baptism, not because he needed to, but as the incarnate Word acting from the human and divine side for us so that we might be sanctified in him, as Torrance so clearly noted.

In any case, McCormack turns to Bulgakov and his dissatisfaction with the traditional view of *enhypostasis* and *anhypostasis*. For Bulgakov, "humanity belongs to what the Logos is essentially—as the personal property that differentiates this hypostasis from the other two."[153] We are told that "the 'hypostasis' of the Logos that takes the place of the human 'hypostasis' in accordance with the Tradition is, for Bulgakov, human—or, to be more precise and accurate it is *also* human."[154] At the end of the day Bulgakov gives McCormack what he was looking for. He says, "The hypostasis of the Logos incarnate is, after all, *Divine*-Human."[155] Yet, according to Torrance's analysis presented above, the hypostasis of the Logos incarnate is the divine Word or Son in whom the humanity of Jesus is grounded.

Above, we noted that Torrance correctly insisted with Barth that God did not need to become incarnate because that was a free new movement of God *ad extra*. McCormack claims that for both Barth and Bulgakov, in different ways, "*a determination for incarnation is proper to the second person of the Trinity.*"[156] In relation to this view McCormack says Florovsky's remark that their view on this matter amounts to the idea that "'the Holy Trinity never existed without Jesus'" is inappropriate because it would imply that "the Logos is eternally embodied" and "that he brings his body with him in entering

---

[153] Ibid., 131.
[154] Ibid.
[155] Ibid., 137. Following Bulgakov, McCormack says "'The Logos, the second hypostasis, is the proper hypostasis of the 'Divine-Humanity' in God'" (ibid.). And Bulgakov also rejected the *enhypostasis* and *anhypostasis* because he, like McCormack, holds that for Chalcedon "there is no space left for a real human hypostasis" (ibid.). This is solved, for McCormack, because Bulgakov supplied the "ontological conditions in God that made possible a real *inward* union of divinity with humanity in time" (ibid.). Those ontological conditions are found in the "eternal 'Divine-Humanity' of the Logos" (ibid.). All of this, as we have seen, Torrance rejected by fully upholding the humanity of Christ within the eternal Logos on the basis of his actual incarnation, without eternalizing his humanity within the immanent Trinity prior to that event in time, in the manner suggested by Buglakov and McCormack.
[156] Ibid., 138.

this world."[157] McCormack insists that neither theologian would say this. But the fact is that the idea that the eternal Son is generated as divine-human relation for the purpose of incarnation says exactly what Florovsky himself claimed it said. And the proof that Florovsky was right can be seen in the very conclusions that McCormack draws here. He says, "the 'hypostasis' of the Logos has an essential determination for incarnation in Jesus; it is directed towards him and has never been divine alone."[158] Even more precisely, McCormack claims that "it is, in fact, the eternal Logos who is the one God-human both in eternity and in time."[159] He thinks this is the most natural way to understand Barth's later Christology. Yet, as noted above, Barth insisted upon acknowledging the Logos *asarkos* in order to recognize and maintain the freedom of God's grace in CD IV/1. This is a crucial point because it coheres with Barth's insistence on a clear and sharp distinction between the immanent and the economic Trinity early and later in his theology. Torrance made very similar statements as when he said that:

> The incarnation must not be understood as involving any surrender of God's transcendence, or any compromising of his eternal freedom, or any renouncing of what he ever was before the foundation of the world, or any imprisoning of his eternal trinitarian relations within the space-time processes of our creaturely world.[160]

What would such "imprisoning" look like? It would look like this: any view of the eternal Logos, the hypostasis of the Logos that makes it "eternally 'compound'"[161] in the manner advanced by Bulgakov. What did this mean? We are told that "If the love of God revealed in Christ is self-giving, self-donating, self-emptying love, if that is its very nature, then it is certainly plausible to suggest that such love requires an 'other' as its 'object.'"[162]

---

[157] Ibid., 139.
[158] Ibid.
[159] Ibid., 261.
[160] Torrance, *Christian Doctrine of God*, 108. Indeed, Torrance insisted that the *homoousion* had a critical function "in regard to what may and what may not be read back from God's revealing and saving activity in history to what he is antecedently, eternally and inherently in himself. It does tell us that what God is antecedently, eternally and inherently in himself he is indeed toward us in the incarnate economy of his saving action in Jesus Christ on our behalf, but it relates that economy ontologically to God in the ineffable Mystery of his Being who remains transcendent over all space and time, so that a significant distinction and delimitation between the economic Trinity and the ontological Trinity must be recognized as well as their essential oneness" (ibid., 97).
[161] McCormack, *The Humility of the Eternal Son*, 141.
[162] Ibid.

But this is just what Torrance and Barth both reject as a compromise of the freedom of God's grace. For both theologians, God did not need to become incarnate because he did not require another outside his own eternal existence as Father, Son, and Holy Spirit to be fully God. That he is God for us is a *new* act of free grace and is not required because of anything within God or outside of God. Following Athanasius, Torrance himself carefully noted that "since God was not always incarnate any more than he was always Creator, the incarnation and the creation are to be regarded as new even for God, although they result from the eternal outgoing movement of his Love."[163] Therefore, "we cannot think of the ontological Trinity as if it were constituted by or dependent on the economic Trinity, but must rather think of the economic Trinity as the freely predetermined manifestation in the history of salvation of the eternal Trinity which God himself was before the foundation of the world, and eternally is."[164] Finally, we cannot speak accurately about the "oneness between the ontological Trinity and the economic Trinity"

> without distinguishing and delimiting it [the economic Trinity] from the ontological Trinity—there are in any case ... elements in the incarnate economy such as the time pattern of human life in this world which we may not read back into the eternal Life of God. On the other hand, the fact that the ontological Trinity has ontological priority over the economic Trinity, does not preclude us from saying that the ontological Trinity is essentially and intrinsically evangelical, for it is precisely the ontological Trinity that God has made known to us in his self-giving and self-revealing as Father, Son and Holy Spirit in salvation history, and it is on the ontological Trinity that the evangelical nature of the economic Trinity entirely depends.[165]

However, we must not forget the all-important point Torrance makes, with Barth, that "we cannot think of the ontological Trinity as if it were constituted by or dependent on the economic Trinity, but must rather think of the economic Trinity as the freely predetermined manifestation in the history of salvation of the eternal Trinity which God himself was before the foundation of the world, and eternally is."[166] It is this that McCormack has done with his attempted "repair" of Chalcedon.

---

[163] Torrance, *Christian Doctrine of God*, 108.
[164] Ibid., 108–9.
[165] Ibid., 109.
[166] Ibid., 108–9.

Listen to some of McCormack's views. Instead of saying that Jesus' self-emptying is a freely predetermined act of God for us (as a free choice), he says we do not have to think of that *kenosis* as a choice at all because "it could, in fact, be contained in the Son's eternal (equally necessary [as is God's triune existence]), response to his eternal generation by the Father."[167] So, when it comes to explaining Christ's suffering and death, he concludes that "what befell Jesus in his last hours was no fate, no accident, no unforeseen victimization. It was in fact the goal of his self-constituting activity."[168] Here McCormack disastrously makes the eternal Son's being and action dependent on an external condition, thus denying God's eternal freedom and the freedom of God's grace. And that's not the end of it. He repeatedly asserts that the second person of the Trinity is "composite" such as when he says, "he is 'composite' not only in time but already as preexistent."[169]

That brings us to his contradictory statements regarding the Logos *asarkos*. First, it will be recalled that Torrance, as noted above, insisted that the Logos of John's Gospel referred to the exclusive deity of the Word or Son in relation to the Father and linked that viewpoint with Mt. 11:27 and Jesus' sayings in John 17. Torrance is precise in stating that "in Jesus Christ there was a hypostatic and personal union between his deity and his humanity. In him there were two natures in one person, and all his words and actions were words and actions of that one person and within that hypostatic union."[170] That means that when the Gospel of John speaks about the Word who was God and was spoken in Israel, it is referring to the "*Word of God, the creator—* Word by whom all things are made. He is the eternal Word, but now that Word, without ceasing to be what it eternally is, becomes a creature."[171] Only thus could Jesus himself as the incarnate Word be our objective reconciliation (atonement) with God the Father. Thus, since God in Christ descended into "our condemned state" and took that upon himself, with Barth, Torrance insisted that in Christ "God the judge made himself also the one judged in our place."[172] Here, Torrance insists that "every human being is loved by Christ and all men and women are involved in him" because "God's eternal love is incarnated in him" so that in his life and death the love of God himself is poured out "upon all humanity."[173]

---

[167] McCormack, *The Humility of the Eternal Son*, 211.
[168] Ibid., 212.
[169] Ibid., 213.
[170] Torrance, *Atonement*, 336–7.
[171] Torrance, *Incarnation*, 60.
[172] Torrance, *Atonement*, 184.
[173] Ibid.

Second, Torrance further insists that in Christ, Jesus did not just suffer and die humanly, but that "it was indeed *God himself* who bears our sins, God become man and taking man's place, standing with humanity under the divine judgement ... [thus] we cannot divorce the action of Christ on the cross from the action of God. The concept of limited atonement divides Christ's divinity from his humanity and thus rests upon a basic Nestorian heresy."[174] These are vitally important insights because they demonstrate that all of Christ's human actions, as actions of the Word who is the subject of incarnation acting for us, are actions of God himself effective for all people and not just for some who are supposedly the elect. Thus, the action of the Word cannot be restricted only to his becoming incarnate without divorcing atonement from revelation and compromising the actual meaning of the hypostatic union. Moreover, for Torrance, there was no hint of a claim that Jesus was generated by the Father as composite, because Torrance knew that such a view could only be the result of illegitimately reading back elements of the economy into the immanent Trinity.

By contrast, McCormack says that for Paul "even the preexistent Christ" is "in some sense composite (i.e. divine and human)"[175] and that reflection on the Logos of John's Gospel *might* invite "reflection on the nature of the relation of two 'natures.'"[176] However, he claims that what happens in Christ's death and resurrection begins as divine and ends as human. But if the pre-existent Christ is generated as "composite," then his humanity is already part of his generated being from the Father and as such is no longer truly human. For McCormack, "God is *essentially* kenotic."[177] For Barth and Torrance *kenosis* is a free act of grace which is not made necessary by God's essence or by some metaphysical necessity such as "ontological receptivity." If it were necessary by virtue of God's essence, then it would no longer be grace according to both Barth and Torrance. There is a serious internal inconsistency in McCormack's position, namely, that if the Son was generated for the purpose of incarnation, then the Son would not be God and could not be God without us. That destroys the concept of grace as a free decision and action of God toward us. Furthermore, to hold that the Son is generated as "composite" conflicts with McCormack's proposal that "the one history of the one God-human begins as divine and ends as human."[178] Why? Because, if the Son was generated by the Father as "composite," there never was a Son of God as such

---

[174] Ibid., 184–5.
[175] McCormack, *The Humility of the Eternal Son*, 214.
[176] Ibid.
[177] Ibid., 215.
[178] Ibid., 258.

who was fully divine in himself without needing to be God for us. This idea of a "composite" second person of the Trinity compromises both Jesus' true deity and his true humanity. As God from God, the Son or Word either was generated thus (as God from God) or he was generated as "composite"; the second alternative blurs the distinction between Creator and creature, while the first does not.

These difficulties and inconsistencies become clearer with McCormack's confused remarks regarding the Logos *asarkos*. His most basic assertion is that at least in the Synoptics, the door is barred "to the 'preexistence' of a metaphysical subject whose being is complete in itself without relation to Jesus (an independent Logos *asarkos*)."[179] However, such a remark is in fact a rejection of the actual existence of the immanent Trinity as Barth and Torrance understood that as God's eternal being and act as the one who loves in freedom. It will be recalled that Barth said that there is nothing higher to God than his being as Father, Son, and Spirit and that he was and is this without us and *without needing us*. That is in line with all classical views of the Trinity. If God in himself needed us, which would be the case if the Son was generated for the purpose of incarnation, then the whole meaning of grace as God's free unconditional love of us would be obliterated. Torrance said and held the same things as Barth by distinguishing the ontological (immanent) from the economic Trinity, as we have seen. McCormack knows that he must hold to some version of a doctrine of the immanent Trinity. But his position that Jesus' human history in some sense *constitutes* his eternal Sonship makes it impossible for him to uphold a proper view of that doctrine. Within his view of Christology, McCormack is willing to espouse "the preexistence of the Spirit-filled Jesus" rather than that "of a 'Son' whose reality has been posited with the help of a cosmologically grounded metaphysics."[180] It is just this kind of thinking that compromises a proper trinitarian view of Christology because Jesus was not simply "Spirit-filled" but, as the eternal Son, he was *one in being* (*homoousios*) with the Father and the Spirit. Thus, it is hardly the case that the important assertions in Mt. 11:27 were cosmologically grounded views based on cosmology. Those statements about the Son's relation to the Father and the Father's relation to the Son were grounded in the revelation that the disciples encountered in Jesus himself as the Son or Word of God incarnate.

There is no doubt that McCormack has obliterated any properly functioning doctrine of the immanent Trinity as when he says "any thought of a vis-à-relation of the Son to the Father in the immanent Trinity must

---

[179] Ibid., 223.
[180] Ibid., 225.

include the humanity of Jesus. For it is the humanity of Jesus that makes it a tenable thought."[181] This assertion is a classic confusion of epistemology and ontology. We cannot know the eternal Son in relation to the Father except through the human Jesus who is the incarnate Son. But when we do know the eternal Trinity, it is *God in himself* whom we know. And the eternal Trinity not only pre-existed creation but the eternal Trinity did not and does not need relation with us or even with Jesus to be the God who loves in freedom, just as Barth and Torrance frequently affirm. However, because McCormack has mistakenly read the missions directly back into the processions, he has thereby abolished the distinction between the immanent and economic Trinity. Torrance captures the issue here perfectly when he says, "the incarnation stands, not for the projection of the human into the divine, but for the projection of the divine into the human, and as such is the rock upon which all mythology is shattered."[182]

What then happens is that McCormack employs his own metaphysics with his view that "ontological receptivity" is what makes the Son who he is with the result that he then claims that "the receptivity of the Logos *is* the ground of the unified subject. Not God *in* a human but God *as* human is the meaning of incarnation."[183] Let us be clear. If the receptivity of the Logos as "ontological receptivity" is the ground of the incarnate Word, then it is that ontological principle and not the gracious action of the eternal God electing us in Christ and acting for us in the incarnation that determines the meaning here. Torrance claims election is God inserting his eternal love into our broken history to save us and restore communion with us in the face of sin, suffering, evil, and death. McCormack thinks election refers to God eternally determining himself for us or giving himself his being in such a way that there never was a Son as such. However, if the Son is God from God, which he is, then it is simply his Sonship that distinguishes him from the Father and Spirit and not the ontological principle of receptivity which, as an ontological principle, undoes his personal acts of knowing and loving within the immanent Trinity and again in the economy.

---

[181] Ibid., 245.
[182] Torrance, *The Trinitarian Faith*, 71.
[183] McCormack, *The Humility of the Eternal Son*, 259. Here McCormack notes that his phrasing is that of T. F. Torrance but that "Torrance himself meant something quite different by it (i.e. the classical *an-* and *enhypostasia*)." Exactly. With those two categories Torrance was able to espouse and hold together both Jesus' true and eternal deity and his full humanity precisely by consistently uniting incarnation and atonement.

Ontological Receptivity

The fact that McCormack has read a logical necessity back into the Trinity then is demonstrated by his use of the category of "ontological receptivity" in order to understand the second person of the Trinity. He wants to reverse Cyril of Alexandria's view that the subject of the incarnation is and remains the Logos (the Word) alone. Because of this, McCormack thinks one who follows Cyril's view must instrumentalize Jesus' passive humanity. Whether that was actually the case with Cyril we can leave to patristic scholars. Here, we can certainly say that that is not how Torrance read Cyril.[184] Both Barth and Torrance grounded Jesus' humanity in his eternal being as the second person of the Trinity employing the categories of *enhypostasis* and *anhypostasis* as we have seen and as McCormack himself noted.

McCormack believes that if we "surrender belief in divine simplicity and impassibility," we can "simply reverse the flow of traffic, making Jesus in the power of the Holy Spirit to be the performative agent of all that is done by the God-human."[185] Jesus then is the single performative agent. But that would mean that "the Logos would have to be understood as relating to the human Jesus *receptively*—which means that the Logos never acted through or upon Jesus but was united to him solely for the purpose of taking all that Jesus did and experienced and therefore *is* 'up' into his own life."[186] This receptivity would make God's being affective. In that way we have an "ontological receptivity." McCormack is quick to point out that this does not

---

[184] For an extended discussion of Cyril's theology, see Torrance, *Theology in Reconciliation*, 156–201. According to Torrance, Cyril held that "being God, the Logos became flesh, and was not in man in the way in which he was in the saints … [since] Christ came *as man* and not as Son of God conjoined to man, and was not just in man, Cyril could think consistently of Christ as him in whom God and man *completely concur*, so that the same person is at once God and man" (157). From this it follows that Cyril "could think of the incarnate Son as acting completely as man, in a perfectly human way, and yet as acting completely as God in a perfectly divine way, without having to posit some kind of conjunction between two persons or two realities or some kind of alternation between divine and human activities. The incarnate Son is one divine-human subject or reality" (ibid., 157–8). For Torrance, Cyril emphasized Christ's human activities and human works and strongly opposed Apollinarianism. Torrance forcefully argues that for Cyril, because "God did not come into man but became man, while remaining God, he lives as man, acting both divinely and humanly, as it befitted him in his one incarnate reality" (ibid., 165). While Torrance noted that Cyril appeared "not to have thought sufficiently into one another the 'anhypostatic' and 'enhypostatic' aspects of the Incarnation," he was nonetheless very clear in opposing any "docetic ideas about the rational soul or human mind of Jesus or his growth from infancy to maturity completely within the measures and laws governing human nature" (ibid., 166).

[185] McCormack, *The Humility of the Eternal Son*, 257–8.

[186] Ibid., 258.

mean such receptivity is "passivity." He claims this is in fact an "active relation ... employed by the Logos 'in weakness'—that is, as receptivity." And this means that "ontological receptivity" can be seen as "one possible expression of divine Lordship, an act by means of which the 'end' for which the Logos is eternally generated is realized concretely in time in taking up all that comes to him through uniting himself with Jesus. Jesus' history is made to be the 'completion' of his own history by his power to receive."[187] Here we do not have two histories with one corresponding to the other; rather, we have "just one history of the one God-human."[188]

To be clear about what is meant here, McCormack is claiming that "The *only* act of the Son of God in relation to his humanity is the act in which he gives it existence in his own being and existence. All subsequent acts of the God-man made possible by *this singular act* are acts performed by the man Jesus."[189] Certainly, McCormack is correct in his desire to move away from a static view of the Chalcedonian teaching just as T. F. Torrance and Karl Barth were. However, this view undermines a most important point stressed by both Torrance and Barth, namely, that all Jesus' human actions are also mysteriously actions of the Son or Word. Indeed, both Torrance and Barth insist that Jesus is not the revealer in his humanity as such because the revealing and reconciling power of the man Jesus comes from his actions as the Word in union with the Holy Spirit. While McCormack does mention the Holy Spirit, as just noted, he also marginalizes the continued action of the Word in and as the man Jesus with this view that the only action performed by the Word is the act of becoming incarnate.

He even makes the confusing claim that since for Barth "The second 'person' of the Trinity is the God-man," so that "even in the act of hypostatic *uniting*, the 'subject' who performs that action is the God-man, Jesus Christ in his divine-human unity."[190] From within the perspectives of Torrance and Barth, this remark makes absolutely no sense because for them it is the eternal Word or Son who is the second person of the Trinity and thus the one who becomes hypostatically united with the man Jesus through the power of the Holy Spirit in the incarnation. If the subject of the hypostatic union is already a "divine-human unity," then that view is completely contrary to

---

[187] Ibid.
[188] Ibid.
[189] Bruce L. McCormack, "Divine Impassibility or Simply Divine Constancy? Implications of Karl Barth's Later Christology for Debates over Impassibility," in *Divine Impassibility and the Mystery of Human Suffering*, ed. James F. Keating and Thomas Joseph White, O. P. (Grand Rapids, MI: Eerdmans, 2009), 150–86, 177. For more on this, see Molnar, *Faith, Freedom and the Spirit*, 252ff.
[190] Ibid., 178.

any traditional view of incarnation as the incarnation of the eternal Word who was and is God from God and not already a "divine-human" unity in pre-temporal eternity.

By contrast, because Torrance recognizes that the eternal Son or Word of the Father is not generated from the Father as "composite" but is God from God, he says of Jesus that during his lifetime he "is the embodiment of the still small voice of God: he is the Word made flesh, the Word that is able to divide soul and spirit asunder. That voice, that Word of God in Jesus penetrated as never before into the secrets of humanity and exposed them."[191] And as Jesus did this, "he produced the most violent reaction that culminated in his crucifixion."[192] This, because,

> the more the truth entered into the innermost centre of man's sin and guilt, the more it involved man in ultimate conflict with God who is truth and love. It was not that Jesus was making mankind more guilty, but that his absolute consistency as holy love, his truth, was exposing the infinite guilt of humanity as he drew it fully and completely upon himself in all its utter violence to bear it and bear it away as the lamb of God in atoning sacrifice.[193]

All this means that,

> since God the Father is not Father apart from the Son, while the Son is not Son apart from the Father, the incarnation of the Holy Love of the Father in Jesus Christ tells us that he works along with the Father in the creating and ordering of the universe. In Jesus Christ none other than the Creator, the ultimate Ground and Source of all being, order and rationality, the Creator Word of God who is God, has himself become man within our creaturely existence and operates creatively within it imparting to all things their form and order.[194]

Torrance goes on to say that since the incarnate Word is God acting for us *as* man, he is able to redeem and reconcile us to God. The Word, through whom God created the universe, became incarnate within the universe without ceasing to be God and made creation's "alienation and lost condition his own and through his reconciling life and atoning passion he brought the

---

[191] Torrance, *Incarnation*, 151.
[192] Ibid.
[193] Ibid., 151–2.
[194] Torrance, *Christian Doctrine of God*, 213.

love and power of God to bear upon its deep-seated disorder so as to make an end of it for ever."[195] In the incarnate Word "the *new creation*" was "effected in the midst of the old, inaugurated in Jesus' birth of the Virgin Mary and consummated in his resurrection from the dead" disclosing the way God's love operates as "*omnipotent Grace*."[196] Thus, by affirming that the subject of the incarnation was the very Son of God, that is, God himself acting for us in history and not a divine-human subject who supposedly became man, Torrance successfully maintained the freedom of God's grace as his free and unconditional love of us by forgiving our sins and experiencing God's own opposition to sin for us in his own person to accomplish our reconciliation with God.

Consequently, because Torrance does not make Jesus' eternal Sonship contingent on his human history as McCormack does, he can say that:

> In the incarnate life of Jesus, and above all in his death, God does not execute his judgement on evil simply by smiting it violently away by a stroke of his hand, but by entering into it from within, into the very heart of the blackest evil, and making its sorrow and guilt and suffering his own. And it is because it is God himself who enters in, in order to let the whole of human evil go over him, that his intervention in meekness has violent and explosive force. It is the very power of God. And so the cross with all its incredible meekness and patience and compassion is no deed of passive and beautiful heroism simply, but the most potent and aggressive deed that heaven and earth have ever known: the attack of God's holy love upon the inhumanity of man and the tyranny of evil, upon all the piled up contradiction of sin.[197]

In short, because Torrance does not restrict the Word's activity only to that one act of incarnation as McCormack does, he can say, with power, that with "the atoning work of Christ seen at work" in his taking our sin upon himself and exposing it for what it is, he could draw out "all its hate and enmity, revealing its true nature as sheer hatred of grace" by bearing it in himself on the cross. His atoning actions were not mechanical actions because they were not merely forensic and transactional. His atoning work was the "activity of the divine person penetrating directly into the hearts of men and women and in an acutely personal way, by way of God's decision of love, opening up people in their decisions and gathering them into communion and union

---

[195] Ibid., 214.
[196] Ibid.
[197] Torrance, *Incarnation*, 150.

with God."¹⁹⁸ He did this, as "only he who is God and man could."¹⁹⁹ Torrance could accomplish all of this precisely because he envisioned God decisively acting for our benefit throughout Jesus' entire life of perfect obedience to the Father for us.

By contrast, instead of allowing the second person of the Trinity to be the active Word of God who speaks to us personally and who enables us to know and love God as the risen and ascended Lord through the power of his Holy Spirit, McCormack thinks all Jesus' actions in eternity and in history are determined by "ontological receptivity." Despite his desire to present us with an actualistic view of Jesus Christ as the one Mediator, this viewpoint allows the idea of "ontological receptivity" to define both divine and human being in Christ, thus undercutting the uniqueness of the hypostatic union, as already noted. For his view of "ontological receptivity," McCormack cites statements from CD IV/2 where Barth speaks of the "history of God in his mode of existence as the Son."²⁰⁰ In his reading, "both 'divine' and 'human' being are 'defined' by this history, for this history constitutes the 'essence' of each."²⁰¹ This viewpoint leads McCormack to the astonishing claim that there is "a single composite hypostasis, constituted in time by means of what I will call the 'ontological receptivity' of the eternal Son to the 'act of being' proper to the human Jesus as human. 'Ontological receptivity,' it seems to me, is the most apt phrase for describing the precise nature of the relation of the 'Son' to Jesus of Nazareth."²⁰² From this it follows that "it is the Son's 'ontological receptivity' that makes an eternal *act* of 'identification' on the part of the Logos

---

¹⁹⁸ Ibid., 152.
¹⁹⁹ Ibid.
²⁰⁰ Ibid., 252 citing Barth, CD IV/2, 106.
²⁰¹ Ibid. It should be noted here that Barth never says that divine and human being are each *constituted* in the history in which "God in His mode of existence as the Son, in whom He humbles Himself and becomes also the Son of Man Jesus of Nazareth," CD IV/2, 106. In fact, Barth argues that the Son's becoming man and his exaltation of human nature into union with God "mutually interpret one another" (ibid.). Thus, he says, "It is in the actual occurrence of this history that we have seen that which particularly interests us in the present context—its movement from below to above, the exaltation of the Son of Man who in His identity with the Son of God comes to God as the bearer of our human essence ... this history itself, and its dynamic, is the reality, the *mysterium*, the sacrament of the being of Jesus Christ ... it is this history which is meant according to our assumption: the act of God in which the Son of God becomes identical with the man Jesus of Nazareth, and therefore unites human essence with His divine essence, and therefore exalts the human into fellowship with the divine; the act of God in which he humbles Himself to exalt man. The Subject Jesus Christ is this history. This is the content of the eternal will and decree of God ... [it is] the history in which He, the Son of God, becomes and is the Son of Man, going into the far country as the Son of God to come home again as the Son of Man" (ibid., 106–7). There is no implication here that divine being is constituted in this act of incarnation for our reconciliation.
²⁰² Ibid.

with the human Jesus to be *constitutive* of his identity as the second 'person' of the Trinity even before the actual uniting occurs."[203] Here, once again, instead of recognizing the incarnation as a new, free, and sheer act of grace as Barth and Torrance did, McCormack has made the incarnation a necessary result of "ontological receptivity." And that's not the end of it, because it is here that McCormack states quite clearly and mistakenly that the second person of the Trinity is *constituted* by his identification with his humanity in the incarnation, even before the incarnation. However, any idea at all that the second person of the Trinity is "composite" within the immanent Trinity as generated from the Father is a denial of grace and makes God dependent upon history to be who he is in eternity. As Torrance so clearly indicated, while "God was always able to become incarnate, he chose to become incarnate in what the Bible calls 'the fullness of time.'"[204] McCormack's view completely undermines a proper doctrine of the immanent Trinity. This confused reasoning leads McCormack to reject the Logos *asarkos* while claiming to accept it. We will consider that in more detail shortly.

Here it is important to stress that his appeal to Barth does not accurately present Barth's view. Torrance also strongly opposed any such view as just described because the eternal Son is not defined *by* his human history; instead, his human history is saving history because it is, as noted above, an act of God in union with Christ's human nature taken from our fallen humanity and healed through his life of perfect obedience. In his view of "ontological receptivity" McCormack leaves out what Barth emphasizes in CD IV/2, namely, that "in the inner life of God, as the eternal essence of the Father, Son and Holy Ghost, the divine essence does not, of course need any actualisation. On the contrary, it is the creative ground of all other, i.e., all creaturely actualisations."[205] Furthermore, Barth states that "Even as the divine essence of the Son it did not need His incarnation, His existence as man and His action in unity with the man Jesus of Nazareth, to become actual." This is because "As the divine essence of the Son it is the predicate of the one God. And as the predicate of this Subject it is not in any sense merely potential but in every sense actual."[206] Then Barth says,

> But his divine essence—and this is the new thing in Jesus Christ from the divine standpoint—needed a special actualisation in the identity of the Son of God with the Son of Man, and therefore in its union

---

[203] Ibid., emphasis mine.
[204] Torrance, *Christian Doctrine of God*, 208.
[205] Barth, CD IV/2, 113.
[206] Ibid.

with human essence. In this union it is not immediately actual. In this union it is addressed to what is of itself totally different human essence. It is directed to a specific goal (*apotelesma*), the reconciliation of the world with God.[207]

In this sense, in agreement with Athanasius and with Torrance, Barth holds that in his divine essence, the Son has to *become* human, and that is what "needs an actualisation which is new even from above, from the divine standpoint. It needs the *novum* of the execution of the eternal will and decree in which God elected man for Himself and Himself for man, giving this concrete determination to His own divine being."[208] For that reason, "all that Jesus does and says as the one Son of God and Son of Man—includes this human *novum* in itself, a new and special actualisation (among all the many actualisations of human essence) in the address and direction of the human to the divine essence of the one Son of God."[209] Barth is here holding together Christ's divine and human actions in the union of divine and human being in him so that he can then say that

> what Jesus Christ does as the Son of God and in virtue of His divine essence, and what He does as the Son of Man and in exercise of His human essence, He does (in this strictest relationship of the one to the other) in such a way that they always actualise themselves as the one and the other: *per efficaciam distinctam utriusque naturae* [through the distinct efficacy of each of the two natures].[210]

Consequently, Barth opposes any dualistic separation of the two natures in Christ. But he also opposes any monistic confusion and reversal of the two natures in Christ. Hence, it follows for Barth that

> in the work of the one Jesus Christ everything is at one and the same time, but distinctly, both divine and human. It is this in such a way that it never becomes indistinguishable. Where Jesus Christ is really known, there is no place for a monisitc thinking which confuses or reverses the divine and the human. Again, there can be only a historical thinking, for which each factor has its own distinctive character. The divine and the human work together. But even in their common working they are not

---

[207] Ibid., 113–14.
[208] Ibid., 114.
[209] Ibid.
[210] Ibid., 115.

interchangeable. The divine is still above and the human below. Their relationship is one of genuine action.[211]

All of these crucial distinctions evaporate with the notion of "ontological receptivity." Once that metaphysical notion is employed, the above and below, the free new acts of God are dissolved into the necessity of being which is by its very nature receptive. The result is that McCormack can then claim that Jesus' human history *constitutes* his eternal being as the Son in such a way that the second person of the Trinity is generated by the Father as composite, namely, as divine-human relation. This very idea, as noted above, obliterates the distinction between the eternal existence the God as Father, Son, and Holy Spirit and God for us in the incarnation and outpouring of the Holy Spirit in the economy of salvation. Even more drastically, however, this notion of "ontological receptivity" becomes the subject with God the Son the predicate, so that it becomes unnecessary and even impossible to envision God the Son *as* God acting for us as the reconciler throughout Jesus' life on earth.

To be clear, against this logical necessity of "ontological receptivity," Torrance insists that the hypostatic union means that there is a real union of natures "within the *one* person of the Son, so that it is only in and through the one person of the Son that we can have personal relations with the Father. And here 'personal' relations is therefore not a psychological expression, but a christological, because christocentric, expression."[212] This crucial point is enabled just because Torrance held that in the incarnation we have an act of grace

> in which God the Son freely descended into our human existence, and freely assumed human being into oneness with his divine being. That was an act of sheer grace. He did not need to do it. He did not owe it either to himself or to man to do it; it is an act grounded only in the pure overflowing love of God. It is in no sense a two-sided event, for even though there is within it, the unity of divine and human natures, act of

---

[211] Ibid., 116.

[212] Torrance, *Incarnation*, 207. It is no accident that McCormack's mistaken view of the eternal Son stemmed from his attempt to understand this psychologically instead of in a strictly christological way. See the article by Alexandra Pârvan and Bruce L. McCormack cited above in n. 115 where they take "Steps Towards a 'Psychological' Ontology of God." McCormack indicates that his next book "will elaborate more fully what [he understands] by a 'psychological ontology' of God," *The Humility of the Eternal Son*, 295.

God and act of man, the whole act of incarnation ... is grounded solely and entirely and exclusively in the act of God's grace.[213]

Thus, hypostatic union "does not mean ... a union between two persons and in that sense a personal union, but precisely the opposite, a union within the *one* person of the Son, so that it is only in and through the one person of the Son that we can have personal relations with the Father."[214]

Enhypostasis/Anhypostasis

Given this view, Torrance can then explain the proper function of *anhypostasis* and *enhypostasis*. His explanation is revealing. Because the incarnation is an act of pure grace "the human nature of Jesus never existed apart from the incarnation of God the Son."[215] That there is only one person in Jesus means that Jesus' human nature had no independent "centre of personal being" which would then be "over against the person of the Son of God."[216] However, since his human existence from its first moment of existence "was in hypostatic union with his Godhead," it had its "*hypostasis* or personal subsistence *in* the personal subsistence of God the Son" because it was *enhypostatic*.[217] It was *anhypostatic* in that it had no other personal center than that of the Son. Torrance insisted that these two categories did not detract from Jesus' full and complete humanity but actually insured them. He says,

> Jesus had a fully human mind and human soul and human will; he lived a fully human life in hypostatic union with his divine life, and in that union with his divine life, his human life had manifested the most singular and unique personality as man ... *enhypostasia* ... preserves the acknowledgement of the full humanity of Jesus, and indeed of his historical person as a man among others, and as one of mankind, a true man.[218]

What Torrance here stresses is that while Jesus is like us in all things but without himself sinning, he is also unique in that only his human nature is

---

[213] Ibid., 206.
[214] Ibid., 207.
[215] Ibid., 229.
[216] Ibid.
[217] Ibid.
[218] Ibid., 230.

uniquely united "to the divine nature in the one person of God the Son."[219] Ultimately, Torrance maintains that

> the doctrine of *anhypostasia and enhypostasia* (put together as one concept) helps us also to understand or express how God the Son was made in the likeness of our flesh of sin, and yet was not himself a sinner; how he became one with us in the continuity of our adamic and fallen existence in such a way as to make contact with us in the very roots of our sinning being, and yet did not himself repeat our "original sin" but vanquished it, and broke its continuity within our human nature.[220]

Anhypostasis then referred to God's unconditional "and amazingly humble act of grace in assuming our humanity in the concrete likeness of the flesh of sin," while *enhypostasis* "speaks of the fact that the person of Christ was the person of the obedient Son of the Father, who in his humanity remained in perfect holy communion with the Father from the very beginning, and so was sinless, and absolutely pure and spotless and holy."[221] In this way he took our sin and guilt upon himself in his life of perfect obedience so that "in our place and on our behalf [he] might expiate our sin and guilt and make propitiation for us before God the Father, thus restoring us to the Father in purity and truth and love."[222]

Torrance does admit that, as Leontius and John of Damascus understood these categories, they did not stress the anhypostatic element which denotes the "assumption in pure grace of our fallen humanity."[223] For this reason, they did not properly stress Christ's enhypostatic humanity in order to "secure the place of the historical Jesus as active agent and mediator, and not simply as instrument, in revelation and reconciliation."[224] Here Torrance insists that a proper view of this matter would take cognizance of the fact that in Christ there were two wills and not just one (Monothelitism). Monothelitism was condemned at the second Council of Constantinople in 680 because the hypostatic union meant that in Christ there was a union of a divine and a human will in the one person of the mediator.

Thus, "Christ was subject to temptation as we are," but since the human will "belonged to the one person of God the Son," Christ was able to "resist"

---

[219] Ibid.
[220] Ibid., 231–2.
[221] Ibid., 232.
[222] Ibid.
[223] Ibid., 211–12.
[224] Ibid., 212.

temptations and "condemn sin in our human nature, and then to bend the will of man back into oneness with the divine will."[225] Importantly, any idea that in Christ God assumed a neutral human nature and not our estranged, fallen, and sinful human nature, would have meant we would be unable to give proper weight to his temptations and thus to his human obedience through which he overcame our sinfulness. This is crucial and it is why Torrance consistently insists on holding together incarnation and atonement in a way that patristic theology did not. Without thinking these doctrines into each other, Torrance maintains one would always undercut the saving significance of Christ's humanity throughout the whole course of his life of obedience to the Father. Precisely on the basis of a properly conceived concept of *enhypostasis*, Torrance expressed a proper view of *kenosis* saying,

> we must think of God as determining himself freely to be our God, directing himself freely to share in the profoundest way in our frail life, in all its limitations and weaknesses, and even in its lostness, all in order to be our God, and to gather us into fellowship with himself. But in this act of unspeakable humiliation, God was not simply using the humanity of Christ as his organ or instrument, while he remained transcendent to it all. *He himself* actually came, the immutable God, humbling himself to become a creature and to suffer as a creature our judgement and death, and throughout all that to maintain his sovereign freedom and initiative, even when he gave himself up to the death of the cross, in an offering as unreserved in his self-giving as it was majestically omnipotent and free in its act of grace.[226]

As an aside, Torrance notes that when Monotheletism was condemned, Pope Honorius I of Rome was anathematized for rejecting the fact that Christ had two wills. It must be noted here that in rejecting the categories of *enhypostasis* and *anhypostasis*, McCormack claims this is necessary to avoid an instrumentalization of Christ's humanity. Yet, as just seen in Torrance's view, he avoids such instrumentalization precisely by employing these two categories. Torrance insists that "by the assertion of the union of the incarnation and atonement, we repudiate the idea that the humanity of Christ was merely instrumental in the hands of God and the idea that the atonement on the cross was a merely forensic transaction, the fulfilment of a legal contract."[227] This view follows from his understanding that the covenant was

---

[225] Ibid.
[226] Ibid., 227.
[227] Torrance, *Atonement*, 182.

a covenant of grace which was fulfilled for Israel and all others in "a unique and utterly vicarious way" in Jesus as the incarnate Word.[228] Here, Torrance insists that "God's eternal election is nothing else than God's eternal love incarnate in his beloved Son, so that in him we have election incarnate. God's eternal decree is nothing other than God's eternal Word so that in Christ we have the eternal decree or Word of God made flesh."[229] Here, Torrance avoids the mistaken historicist view of McCormack which first expressed itself with his view that election is the ground of God's triunity and still expresses itself with the idea that the eternal Son is somehow constituted by Jesus' human history. And Torrance does this precisely by recognizing and maintaining the freedom of God's grace.

It is worth mentioning here that part of the problem associated with the idea that in order to maintain Jesus' full humanity it must be understood as somehow constitutive of his eternal Sonship can also be traced to the fact that such a view unwittingly employs what Torrance called a container notion of space. Torrance explained this by referring to Calvin's idea that "the Son in his complete transcendence became man, and remains transcendently the Son of God, while also man in the form of a servant."[230] Torrance helpfully explains that Calvin's view (the so-called "*extra-Calvinisticum*") could best be understood by accepting the teaching of the Greek fathers when they rejected "the pre-Christian Greek conceptions of space as a 'container', or 'receptacle'" because then space would be understood to mean that it was a "container which contains things inside it."[231] This would mean that if this thinking was applied to the incarnate Word, then what is contained and what contains would be understood to have "a relation of interdependence" as "between the container and its contents."[232] Torrance insists that the fathers relied on the biblical view that "the heaven of heavens cannot contain thee," with the result that the incarnate presence of God in Jesus Christ "could not be construed in terms of any container notion of space" because "God is present with us 'without leaving the throne of the universe', and that 'the Son of God became man, was born of the virgin Mary', and so forth, without leaving his rule over the universe."[233]

Here, Torrance insisted, with the early church, that God's relations with us in the incarnation must be understood relationally and thus without

---

[228] Ibid., 182–3.
[229] Ibid., 183.
[230] Torrance, *Incarnation*, 216.
[231] Ibid., 217.
[232] Ibid.
[233] Ibid., 218.

employing this container notion of space, which would have to mean that history would determine Jesus' eternal Sonship in some way. That would obliterate the truth that God came to us in Christ within space and time, "yet in such a way that he did not cease to be the creator transcendent over all space and time."[234] In sum, by insisting that the incarnation cannot be understood in a way which would deny the Son's "eternal transcendence to the creature, by making him a prisoner of time or the time series," Torrance held that the Calvinists maintained that "the Word cannot be subordinated to the flesh it assumes nor can it be limited by the creaturely reality with which it is united, and so be altered in its transcendent and divine nature."[235] Torrance thus claimed that any such view would be "a form of monophysite error in which the human nature of Christ was being absorbed in his divine nature."[236]

Torrance here makes an important distinction absent from McCormack's position, namely, that "with the incarnation of the Word, we must never think of the Word apart from the man Jesus, with whom the Word is for ever united, and from whom the Word is never apart."[237] However, if this is understood relationally, then one would never say that the Word's existence is constituted in any sense by his human nature, even by way of anticipation, because God did not cease being the eternal God even as incarnate in Jesus Christ. In other words, the eternal Word is not interdependent with the humanity of Jesus. While we can only know the eternal Word of God through our union with the human Jesus as the incarnate Word, one cannot confuse this epistemological fact with ontology by then claiming that the missions must be read back into the processions as McCormack has done. That is precisely the point that Torrance avoided by rejecting the receptacle concept of space. This confusion by McCormack is clearly evident in his statement that,

> If, in Jesus Christ, God has elected to become human, then *the human history of Jesus Christ is constitutive of the being and existence of God in the second of God's modes* to the extent that the being and existence of the Second Person of the Trinity cannot be rightly thought of in the absence of this human history.[238]

---

[234] Ibid.
[235] Ibid., 220.
[236] Ibid.
[237] Ibid.
[238] Bruce L. McCormack, *Orthodox and Modern: Studies in the Theology of Karl Barth* (Grand Rapids, MI: Baker Academic, 2008), 223. For more on this, see Molnar, *Faith, Freedom and the Spirit*, 244ff.

Returning to McCormack's view of "ontological receptivity," we recall that for him this means that it is the Son's ontological receptivity "that makes an eternal *act* of 'identification' on the part of the Logos with the human Jesus to be constitutive of his identity as the second 'person' of the Trinity" such that "a determination for incarnation ... is essential to the eternal Son."[239] If that is true, then to that extent the Son could not exist without incarnation, as noted above. This view is in conflict with the fact that incarnation was an act of free grace and was not demanded by the Son's eternal essence in any respect. As already noted, this view essentially makes God a dependent deity, a God who is dependent on the world. George Hunsinger captured this issue perfectly when he wrote that "The Father does not eternally generate the Son for the purpose of pre-temporal election. If election were the purpose of the Son's eternal generation by the Father ... The Trinity would *necessarily* be dependent on the world ... the Son would be subordinated to an external end."[240]

Logos Asarkos

By making incarnation an essential determination of the Son, McCormack finally rejects the Logos *asarkos* despite his claim that he does not. Listen to his words. He claims the bishops of Chalcedon were mistaken when they identified "the 'person' in whom both natures were said to subsist with the preexistent Logos *as such*."[241] He says they were mistaken for three reasons. First, he argues, "the Bible knows nothing of an *independent* Logos *asarkos*—a Logos 'as such.'"[242] Now this certainly seems to be a flat rejection of the Logos *asarkos*. But McCormack immediately insists that this position does not deny that there was a Logos *asarkos* prior to the incarnation. However, in accordance with his having read a logical necessity back into the Trinity with his view of "ontological receptivity," he then says that "the *true* Logos *asarkos* was never without a determination for incarnation" because "he was already, as generated by the Father, a 'composite' entity in anticipation of the incarnation to come."[243]

---

[239] McCormack, *The Humility of the Eternal Son*, 252.
[240] George Hunsinger, "Election and the Trinity: Twenty-Five Theses on the Theology of Karl Barth," *Modern Theology* 24 (2) (April 2008), 192, emphasis mine.
[241] McCormack, *The Humility of the Eternal Son*, 253.
[242] Ibid.
[243] Ibid.

In that very assertion, there is no doubt whatsoever that McCormack does in fact reject the Logos *asarkos* because if the Logos was never without a determination for incarnation, then the Logos *asarkos* never existed and never could have existed without being *incarnandus* (which in fact is the beginning of God's ways and works *ad extra*). McCormack says as much more than once in his book. Thus, for instance, he says, "if the Logos is (effectively) *incarnandus* in the eternal event of his generation by the Father, then clearly there is no unknown X behind election. God simply wills what he already is as kenotic love."[244] And, instead of saying that it is the Logos *asarkos* who becomes *incarnandus* and then *incarnatus*, McCormack says that "there is no 'moment' in which the Logos was not already determined for incarnation because the relation to Jesus is intrinsic to him."[245] Moreover, he also says that "the Logos remains *incarnandus* (which also means *asarkos*—without flesh) for so long as the incarnation has yet to take place as an event in human history."[246] However, *incarnandus* does not mean *asarkos* in the same way as Barth had in mind when he said the Logos *asarkos* was a necessary idea in the strict doctrine of the Trinity and in Christology in order to affirm the freedom of God's grace. The eternal Word without flesh is the second person of the Trinity who is and would be the eternal God with or without creation and incarnation. McCormack sees the transition from *incarnandus* to *incarnatus*, while Barth and Torrance see the transition from *asarkos*, to *incarnandus* to *incarnatus* in such a way that the eternal being and act of the trinitarian Persons remains utterly and sovereignly unique to God alone. McCormack equates *incarnandus* with *asarkos* because he included the history of Jesus "in the ontological constitution of the second 'person' of the Trinity in pretemporal eternity."[247] That is exactly wrong from within a properly functioning doctrine of the immanent Trinity. Therefore, there is no doubt that McCormack reduces the Logos *asarkos* to the Logos *incarnandus*.[248]

McCormack is more than a little ambiguous on this score. So, for instance, he can say, "It is necessary to affirm the eternal generation of the Son if he is

---

[244] Ibid., 287.
[245] Ibid., 282.
[246] Ibid.
[247] Ibid., 283.
[248] Among contemporary theologians, George Hunsinger has offered the clearest and most accurate description of how the Logos *asarkos* should be understood both in Barth's theology and in any properly functioning trinitarian theology and Christology. See George Hunsinger, *Reading Barth with Charity: A Hermeneutical Proposal* (Grand Rapids, MI: Baker Academic, 2015), 16–32 et al.

to be recognized as 'truly God' and not merely the first among creatures."²⁴⁹ With that I wholeheartedly agree. However, for the Son, McCormack has substituted a "composite" reality, namely, an essential relation to the human Jesus that constitutes his Sonship. Thus, he also erroneously argues that "the relation that joins the Logos to Jesus is one that is essential to the second 'person' of the Trinity. There is no 'moment' in which the Logos was not already determined for incarnation."²⁵⁰ What McCormack fails to notice or to acknowledge here is that he has obliterated God's *free decision* to move *ad extra* as Creator and then as the Son who becomes incarnate for us and for our salvation. Those were *new* actions for God and for us, and they simply cannot be construed as essential determinations of the immanent Trinity without dissolving God into what God does for us and in relation to us. But because it is the principle of "ontological receptivity," as discussed above, that determines the Son's relation to the Father and to us, the whole notion of a free decision on God's part in this matter is completely undermined.

McCormack emphatically denies that his position evacuates the history of Jesus of its significance because, he says, "a determination for incarnation is not yet a realized incarnation."²⁵¹ But the problem here is that while God does determine himself for incarnation, that was and is a *free decision* of the triune God who eternally exists and Father, Son, and Holy Spirit and would so exist even if he never made that determination. Thus, for McCormack, the determination is the result of a logical necessity, namely, "ontological receptivity," such that "*incarnandus* also means *asrkos*."²⁵² By contrast, for Barth, Torrance, and the early church it was the Son or the eternal Word (Logos) who was begotten of the Father. It was the Word (not a composite figure) that was and is the Logos *asarkos* who, in a free decision with the Father and Spirit, as the beginning of God's ways and works *ad extra*, determined to be Creator, Reconciler, and Redeemer. McCormack's failure here is due to the fact that he has included the history of Jesus "in the ontological constitution of the second 'person' of the Trinity in pretemporal eternity."²⁵³ From this he reaches the astonishing conclusion that "whether then one says that the self-constituting act of God consists in the divine processions or in the trinitarian history of Jesus matters little so long as one says both."²⁵⁴ This is an astonishing conclusion because, as stated, this represents a complete collapse of the

---

[249] Ibid., 256-7.
[250] Ibid., 282.
[251] Ibid.
[252] Ibid.
[253] Ibid., 283.
[254] Ibid.

immanent into the economic Trinity since he is clearly claiming that there could be no processions within the eternal Trinity without the history of Jesus constituting his being as the Son of the Father. That's exactly what cannot be said if God truly is free as the eternal Trinity. I have already explained that he takes this all to mean that the history of Jesus begins as divine and ends as human, but that is also incorrect because he claims the Son was generated as "divine-human relation." If that is in any sense true, then the Son cannot really have a fully divine beginning within the immanent Trinity!

McCormack has completely broken with the Bible and the early church tradition because even in Jn 3:16 it speaks of God's only Son coming into the world and the Nicene Creed explicitly says that it is the eternal Son who is begotten before all worlds. The Son was begotten and not made. Moreover, in the very first verse of John's Gospel, the words could not be clearer, i.e., "In the beginning was the Word, and the Word was with God and the Word was God." Not only did God create the world through this eternal Word, but it is this Word who became flesh (Jn 1:14) and whose glory was seen as "the glory as of the Father's only Son, full of grace and truth." Beyond this, when it is said that "No one has ever seen God. The only Son, God, who is at the Father's side, has revealed him," the meaning could not be clearer. The Word was and is God. The Son is the Word and was and is God as his only Son. Furthermore, in the key text from Mt. 11:27 with a parallel in Lk. 10:22, Jesus is said to have claimed that "All things have been handed over to me by my Father. No one knows the Son except the Father, and no one knows the Father except the Son and anyone to whom the Son wishes to reveal him." Torrance makes the extremely important point regarding these texts, namely, that this relationship between the Father and Son in eternity is a "closed circle,"[255] and

---

[255] See Torrance, *Incarnation*, 127–8. Torrance notes that this relation of knowing between the Father and Son "involved a mutual relation of *being* between them as well, and not only between the eternal Son and the Father but between the incarnate Son and the Father. This implies that we are given access to the closed circle of divine knowing between the Father and the Son only through cognitive union with Christ, that is only through an interrelation of knowing and being between us and the incarnate Son, although in our case this union is one of participation through grace and not one of nature," *The Trinitarian Faith*, 58–9. Torrance makes another important point insisting that "we do not know the Father first and then come to know the Son; nor do we know the Son first and then come to know the Father … If we begin with the conviction that Christ is God, we inevitably apply a preconceived idea of God to our understanding Christ. But if we know Christ only as the Son of the Father, and only as in and through him we know God, then our knowledge of Christ the Son and our knowledge of God the Father coincide" (ibid., 60). Because our knowledge of God is of the Father through the Son in their mutual relationship and because the Holy Spirit is one in being with the Father and the Son, it is only through the incarnate Son that we also know of the Holy Spirit through union with Christ in his humanity as the incarnate, ascended, risen, and coming Lord.

we have no way of entering this except through conceptual union with Christ in faith as he enables that union since, as it clearly says in Jn 1:12 that, while his own people did not accept him, Jesus, the incarnate Son, gave the power to become children of God "to those who believe in his name." That power came from him who is God acting for us without ceasing to be God in his incarnate Word.

Considering all of this, for one to say that the second person of the Trinity was generated from the Father as "composite" explicitly denies the all-important truth that it is the Word who really was God and that it is that Word who is the only Son of the Father.[256] This is denied by making his mission part of his eternal generation. Such a move makes the eternal Trinity dependent on an external event, and that, as already noted, opens the door to a "dependent deity" which undermines the freedom of the immanent Trinity. McCormack leaves no doubt about his view arguing that "the preexistent Logos *as such* is a pure postulate, a human invention, alleged to be complete in itself without regard for its activity *ad extra*."[257] Furthermore, he claims that the Logos *as such* is an "an 'idol' by any other name" because, in his view, the Bible only knows "a Son who has his being in his sending and the mission to which it gives rise" and this is the case because "in this sending … his mission is built into his eternal generation. *As eternally generated,* he already has a relation to Jesus of Nazareth."[258] All of these assertions flatly undermine the unique eternal relation between the Father and Son in eternity as stated both in the Bible and at Nicaea and beyond.

---

[256] Consider the following remark from Barth as he ponders Jesus' Lordship: "grounded in Himself, and apart from what He means for us, Jesus Christ is what He means for us, and that He can mean this for us because quite apart therefrom He is it antecedently in Himself" (CD I/1, 424). Thus, "Jesus Christ does not first become God's Son when he is it for us. He becomes it from eternity; He becomes it as the eternal Son of the eternal Father" (ibid., 427). Notice that for Barth, as for the entire tradition stemming from Nicaea, it is the Son who is eternally begotten of the Father and not a divine-human composite.

[257] McCormack, *The Humility of the Eternal Son*, 253.

[258] Ibid. In his Conclusion, McCormack says the promise of his book has been kept because he has maintained "the integrity of God and human in their uniting in Christ" (293). Then he says, once again, that God the Son's nature is "teleologically ordered" and that "he was eternally generated for his mission in time and beyond it" (ibid.) What has been demonstrated in this chapter is that he has not maintained the integrity of the God confessed in the Nicene-Constantinopolitan Creed by making God's eternal being and act dependent on an external condition, and he has not maintained the integrity of the humanity of Christ precisely because he confuses that humanity with the eternal generation of the Son from the Father within the immanent Trinity by reading the missions back into the processions and claiming that the second Person of the Trinity was generated as a divine-human composite.

For this reason, McCormack mistakenly thinks "eternal generation is itself a teleologically ordered activity" so that "the 'preexistent Son' then has an essential relation that defines him as *this* 'person' of the immanent Trinity and it is this relation that is characterized—both in eternity and in time—by 'receptivity.'"[259] McCormack goes on to say that it is just because the Council of Chalcedon equated the Logos *as such* (an *independent* Logos *asarkos*) with the second person of the Trinity that they then needed the *enhypostasis* and *anhypostasis* because espousal of a Logos *as such* has to mean that "No real relation of the humanity of Christ to the 'person of the union' is possible." McCormack thus claims that with that traditional view of the Logos, Jesus' human mind and will could not behave spontaneously as in all human activity. He then claims that "Chalcedon's talk of two 'natures' ... needs to be surrendered."[260] This leads him to redefine the meaning of the hypostatic union saying that "it can accommodate the suggestion that the Son has an eternal relation to Jesus that has now been actualized (rendered concretely real) through uniting in time."[261]

Amazingly, in responding to criticisms of his position leveled by Rowan Williams, McCormack claims that he no longer holds the view that "triunity is a 'function' of the divine election."[262] But then he claims that "'The eternal act in which God gives to himself his own being as Father, Son and Holy Spirit and the eternal act in which God chooses to be God in the covenant of grace is *one and the same act.*'"[263] Thus, there is no before and after in

---

[259] Ibid.
[260] Ibid., 254.
[261] Ibid., 255. Citing Marilyn McCord Adams, McCormack notes that she said, "So far as I know, no one ... has envisioned the Divine Word's possessing human nature essentially in such a way that the Divine Word could not exist without being human. Most Christian theologians would agree; not only is this false; it makes no sense" (McCormack, *The Humility of the Eternal Son*, 253–4). McCormack's response is that "Bulgakov clearly did. Barth and von Balthasar moved in this direction too" (ibid.). Amazingly, McCormack once again contradicts himself claiming that "I have retained the need for a preexistent Logos who 'descends' into this world and unites himself with Jesus and who does so in a continuous activity that begins with the conception of Jesus" (ibid., 268). If the Son or Word is generated as "composite" and if the Logos *asarkos* is in fact the Logos *incarnandus* as McCormack argues throughout this book, then the subject of the incarnation is, as he also says, incomprehensibly, a divine-human subject. So, his reference to a preexistent Logos who "descends" into this world is meaningless because it is not really referring to the Logos *asarkos* at all which he considers an idol, but to a "divine-human" composite in the form of the Logos *incarnandus*. It will be recalled that McCormack claims that "even in the act of hypostatic *uniting*, the 'subject' who performs that action is the God-man, Jesus Christ in his divine-human unity" (McCormack, "Divine Impassibility," 177). This is far from the New Testament and the Nicene view of the Word or Son of the Father and very far from the view of Athanasius, Cyril, Barth, and Torrance as I have shown.
[262] Ibid., 284.
[263] Ibid.

God, and in his view of Barth's theology, there is "no 'state of being [in God] above and prior to the decision to be incarnate in time.'"²⁶⁴ However, Barth directly insisted that:

> We know God's will *apart* from predestination only as the act in which, from all eternity and in all eternity, God affirms Himself. We must guard against disputing the eternal will of God which precedes even predestination. We must not allow God to be submerged in His relationship to the universe or think of Him as tied in Himself to the universe ... we confess the eternal will of the God who is free in Himself, even in the sense that originally and properly He wills and affirms and confirms Himself.²⁶⁵

And Barth clearly held that God did not *need* to give himself his being saying that God,

> does not need his own being in order to be who He is: because He already has His own being and is Himself ... If, therefore, we say that God is *a se*, we do not say that God creates, produces or originates Himself ... He cannot 'need' His own being because he affirms it in being who He is²⁶⁶

Moreover, Barth makes a number of other statements that clearly oppose what McCormack says here. First, he says that the love of the eternal Trinity is "free and unconstrained in God Himself" and only thus,

> is it free in its realisation towards man. That is, in His Word becoming flesh, God acts with inward freedom and not in fulfilment of a law to which He is supposedly subject. *His Word would still be His Word apart from this becoming, just as Father, Son and Holy Spirit would be none the less eternal God, if no world had been created.*²⁶⁷

Second, Barth asserted that "Even as the divine essence of the Son it did not need His incarnation, His existence as man ... to become actual. As the divine essence of the Son it is the predicate of the one God. And as the predicate of

---

²⁶⁴ Ibid.
²⁶⁵ Barth, CD II/2, 155, emphasis mine.
²⁶⁶ Barth, CD II/1, 306.
²⁶⁷ Barth, CD I/2, 135, emphasis mine.

this Subject it is not in any sense merely potential but in every sense actual."[268] Third, for Barth "The Word is what He is even before and apart from His being flesh. Even as incarnate He derives His being to all eternity from the Father and from Himself, and not from the flesh."[269] All of these statements of Barth categorically oppose the position advocated by McCormack and his followers. For instance, Kevin Hector claimed to uphold God's freedom in the manner suggested by Barth, but then embraced McCormack's thinking by also saying that "properly speaking, God has no being-in-Godself apart from the covenant."[270] However, this statement clearly obliterates the reality of the immanent Trinity in the sense advanced by Barth. Barth opposed such views insisting that Jesus Christ "was not at the beginning of God, for God has indeed no beginning. But He was at the beginning of all things, at the beginning of God's dealings with the reality which is distinct from Himself … He was the election of God's grace as directed towards man."[271]

---

[268] Barth, CD IV/2, 113.
[269] Barth, CD I/2, 136.
[270] Kevin Hector, "Immutability, Necessity and Triunity: Towards as Resolution of the Trinity and Election Controversy," *Scottish Journal of Theology* 65 (1) (2012), 74. This idea is discussed in detail in Molnar, *Faith, Freedom, and the Spirit*, 166ff.
[271] Barth CD II/2, 102.

Conclusion

This has been a constructive work in systematic theology. Its main focus was on Christology with a view toward seeing how a properly understood Christology illuminates a proper view of justification by grace along with a proper view of God and God's relations with us in history. Toward that end I relied heavily on the work of Thomas F. Torrance while also referring to the work of Karl Barth at crucial points along the way. My goal was to illustrate that there could be substantial agreement between Roman Catholics and Protestants regarding such crucial theological themes as nature and grace, revelation, theological anthropology, and the doctrine of God, especially as this relates to contemporary approaches to liberation theology if and to the extent that they allowed Jesus Christ in his uniqueness to be the first and final word in their theology.

In the first chapter, we explored in detail the difference it makes for several key aspects of theology if grace is understood decisively as the grace of Jesus Christ. That means, as Torrance never ceased to remind us, that grace, as God's forgiveness and mercy, not only is God's own personal act of coming to us in his revelation to Moses and in the forgiveness experienced in Israel but it is identical with God's personally coming to us in the incarnation. In that event, from his birth to his death on the cross and in his resurrection and ascension, Jesus Christ is truly God with us. He is the Giver of grace. He not only forgives our sin but promises us a new life through union with him as the risen and ascended Lord who lives now in his true divinity and true humanity as a new creature who is no longer subject to sin, suffering, evil, and death. In him we have the promise of eternal life when he returns to judge the living and the dead. Because he is the grace of God, grace cannot be understood as a divine quality which could be detached from Jesus, the risen Lord, personally acting here and now through the power of his Holy Spirit. It is not a quality that inheres in us as human beings. The moment such conceptuality is introduced, theologians are then mistakenly inclined to look within themselves to understand who God is as well as the meaning of revelation, faith, grace, and salvation itself.

In that chapter, I compared the views of nature and grace offered by two of the twentieth century's most important figures, Thomas F. Torrance and Karl

Rahner. After presenting a detailed overview of Torrance's understanding of nature and grace in light of God's revelation in Jesus Christ, I then developed Karl Rahner's view with the aid of key insights on nature and grace from William V. Dych, a prominent commentator on Rahner's theology. The most important points of the chapter concerned the fact that Torrance applied a careful view of the doctrine of justification by grace through faith to his theological anthropology, Christology, and his view of God, while Rahner tended to focus on us first with our transcendental experiences of our horizon in order to understand these matters. The results of the comparisons were indeed startling because Torrance took the problem of sin seriously in a way that Rahner did not. And he could do that because he understood the meaning of sin exclusively in light of the fact that it was and is forgiven sin just because he decisively connected the doctrines of incarnation and atonement.

Among other things, this led Torrance to insist that since Jesus himself is the Way, the Truth, and the Life (Jn 14:6), there is no authority for believing in him other than himself. Because of that, one could never consider salvation by equating that with obedience to the moral law, obedience to conscience, or obedience to the teaching authority in the church, or even obedience to the Ten Commandments. None of these authorities has the power to save us or to unite us to the God of grace who comes to us in Jesus Christ. Because the truth of our knowledge of God and the truth of the Gospel is and remains always grounded exclusively in Christ himself, it is only in obedience to him that we live in true freedom as children of God. As stated in Jn 1:11-14, Jesus

> came to what was his own, but his own people did not accept him. But to those who did accept him *he gave power* to become children of God, to those who believe in his name, who were born not by natural generation nor by human choice nor by a man's decision but of God. And the Word became flesh and made his dwelling among us, and we saw his glory, the glory as of the Father's only Son, full of grace and truth.

The power to know God's grace as truth then can only come directly from Christ himself to us through faith in him. That requires conceptual union with Christ himself to know of our salvation. That also requires that we realize that our righteousness (right relation with God and our neighbors) cannot be achieved through obedience to the moral law since that could just be a way to avoid the need to rely totally on grace alone to know God and to live our true freedom as freedom from sin as self-will, which is identical with our free-will. When this set of ideas is compared to the views of Rahner, one can see that his view of nonconceptual knowledge of God grounds such knowledge in us and leads him to uphold his view that we have an obediential potency for God as well as a supernatural existential. These twin ideas lead to his view of anonymous Christianity, which is essentially a Christianity without Christ. In that important chapter I contrasted his views, which Torrance would claim have more and a little tinge of Pelagianism to them, with the views of Torrance.

I demonstrated in detail that because Torrance rigorously held that knowledge of the Truth had to mean knowledge of God's *being* which we directly meet and can know *conceptually* only in our encounter with Christ himself, he rejected nonconceptual knowledge of God. This led him to espouse his powerful view of cheap and costly grace in order to illustrate that when grace is not detached from Christ, the Giver of grace, then, in light of the cross, we see that in ourselves we are disclosed sinners in need of forgiveness. From this it follows that we do not have an obediential potency for grace since that power comes directly from the Holy Spirit uniting us to Christ the risen Lord conceptually and ontologically. Neither of these facts is properly seen or understood when, with Rahner, we pursue an *a priori* view of Christology in which grace is detached from Christ and ascribed to us in our supposed "searching Christology," which he thinks can be seen through an analysis of anthropology, which supposedly exists in a mutually conditioning relationship with Christology. We explored in detail why and with what implications Torrance directly rejected all such thinking. The point of that chapter was and is that if grace is not detached from Christ, the Giver of grace, then both Catholics and Protestants would be firmly united in their acknowledgment of Jesus Christ as the Way, the Truth, and the Life. If that were to happen, then Catholics and Protestants together would be free to engage in repentant rethinking of each of their theological positions in light of that particular truth, which alone unites them and frees them from all forms of legalism, authoritarianism, and license.

In Chapter 2, I revisited Torrance's view of the doctrine of justification by grace in order to contrast his view of divine and human freedom with the views of a number of prominent contemporary theologians engaging in forms of liberation theology. My goal was to show the difference it makes not only for theological method but for a properly functioning Christology when true freedom is sought and found decisively in Christ as the only one who can set us free from our free-will, which is our self-will. Self-will for Torrance means that by nature, since the Fall, we all tend to be self-reliant and thus we all tend to act autonomously in relation to God. That is a major problem because God did indeed create us to find our happiness in him and not in ourselves or in what we think is important and necessary. Sin always is the attempt to decide good and evil for ourselves instead of recognizing that God alone is good, and goodness as well as true freedom from self-reliance can only come from genuine union with God through God's own reconciling grace which meets us in his Word and Spirit.

These are crucial points because what is demonstrated in that chapter is that much liberation theology begins with the assumption that the fight against oppression and for liberation is and must be the starting point for a theology of liberation. I argued that any such starting point always leads to a form of self-justification, which exacerbates our sinfulness by continually pointing us back to ourselves and our social, political, and religious attempts to create a better world. The point of that chapter was and is that true freedom understood evangelically is and always remains grounded in Christ alone who sets us free. Crucial here is Jesus' interaction with his fellow Jews who refused to believe in him, saying to them, "You belong to what is below, I belong to what is above. You belong to this world, but I do not belong to this world. That is why I told you that you will die in your sins. For if you do not believe that I AM, you will die in your sins" (Jn 8:23-24). To those who believed in Jesus he said, "If you remain in my word, you will truly be my disciples, and you will know the truth, and the truth will set you free" (Jn 8:31). In applying the name of God revealed to Moses in Ex. 3:14 to himself, Jesus clearly was claiming to be identical with God and then said to his fellow Jews who were rejecting him that they were slaves of sin and needed to be set free from that. They replied that their father was Abraham. Jesus responded, "If you were Abraham's children, you would be doing the works of Abraham. But now you are trying to kill me, a man who has told you the truth that I heard from God; Abraham did not do this" (Jn 8:39). Then Jesus told them they were doing the works of their father, namely, the devil, the father of lies, precisely because they refused to believe in him!

Considering this, true freedom means and must mean that Jesus himself is the liberator, namely, the only one who can set us free to love God and, on that basis alone, to love our neighbors by fighting against all that oppresses them and us, such as racism, sexism, and exploitation of every kind. What I demonstrated in this chapter is that whenever theologians begin thinking about liberation *from* our actions for liberation and against oppression, then they always "use" Jesus as a means to their social, political, or religious goals. When that occurs, Jesus' significance for faith and knowledge of the truth is completely lost because he is in practice and in fact subordinated to one's social, political, or religious goals. In effect we become the first and final word in theology and God himself is subordinated to our ideology. That is a recipe for sin precisely because in that very activity and its results, the creature now has been substituted for God the Creator, who is and remains Lord of all we think, say, and do. But God is the Lord who became incarnate in Jesus Christ precisely to free us from the misguided attempt to rely on ourselves instead of upon God's forgiving grace, which alone can and does free us to hear the Word of God and to obey God alone.

In this chapter, I relied on Torrance's important view that taking justification seriously means that "the ground is completely taken away from [our] feet and along with that would go" our invented ideas of God which we construct by relying on ourselves to right the human situation by obeying the moral law instead of God himself. This is why I follow Torrance, who held that we cannot substitute our reliance on the moral law or religion to be in right relation to God and others. This is the case because our real need is for Jesus Christ himself and for us to rely exclusively upon him as the only one who justifies and sanctifies us. In that way, he alone frees us, for the truth which is and always remains identical with God himself and never comes under our control.

In order to develop the implications of this set of ideas, I explain that for Torrance Christ liberates us from our free-will, which is in fact identical with our self-will. From this I explain why Torrance rejects all ideas of conditional salvation, why he holds the doctrines of incarnation and atonement together, and why it was not Jesus' death that constituted atonement but Jesus Christ as the Son of God offering himself in sacrifice to God vicariously on our behalf. That means everything depends on who Jesus was as God himself acting from the divine and human side to reconcile the world to God. Whenever this freedom that comes from Christ alone is ignored or marginalized, then and there we are led directly into forms of legalism or moralism and miss the actual meaning of our justification and sanctification in Christ by espousing some form of self-justification. I argued that it is just because Christ is and remains at the center of theology precisely because he himself is God acting for us here and now from the divine and human side that we, as the sinners we are apart from him, then use the moral law to determine our goodness before God. Consequently, in that way we rely on our "moral awareness," and in that very action we separate ourselves from God by autonomously relying on ourselves in that moral awareness. In that approach we then assume that it is precisely by loving our neighbors that we think we fulfill our duty toward God. Unfortunately, however, it is exactly in that way that, in the very name of theology, we cut ourselves off from God and the freedom that is ours by relying on him alone as the one who justifies and sanctifies us.

After presenting a complete picture of the freedom of grace in Torrance's theology, I then considered the implications of his view of justification for contemporary approaches to liberation theology by exploring in detail Elizabeth Johnson's feminist liberation theology and Rubén Rosario Rodríguez's attempt to explain liberation directly from experiences of liberation precisely by separating the Holy Spirit from the Word with his view that we can discover the Holy Spirit in works of liberation. This is a problem since an actual experience of the Holy Spirit will always mean that the Spirit unites us directly with Christ himself as the one who alone liberates us for knowledge of the Father in his forgiving grace. This is what is recognized in faith which involves knowledge of the truth. So, while Rosario Rodríguez thinks that our participation in liberation is in itself already in some sense a "salvific work," I demonstrate that this very view is just another form of self-justification which leaves us far from the freedom that comes from Christ alone in the power of his Holy Spirit. Then I discussed another contemporary approach to a kind of liberation theology embodied in the work of Hanna Reichel, who constructs her theology by means of a dialogue between Marcella Althaus-Reid and Karl Barth. Althaus-Reid was presented as representative of what is called constructive theology, while Barth was presented as a representative of systematic theology.

I explained that while Reichel thinks that both theologians have in common a view of God as "wholly Other," she was very much mistaken for one simple reason. That reason was and is that the "wholly Other" Barth had in view throughout his work was the eternal Trinity who could only be known through union with Christ in faith and in complete dependence on the Holy Spirit uniting us to Christ and thus to the Father. Hence, for Barth faith, love, and hope are always specifically understood from Christ himself as the one in whom we believe and the one who enables us to love God and our neighbors. Christ coming again to judge the living and the dead is also the object of hope for Christians. I demonstrated that for Hanna Reichel, following Althaus-Reid, each of these theological categories becomes distorted precisely because they are employed as ways of relating with God by relying on our own experiences of faith, love, and hope in a general way. The end result is that Reichel presents us with a "bi-sexual" Jesus and a "queer God" because she thinks it was acceptable to follow Althaus-Reid and understand theology from the perspective of sex and specifically in light of what she described as "queer holiness." I contrasted her conclusions with Barth's view that any attempt to ground theology in reason or experience always ends with the hypostatization of the human, which then pits us against the freedom of God for us that is there for all in Christ himself.

Finally, I discussed at some length the view of liberation theology presented by James Cone in his landmark book, *A Black Theology of Liberation*. I explained that, on the one hand, Cone was right to claim that Christ must be at the center of all Christian theology. On the other hand, I then demonstrated that because he insisted that Christ himself had to be understood "in light of the black perspective," he too, undermined the actual centrality of Christ for black theologians and for all people. I demonstrated that because Torrance was right to insist that Jesus Christ, the incarnate Son of God, had to be considered an ultimate, indeed, the ultimate, there was no ground for believing in him other than Jesus himself. That obviously could not mean that we have to totally abandon our perspectives; that cannot be done. However, I argued that no human perspective can or could become the starting point or criterion for the truth that comes to us in and from Jesus himself since he really is the Way, the Truth, and the Life. It is from him that we are made free to know God as he truly is. It is because he loved us while we were still sinners that, through the action of the Holy Spirit, our minds are reconciled to God, and we are enabled to have the mind of Christ to know God the Father.

I argued then that it is because of God's unconditional love of us *as* the incarnate Word that we become free to love God and, on that basis, to fight against racism and all other forms of oppression. While the truth for Christians is identical with Jesus himself who discloses that truth to us, I explained that Cone transmutes that truth in light of what he calls "black reality." So, he claimed that "truth for the black thinker arises from a passionate encounter with black reality." The problem with this view is that truth is the same for everyone since it is and always remains identical with God himself as he meets us in his incarnate Word and through the Holy Spirit. Because Cone mistakenly alleges that "truth is not objective," he ends up confusing theological truth with differing racial perspectives. Thus, he erroneously claimed that God is not the "God of white religion but the God of black experience." I argued that the eternal Trinity can be equated with neither of these views because God has no race and no gender. And to conceptualize God as the God of black or white religion is to conceptualize God by projecting our experiences into God instead of allowing revelation that meets us directly in Christ himself to transform our knowledge so that we can know God through God himself since in Christ we are, as Torrance claimed, face to face with God.

In the final chapter, I tackled the question of whether the Council of Chalcedon needed to be repaired in order to recognize and maintain the full humanity of Jesus Christ, the incarnate Son. I considered the views of Bruce

McCormack, who claims that such traditional notions as divine simplicity and impassibility, along with the concepts of *enhypostasis* and *anhypostasis*, had to be discarded today in order to recognize and maintain the full humanity of Jesus Christ. He claimed that when that humanity is grounded in the eternal Logos, then Jesus' full humanity is undermined. The repair that is then proposed is one that leads to the view that we must think of Jesus' human history as in some sense *constitutive* of his being as the eternal Son of the Father. I relied on the views of Thomas F. Torrance and Karl Barth to demonstrate in detail that both theologians help us uphold the full deity as well as the full humanity of Jesus precisely on the basis of the Chalcedonian teaching.

Among other things, this chapter illustrated that with McCormack's reduction of the Logos *asarkos* to the Logos *incarnandus*, he carries out his initial insight that the Logos *asarkos* is "an 'idol' by any other name," while simultaneously claiming that he does not reject the Logos *asarkos*, as Robert Jenson did. This led to the bizarre notions that the second person of the Trinity "is eternally generated as divine-human relation" and that the second person of the Trinity was generated by the Father for the purpose of incarnation. These are views that were flatly rejected in the early church with the recognition that the God who meets us in his Word and Spirit is *free* in himself and never becomes dependent on anything external to himself, as he would if the Father's generation of the Son was contingent on the Son's future incarnation, suffering, and death. Failure to acknowledge that freedom of God undermines a properly functioning doctrine of the Trinity and ends up compromising both Jesus' true deity and his true humanity.

Thus, this chapter showed that McCormack's "repair" of Chalcedon is not a repair at all, but a view that consistently undermines both Jesus' true deity and his true humanity. From at least the fourth century on, Jesus was explicitly recognized in the Nicene Creed as the pre-existent Son who was begotten of the Father before all worlds; he was God from God, true God from true God and thus begotten and not made. It is therefore the Son who was and is God from God. Therefore, anyone reflecting on the teaching of the Council of Chalcedon would also have to accept this crucial teaching of the Council of Nicaea. Then, one could never claim that the second person of the Trinity was generated as "divine-human relation" since the second person of the Trinity was the eternal Son, the Logos *asarkos*. It was the divine Son of the Father who was and is eternally begotten of the Father, not his humanity. In that chapter I explained that it was just because McCormack mistakenly claimed that the Father generated the Son for the purpose of incarnation that he inadvertently compromised the freedom of God's grace with dire consequences for Christology as well as the doctrine of God. Relying on the views of Torrance, I was able to demonstrate positively that if divine simplicity, impassibility and passibility, as well as the categories *enhypostasis* and *anhypostasis* are all rightly understood, they clearly enable us to recognize Jesus in his uniqueness as truly divine and truly human without confusing, mixing, or separating his two natures. One can thus avoid Monophysitism (Eutychianism) as well as Nestorianism in Christology precisely on the basis of the Chalcedonian teaching without the need to "repair" it in the manner suggested by McCormack.

Select Bibliography

Barth, Karl. *Church Dogmatics*. 4 vols. in 13 pts.
Barth, Karl. Vol. 1, pt. 1: *The Doctrine of the Word of God*. Edited by G. W. Bromiley and T. F. Torrance. Translated by G. W. Bromiley. Edinburgh: T&T Clark, 1975.
Barth, Karl. Vol. 1, pt. 2: *The Doctrine of the Word of God*. Edited by G. W. Bromiley and T. F. Torrance. Translated by G. T. Thomson and Harold Knight. Edinburgh: T&T Clark, 1970.
Barth, Karl. Vol. 2, pt. 1: *The Doctrine of God*. Edited by G. W. Bromiley and T. F. Torrance. Translated by T. H. L. Parker, W. B. Johnston, H. Knight, and J. L. M. Harie. Edinburgh: T&T Clark, 1964.
Barth, Karl. Vol. 2, pt. 2: *The Doctrine of God*. Edited by G. W. Bromiley and T. F. Torrance. Translated by G. W. Bromiley, J. C. Campbell, Iain Wilson, J. Strathearn McNab, Harold Knight, and R. A. Stewart. Edinburgh: T&T Clark, 1967.
Barth, Karl. Vol. 4, pt. 1: *The Doctrine of Reconciliation*. Edited by G. W. Bromiley and T. F. Torrance. Translated by G. W. Bromiley. Edinburgh: T&T Clark, 1974.
Barth, Karl. Vol. 4, pt. 2: *The Doctrine of Reconciliation*. Edited by G. W. Bromiley and T. F. Torrance. Translated by G. W. Bromiley. Edinburgh: T&T Clark, 1967.
Cone, James H. *A Black Theology of Liberation Fiftieth Anniversary Edition*. New York: Maryknoll Orbis Books, 2020.
Duffy, Stephen. "Experience of Grace," in *The Cambridge Companion to Karl Rahner*. Edited by Declan Marmion and Mary E. Hines. Cambridge: Cambridge University Press, 2005, 43–62.
Dych, William V. *Karl Rahner*. Collegeville, MN: The Liturgical Press, 1992.
Frye, Roland. "Language for God and Feminist Language: Problems and Principles," *Scottish Journal of Theology* 41 (4), 1988, 441–69.
Galvin, John P. "The Invitation of Grace," in *A World of Grace: An Introduction to the Themes and Foundations of Karl Rahner's Theology*. Edited by Leo J. O'Donovan. New York: Crossroad, 1981, 64–75
Haught, John. *What Is God: How to Think about the Divine*. New York: Paulist Press, 1986.
Hector, Kevin. "Immutability, Necessity and Triunity: Towards as Resolution of the Trinity and Election Controversy," *Scottish Journal of Theology* 65 (1), 2012, 64–81.
Hilary, St. of Poitiers. *On the Trinity*, Church Fathers. Translated by E. W. Watson, L. Pullan, et al. Edited by W. Sanday. A Select Library of Nicene and Post-nicene Fathers of the Christian Church. Second series. Edited by Philip Schaff and Henry Wace. Volume IX. Grand Rapids, MI: Eerdmans, 1997.

Hunsinger, George. "Election and the Trinity: Twenty-Five Theses on the Theology of Karl Barth," *Modern Theology* 24 (2), 2008, 179–98.

Hunsinger, George. *Reading Barth with Charity: A Hermeneutical Proposal*. Grand Rapids, MI: Baker Academic, 2015.

Johnson, Elizabeth A. *She Who Is: The Mystery of God in Feminist Theological Discourse*. New York: Crossroad, 1992; reissued in 2002 as a Tenth Anniversary Edition and in 2017 as a Twenty-Fifth Anniversary Edition.

Johnson, Elizabeth A. *Quest for the Living God: Mapping Frontiers in the Theology of God*. New York: Continuum, 2008.

Jones, Paul Dafydd. "Liberation Theology and Karl Barth in the Shadow of the Alt-Right," in *Karl Barth and Liberation Theology*. Edited by Kaitlyn Dugan and Paul Dafydd Jones. London: T&T Clark, 2023, 213–34

Kimel, Alvin F. Jr. Editor. *Speaking the Christian God: The Holy Trinity and the Challenge of Feminism*. Grand Rapids, MI: Eerdmans, 1992.

McCormack, Bruce Lindley. *Orthodox and Modern: Studies in the Theology of Karl Barth*. Grand Rapids, MI: Baker Academic, 2008.

McCormack, Bruce Lindley. "Divine Impassibility or Simply Divine Constancy? Implications of Karl Barth's Later Christology for Debates over Impassibility," in *Divine Impassibility and the Mystery of Human Suffering*. Edited by James F. Keating and Thomas Joseph White, O.P., 150–86. Grand Rapids, MI: Eerdmans, 2009.

McCormack, Bruce Lindley. "The Lord and Giver of Life: A 'Barthian' Defence of the *Filioque*," in *Rethinking Trinitarian Theology: Disputed Questions and Contemporary Issues in Trinitarian Theology*. Edited by Robert Wozniak and Giulio Maspero. London: T&T Clark, 2012, 230–53

McCormack, Bruce Lindley. "The Passion of God Himself: Barth on Jesus's Cry of Dereliction," in *Reading the Gospels with Karl Barth*. Edited by Daniel L. Migliore. Grand Rapids, MI: Eerdmans, 2017, 155–72

McCormack, Bruce Lindley. *The Humility of the Eternal Son: Reformed Kenoticism and the Repair of Chalcedon*. Cambridge: Cambridge University Press, 2021.

Molnar, Paul D. "Some Dogmatic Implications of Barth's Rejection of Ebionite and Docetic Christology," *International Journal of Systematic Theology* 2, 2000, 151–74.

Molnar, Paul D. "Love of God and Love of Neighbor in the Theology of Karl Rahner and Karl Barth," *Modern Theology* 20 (4), 2004, 567–98.

Molnar, Paul D. *Thomas F. Torrance: Theologian of the Trinity*. Farnham Surrey: Ashgate, 2009.

Molnar, Paul D. "The Obedience of the Son in the Theology of Karl Barth and of Thomas F. Torrance," *Scottish Journal of Theology* 67 (1), 2014, 50–69.

Molnar, Paul D. *Faith, Freedom and the Spirit: The Economic Trinity in Barth, Torrance and Contemporary Theology*. Downers Grove, IL: IVP Academic, 2015.

Molnar, Paul D. *Divine Freedom and the Doctrine of the Immanent Trinity: In Dialogue with Karl Barth and Contemporary Theology* 2nd Edition. London: T&T Clark, 2017.

Molnar, Paul D. *Freedom, Necessity, and the Knowledge of God: In Conversation with Karl Barth and Thomas F. Torrance.* London: T&T Clark, 2022.

O'Donovan, Leo J. Editor. *A World of Grace: An Introduction to the Themes and Foundations of Karl Rahner's Theology.* New York: Crossroad, 1981.

Pârvan, Alexandra and Bruce L. McCormack. "Immutability, (Im)Passibility, and Suffering: Steps towards a 'Psychological' Ontology of God," *Neue Zeitschrift für Systematische Theologie und Religionsphilosophie* 59 (1), 2017, 1–25.

Rahner, Karl. *The Trinity.* Translated by Joseph Donceel. New York: Herder and Herder, 1970.

Rahner, Karl. *Foundations of Christian Faith: An Introduction to the Idea of Christianity.* Translated by William V. Dych. New York: Seabury, 1978.

Rahner, Karl. *The Love of Jesus and the Love of Neighbor.* Translated by Robert Barr. New York: Crossroad, 1983.

Rahner, Karl. *Theological Investigations.* 23 vols.

Rahner, Karl. Vol. 1: *God, Christ, Mary and Grace.* Translated by Cornelius Ernst, O.P. Baltimore: Helicon Press, 1961.

Rahner, Karl. Vol. 4: *More Recent Writings.* Translated by Kevin Smyth. Baltimore: Helicon Press, 1966.

Rahner, Karl. Vol. 5: *Later Writings.* Translated by Karl-H. Kruger. Baltimore: Helicon Press, 1966.

Rahner, Karl. Vol. 6: *Concerning Vatican Council II.* Translated by Karl-H. and Boniface Kruger. Baltimore: Helicon Press, 1969.

Rahner, Karl. Vol. 9: *Writings of 1965–1967.* Translated by Graham Harrison. New York: Herder and Herder, 1972.

Rahner, Karl. Vol. 11: *Confrontations 1.* Translated by David Bourke. New York: Seabury Press, 1974.

Rahner, Karl. Vol. 13: *Theology, Anthropology, Christology.* Translated by David Bourke. London: Darton Longman & Todd, 1975.

Rahner, Karl. Vol. 16: *Experience of the Spirit: Source of Theology.* Translated by David Morland. New York: Seabury Press, 1976.

Rahner, Karl. Vol. 17: *Jesus, Man, and the Church.* Translated by Margaret Kohl. New York: Crossroad, 1981.

Rahner, Karl. Vol. 18: *God and Revelation.* Translated by Edward Quinn. New York: Crossroad, 1983.

Rahner, Karl and Weger, Karl-Heinz. *Our Christian Faith: Answers for the Future.* Translated by Francis McDonagh. New York: Crossroad, 1981.

Reichel, Hanna. *After Method: Queer Grace, Conceptual Design, and the Possibility of Theology.* Louisville, KY: Westminster John Knox Press, 2023.

Rosario Rodríguez, Rubén. *Dogmatics after Babel: Beyond the Theologies of Word and Culture.* Louisville, KY: Westminster John Knox Press, 2018.

Tillich, Paul. *The Shaking of the Foundations.* New York: Charles Scribner's Sons, 1948.

Torrance, Thomas F. *Theology in Reconstruction*. London: SCM Press, 1965.

Torrance, Thomas F. *God and Rationality*. London: Oxford University Press, 1971; reissued Edinburgh: T&T Clark, 1997.

Torrance, Thomas F. "Truth and Authority: Theses on Truth," *Irish Theological Quarterly* 39 (3), 1972, 215–42.

Torrance, Thomas F. *Theological Science*. Oxford: Oxford University Press, 1978.

Torrance, Thomas F. *The Ground and Grammar of Theology*. Charlottesville, VA: University Press of Virginia, 1980.

Torrance, Thomas F. *Transformation & Convergence in the Frame of Knowledge: Explorations in the Interrelations of Scientific and Theological Enterprise*. Grand Rapids, MI: Eerdmans, 1984.

Torrance, Thomas F. *The Trinitarian Faith: The Evangelical Theology of the Ancient Catholic Church*. Edinburgh: T&T Clark, 1988; reissued in a Second Edition in the Cornerstone Series with a New Critical Introduction by Myk Habets, 2016.

Torrance, Thomas F. "The Christian Apprehension of God the Father," in *Speaking the Christian God: The Holy Trinity and the Challenge of Feminism*. Edited by Alvin F. Kimel, Jr. Grand Rapids, MI: Eerdmans, 1992.

Torrance, Thomas F. *The Mediation of Christ*. Colorado Springs: Helmers & Howard, 1992, 120–43.

Torrance, Thomas F. "The Atonement: The Singularity of Christ and the Finality of the Cross: The Atonement and the Moral Order," in *Universalism and the Doctrine of Hell: Papers Presented at the Fourth Edinburgh Conference in Christian Dogmatics, 1991*. Edited by Nigel M. de S. Cameron. Carlisle: Paternoster Press; Grand Rapids, MI: Baker Book House, 1992, 225–56.

Torrance, Thomas F. *Trinitarian Perspectives: Toward Doctrinal Agreement*. Edinburgh: T&T Clark, 1994.

Torrance, Thomas F. *The Doctrine of Grace in the Apostolic Fathers*. Eugene, OR: Wipf & Stock, 1996.

Torrance, Thomas F. *Conflict and Agreement in the Church Vol. I, Order and Disorder*. Eugene, OR: Wipf and Stock, 1996.

Torrance, Thomas F. *The Christian Doctrine of God, One Being Three Persons*. Edinburgh: T&T Clark, 1996; reissued in a Second Edition in the Cornerstone Series with an Introduction by Paul D. Molnar, 2016.

Torrance, Thomas F. *Space, Time and Resurrection*. Edinburgh: T&T Clark, 1998; reissued in Cornerstones Series with an Introduction by Paul D. Molnar, 2019.

Torrance, Thomas F. *The Doctrine of Jesus Christ*. Eugene, OR: Wipf and Stock, 2002.

Torrance, Thomas F. *The Person and Life of Christ*. Edited by Robert T. Walker. Downers Grove, IL: InterVarsity Press, 2008.

Torrance, Thomas F. *Atonement: The Person and Work of Christ*. Edited by Robert T. Walker. Milton Keynes: Paternoster; Downers Grove, IL: IVP Academic, 2009.

Name Index

Abraham 78, 188
Adams, Marilyn McCord 182
Althaus-Reid, Marcella x, 103, 105–7, 109–11, 190
Anselm 5, 8, 25, 47
Apollinaris 139, 156
Aquinas, Thomas 5–6, 8–10
Athanasius 2, 128, 138, 142–3, 146, 148, 150, 159, 170, 182
Augustine 2

Balthasar, Hans Urs von 182
Barth, Karl vi, x–xi, 1, 19, 51–3, 55–7, 59–60, 69, 72, 81, 87–92, 94–6, 103–12, 118–19, 127–39, 145–6, 150–65, 168–70, 176, 178–9, 181–5, 190
Bonhoeffer, Dietrich viii, 57, 59, 61
Bulgakov, Sergius 139, 150, 156–8, 182
Bultmann, Rudolf 14–16, 34, 36, 43, 60, 69–70, 76, 96, 117–18, 122

Calvin, John 8, 78, 133–4, 136, 175
Cone, James H. x–xi, 112–24, 191
Cyril of Alexandria 138, 140, 146, 156, 164, 182

Daly, Mary 81
DeLubac, Henri 27
Duffy, Stephen 43–4
Duns Scotus 6
Dych, William V. viii, 20, 27–8, 31, 35–7, 41–3, 47–8, 186

Epiphanius 142

Florovsky, Georges 2–3, 157–8
Frye, Roland 89

Galvin, John P. 32

Haught, John 61
Hector, Kevin 184
Heidegger, Martin 28, 35
Hilary, St. of Poitiers 82
Honorius I, Pope 174
Hunsinger, George 177–8

Isaac 78

Jacob 78
Johnson, Elizabeth A. ix, 79–92, 190
Jones, Paul Dafydd 88

Kant, Immanuel 5–9
Kaufman, Gordon 80, 88, 118
King, Martin Luther 100, 117

Luther, Martin 14, 66

Maréchal, Joseph 8
McCormack, Bruce L. xi, 127–32, 134–6, 138–40, 142–3, 146–53, 155–65, 167–9, 171, 174–84, 192–3
McFague, Sallie 80, 88
Molnar, Paul D. 4, 19, 25–6, 60, 72–3, 91–2, 129, 134, 137, 145, 165, 176, 184
Moses 51, 143, 185, 188

Nazianzen, Gregory 134, 142

Origen 128, 139
Owen, John 148

Pannenberg, Wolfhart 122
Pârvan, Alexandra 131, 150, 171
Paul, St. 1–2, 31, 37, 54, 75, 78, 119, 161

Name Index

Rahner, Karl vi–viii, 1, 7–8, 19–39, 41–8, 60, 71–2, 75, 84–5, 88–90, 92, 110, 112, 186–7
Reichel, Hanna x, 103, 105–12, 190
Robinson, John viii, 25–9, 34, 36, 43, 60–1, 117–18
Rosario Rodríguez, Rubén x, 93–4, 97–102, 190

Schleiermacher, Friedrich 29, 146

Tillich, Paul viii, 25–9, 34, 36, 43, 61, 114, 118–20
Torrance, Thomas F. vi–xi, 1–22, 24–48, 51–82, 84–8, 90–9, 102, 106–13, 115–18, 121–2, 127–9, 131, 133–6, 138–52, 155–76, 178–80, 182, 185–7, 189, 191–3

Virgin Mary 143, 150, 167, 175

Williams, Rowan 182

Subject Index

absolute xi, 114, 130–2
   being 23, 36
   blank 112
   certainty 94–5
   changelessness 131
   closeness of God 33
   consistency 166
   dependence 29
   disciplinary coherence 109
   entitative modification 30
   freedom 28
   freeness 60
   future 87
   grace 74
   historical presence and mystery 43
   priority 67, 99
   Savior 7
   self-communication see self-communication
   significance 113
   spirit 21
   subject 74
   perfection 81
   truth 43
analogy 41, 92
Anhypostasis (*anhypostasia*) 18, 132, 136–7, 139, 141, 150, 152, 155–7, 164, 172–4, 182, 192–3
Anonymous Christianity (Anonymous Christian) vii, 25, 34, 53, 187
Anthropology (theological) vii, 7, 19, 38–9, 41, 44, 46, 51–3, 56, 65, 71–3, 88, 94–6, 112, 128, 185–7
Apollinarian (Apollinarianism) 55, 138–9, 156–7, 164
Arians (Arian, Arianism) 41, 89, 118, 143

ascension 4, 53, 185
atonement ix, 7, 16, 24, 29, 47, 54, 63, 69, 72, 75–6, 142–3, 147–9, 153, 160–1, 174

baptism 78, 102, 157
beatific vision 41
Black Theology x, 112–15, 118–19, 191

Calvinists 13, 176
causality 40–2
   quasi-formal causality 42
Chalcedon (Chalcedonian) vi, xi, 3, 127–8, 130, 135, 138, 140, 147–51, 153, 155–6, 157, 159, 165, 177, 182, 191–3
Chalcedonian Christology (teaching) 127, 138, 140, 147–8, 156, 165, 192–3
   searching Christology 38, 187
charis 1–3, 31
Christ, Jesus
   Anhypostasis see *Anhypostasis*
   Enhypostasis see *Enhypostasis*
   Liberator ix, 94, 97, 102, 124
   vicarious humanity viii, 15, 29, 34, 62, 64, 66, 69, 71, 76–9, 84, 109, 116, 120, 125, 147, 175, 189
   virgin Mary 143, 150, 167, 175
Christology vi–vii, 3–4, 7, 16, 19, 34, 38–9, 51, 57, 60, 65, 93–4, 96–7, 112–14, 117, 127–32, 136–8, 140, 142, 145, 147, 158, 162, 165, 178, 185–7, 193
   Docetic Christology 60, 129, 131, 137
   Ebionite Christology 60, 129, 131, 137
   existentiell Christology 34

from below/from above 129, 136, 142
transcendental Christology 38
communion 4, 18, 51, 53, 142–3, 163, 167, 173
conversion ix, 14, 68, 79, 82–6, 109
creation 12, 31, 35, 55, 58, 120, 128, 134–5, 141, 159, 163, 167, 178
new creation 46, 55, 167
cross viii, 2, 7, 15, 25, 27, 30, 33–5, 45, 52–3, 56, 58, 60–1, 62–4, 66–9, 74–5, 77–8, 86–7, 93, 96, 102, 109–10, 112, 124, 161, 167, 174, 185, 187

deity 2, 134–5, 147
  dependent deity 177, 181
  of Christ 16, 95, 127, 148–9, 160, 162–3, 192
  speculative deity 111
determinism 2
Deus pro nobis (God for us) 153
divine
  causation 40
  impassibility xi, 130–2, 136, 138–40, 146–7, 164–5, 192–3
  name ix, 7, 21–7, 37, 48–9, 82, 86–9, 91–2, 108, 110–1, 138, 143, 181, 186, 188
  passibility 147, 150, 193
  simplicity xi, 130–2, 136, 138, 140, 164, 192–3
divinization (deification, divinized) 2–3, 30
Docetism 59, 137
dogmatic theology 7, 106
dogmatics 7, 59, 93

election 11, 55, 70, 108, 129, 141, 145, 163, 175, 177–8, 182, 184
Enhypostasis (*enhypostasia*) xi, 18, 132, 141, 136–7, 151, 155, 157, 163–4, 172–4, 182, 192–3
eschatological 4, 113
Eschatology 112
eternity 93, 129, 132, 135, 144–5, 149–50, 152, 154, 158, 166, 168–9, 178–84
Eucharist 186
Eutychianism 127, 193
event 15, 21–2, 46, 69, 74, 76, 117–18, 129, 136–7, 144, 146, 152, 157, 171, 178, 181
Extra-Calvinisticum 175
extrinsicism 30

Faith vii, viii–x, 1–2, 5–8, 10–15, 17, 20, 23–4, 29, 34, 37, 44–9, 54–7, 61, 64–9, 73–4, 77–8, 80, 82–8, 90, 92–3, 96, 100–2, 105–11, 117–19, 124–5, 142, 181, 185–6, 188, 190
  legalizing (legalistic) vii, 13, 62, 65–6, 70
fallen humanity 147, 169, 173
Father (God as Father) ix, xi, 2–3, 5–7, 11–12, 15, 17–20, 23–7, 29, 31, 34, 36, 39, 41, 48–9, 51–3, 55–6, 61, 64, 66–7, 72, 74, 78–89, 91–3, 95, 100–2, 104–6, 108–9, 111–12, 118, 120–1, 124, 127, 129, 132–6, 138, 140–5, 148–51, 153–4, 159–63, 166, 168–9, 171–4, 177–84, 190–2
fellowship 29, 52, 55, 72, 143, 168, 174
feminist theology 68, 81, 107, 190
forgiveness 23, 33–4, 48, 66, 74–5, 94, 108, 144, 146, 149, 185, 187
freedom viii, 13–14, 17–18, 21, 27–8, 31–4, 39, 42, 53, 59, 64, 68, 72, 75–7, 83–6, 92, 95, 98–100, 103, 106, 109–10,

115, 118–20, 122, 125, 129,
  134–5, 143, 150, 152, 155,
  158–60, 162–3, 167, 174–5,
  178, 181, 183–4, 186–90, 192

gender and language for God ix,
  16, 45, 79–80, 82–4, 93,
  108, 123
genus tapeinoticum 155
Gnostic 89
God see Trinity
God with us 143, 185
gospel 54, 95–6, 113, 115
grace vi–x, 1–14, 17–24, 27–44,
  46–8, 51–5, 57–66, 68–77,
  83–8, 90, 93, 95–9, 101–2,
  114–15, 117–19, 121–5,
  128–30, 134–5, 141, 143,
  152, 155, 158–62, 167, 169,
  171–5, 177–8, 180, 182,
  184–90, 192
  cheap grace 27, 34, 60–1, 65,
    68–9, 77, 93, 108, 187
  costly grace viii, 27, 58–9, 61,
    65–6, 68, 87, 93, 95, 108,
    187
  created grace 2, 29–30, 39, 41
  deification see divinization
  deifying 3, 41, 73
  ground of being 27, 87
  infused grace (*fides infusa*) 1, 4–5,
    9, 39, 66
  inseparability of Gift and Giver
    vii, 1–3, 6, 10, 22, 28, 31,
    35–6, 39, 41, 43–4, 46, 61,
    72, 104–5, 107, 112, 125,
    185, 187
  priority of grace 10–11, 18, 141,
    155

harmartiology 112
historicist 175
holy mystery 26, 33, 36, 48–9, 83–5,
  87, 90

Holy Spirit viii, x, 2–5, 7, 12, 17,
  19, 23–7, 29–30, 32, 34,
  36–8, 44, 48–9, 51, 55–6,
  61–2, 65, 78, 80–1, 83–105,
  108–9, 111, 113, 117–18,
  120–1, 127–9, 132, 135–6,
  141–3, 147–8, 151, 155–7,
  159, 164–5, 168, 171,
  179–80, 182–3, 185, 187,
  190–1
homoousion (*homoousios*) x, 3, 41,
  55–6, 87, 93–4, 157–8, 162,
  172
horizon 20, 90, 186
humanitas Christi 145
hypostasis 137, 140, 145, 150, 155–8,
  168
  *enhypostasis/anhypostasis/
    enhypostatic/anhypostatic*
    xi, 18, 132, 136–7, 151–2,
    155–7, 164–5, 172–4, 182,
    192–3
  hypostatic union 2, 12, 16–18, 77,
    137, 141–2, 144–5, 147,
    149–50, 155, 157, 160–1,
    165, 168, 171–3, 182

"I am" sayings 51, 95, 143, 188
idealism 21, 113
identity vi, 3, 10, 20, 22–3, 29, 33,
  35–6, 40, 44, 46, 81, 87,
  90–1, 94, 103, 111, 113,
  125, 133, 154–5, 168–9,
  177
image of God 26
Incarnation ix–xi, 7, 12, 19, 24,
  29, 39–40, 45, 47, 53–5,
  59, 63, 65, 67, 70, 72,
  80–1, 89, 93, 129, 134–6,
  138, 141–2, 145, 147,
  149–53, 155–9, 161–9,
  171–2, 174–9, 182–3,
  185–6, 189, 192
incomprehensible mystery 21

Jesus' history/Jesus of history/
   historical Jesus 4, 18, 37–8,
   68, 83, 95, 116–17, 122,
   165, 173
Judgment vii, 7, 12–13, 46, 48, 55, 65,
   73–4, 76, 108, 161, 167, 174
justification by faith (by grace) see
   grace

kenosis 111, 131, 150, 160–1, 174
knowledge
   a posteriori knowledge 17
   a priori knowledge 7, 16, 21–4,
      38–9, 187
   innate knowledge 36, 53
   knowledge of God vi–vii, 5–6,
      8–10, 19–25, 27–9, 38,
      44–5, 47–9, 53–4, 56,
      71–3, 75, 77, 80, 83–6,
      88–92, 95, 97–8, 101,
      105–6, 108, 111, 118, 121,
      142, 180, 186–7
   natural knowledge of God 23,
      27–9, 38, 58
   non-conceptual knowledge 7–10,
      20, 22–3, 25, 44, 47, 67,
      72–4, 92, 187
   non-objective knowledge (non-
      objective luminosity) 20,
      47–8
   objective knowledge (objective
      facts) xi, 3, 11, 14–15, 21,
      24–5, 28, 45, 48, 62, 68–71,
      96, 99, 114–15, 149, 160,
      191
      primary objectivity 103–4
      secondary objectivity 104
   pre-thematic knowledge 90
   unthematic knowledge 20–3,
      25, 37, 44, 47

Liberation vi, viii–xi, 53, 58, 62,
   65, 68, 77, 82, 86, 88,
   93–4, 97–103, 112–13, 115,
   117–25, 185, 187–8, 190–1

liberalism 8, 113
Logic of grace/Logic of Christ see
   grace
Logical necessity 123, 155, 164, 171,
   177, 179
Logos 131, 137–41, 146, 150, 152,
   154–8, 160–5, 168, 177,
   179, 182, 192
Logos as such 138, 177, 181–2
logos asarkos xi, 129, 136, 138, 150,
   154, 158, 160, 162, 169,
   177–9, 182, 192
logos incarnandus xi, 136, 150, 178–9,
   182, 192
logos incarnatus 138, 150, 178
Lordship 165, 181
love 2, 9, 11, 13, 18, 24, 31–6, 39, 43,
   51, 53, 55, 59, 62–4, 66–8,
   70–2, 74, 76, 78, 80–1,
   84–5, 87, 90, 93, 96–8,
   100–4, 107–11, 118–22,
   128–9, 132, 135, 141–3,
   147, 151–2, 158–60, 162–3,
   166–8, 171, 173, 175, 178,
   183, 188, 190–1
love of God x, 13, 32, 35, 64, 70,
   72, 74, 84, 93, 98, 103–4,
   108–10, 118, 128–9, 132,
   158, 160, 171
love of neighbor ix, 70, 71–3, 101,
   110
luminosity 42–3, 48

matrix 81, 87–8
medieval thought (synthesis,
   theologians, theology) 4,
   6–7, 9, 39–41
Messiah 116, 123
metaphor (metaphorical) 83, 92
metaphysics (metaphysical) 129–30,
   132, 135–6, 142, 162–3, 171
miracle (miraculous) 37, 74–5, 132
mission of the Son 78, 133–4, 163, 181
missions see Trinity
modalism 102

mode of being 133, 136–7, 152
monophysitism (monophysite) 147, 149, 176, 193
Mother (God as Mother or Mother-Sophia) 26, 87–91
mutual conditioning 19, 72
mystery 21–7, 30, 33, 36–8, 43, 48–9, 82–5, 87, 90, 92, 113, 115, 129, 142, 151, 157
mysticism 146
mythology 15, 26–7, 55, 84, 118

nameless (God as nameless mystery) 21–7, 49
natural theology 19, 30, 40, 75
nature 1–5, 8, 16–17, 19–21, 23, 25–33, 35–6, 38, 40–1, 43, 47, 54, 58, 62–3, 67, 73, 78–9, 82, 104, 120, 132, 136–7, 139–41, 143, 145, 147–9, 155–6, 158, 164, 167–9, 171–4, 176, 180–2, 185–7
necessity 123, 154–5, 161, 164, 171, 177, 179
Neo-Protestantism 8
Nestorianism (Nestorian) 144, 156, 161, 193
"new theologians" (new theology) viii, 10, 27, 31, 60–2
Nicaea (Nicene) vi, 52, 65, 67, 81–2, 87, 89, 92, 101–2, 105, 109, 120–1, 127, 136, 180–2, 192
nineteenth-century theology 8
nominalism 6

obedience vii–viii, 10–11, 13–14, 29, 34, 64, 66, 68–9, 73, 76–8, 83–4, 98–100, 109, 121, 123, 129, 132–4, 141–2, 147, 150–2, 154–5, 168–9, 173–4, 186
obediential potency 23, 30, 33, 187
One Mediator 25, 62, 146, 168

ontological receptivity 131, 133, 136, 161, 163–5, 168–9, 171, 177, 179
ontology 28, 131–2, 135, 163, 171, 176

Pantheism (pantheistic) 4
Passibility (passible) 140, 147, 193
Patriarchalism ix, 68, 80, 86, 93
Pelagianism (Pelagian) 13, 30, 39, 117, 120, 187
philosophy (philosophical) 20, 44, 46–7, 71, 130, 138
pietism 13, 146
pneumatology (pneumatological) see also Holy Spirit 87, 97
predestination 183
pride 83–4, 87
process theology 131
processions see Trinity
projection (mythological, idolatrous) x, 45, 48, 55, 84, 118, 122, 163
"prop-God" viii, 57, 59
pure nature 98, 147

queer theology (queer experience, queer virtue, queer grace, queer holiness, queer God) x, 103–7, 109, 111–2, 190

reconciliation 23, 29, 34, 75, 77, 80, 86, 89–90, 95–6, 105, 110, 119, 124, 142, 144, 147–9, 160, 164, 167–8, 170, 173
redemption 4, 12, 39, 141
  co-redemption 41, 67
relationality (relational) 92, 130, 175–6
religionless Christianity viii, 57
resurrection 2, 4, 12, 27, 33, 35, 37, 44–7, 53, 61–2, 67, 69, 86, 90, 95, 108–9, 117, 122, 141–3, 161, 167, 185
  empty tomb 46

revelation vii, x, 3, 7, 10-1, 19-20, 22-5, 27-8, 30, 32-3, 35, 37-8, 40, 42, 44-9, 51, 56-7, 61, 67, 69, 74-5, 80-1, 83-4, 87-95, 97, 99-101, 103-4, 107, 109, 111-13, 115-16, 120, 128-9, 131-2, 134, 138, 142-5, 151, 153, 161-2, 173, 185-6, 191
revelation as offense or offensive 57, 74, 113
transcendental revelation 22
unveiling 22, 89

sacrament (sacramentally, sacramental) 17, 40, 100-2, 104, 168
salvation ix, 2-3, 7, 13-15, 23-5, 32, 34-5, 39, 47-9, 53, 55, 62-3, 67-8, 76, 78, 83, 86, 91, 96, 103, 107-9, 112, 116, 119, 125, 140, 159, 171, 179, 185-6, 189
Savior 7, 36, 56, 62-4, 68-9, 71, 77, 117, 124
scientific objectivity (scientific theology) 62, 105-7
self-acceptance 24, 34, 36, 46-7, 49
self-communication 19-20, 23, 31, 33-4, 36-7, 41-3
self-justification ix-x, 13, 30, 51, 53, 57-8, 69-70, 73, 77, 93, 102, 108, 110, 117, 121, 125, 188-90
self-revelation see revelation
self-sufficiency (human) 33
self-sufficient (God) 111
self-transcendence 22, 37, 36, 48, 73
simplicity see divine
sin (as self-will/free-will) viii, ix, xi, 1, 29, 32-5, 45, 52-5, 57, 63, 71-3, 78-80, 83, 86, 93-4, 96, 98, 100, 102, 106-8, 112, 115, 120-1, 123-5, 149, 163, 166-7, 173-4, 186-7, 189

sonship 45, 81, 144-5
Sophia 88-9, 91
soteriology 112
sovereignty 24, 39, 129
space 58-9, 146, 149, 157-8, 175-6
container/receptacle concept 175-6
subjectivism 9, 14, 25, 27, 41, 56, 69, 92, 114
supernatural existential vii, 23, 30-3, 36-8, 42, 47, 187
symbol ix, 57, 80, 83-4, 86, 92-3, 109, 113, 115, 119, 122-4

theological anthropology vii, 7, 51-2, 73, 185-6
theological ontology 131
theosis 2-3
thinking
from a center in God 60, 65, 107
from a center in oneself 65, 107
repentant rethinking 45, 75, 78, 187
time 113, 122, 129-31, 133-5, 145-6, 148-51, 153-4, 157-60, 165-6, 168-70, 176, 181-3
totalitarianism 98-9
transcendental experience vii, 8, 20, 22-3, 28, 30, 32-5, 37, 43-4, 46, 48-9, 186
transcendental method 44, 129
transcendental revelation see revelation
transcendental Thomists 6, 8, 48
transcendentality 32, 42, 44
Trinity
economic Trinity 16, 19-20, 24, 26, 81, 104, 117, 120, 127, 129, 133-4, 136, 150, 152, 158-9, 162-3, 180
immanent Trinity 20, 23, 81, 89, 92, 103-4, 117-18, 120, 127-9, 132, 134-5, 143, 152,

157–8, 161–3, 169, 178–82, 184
missions 127, 133–4, 149–50, 152, 163, 176, 181
processions 128, 133–4, 149, 152, 163, 176, 179–80, 182
triune God x, 4, 9, 11, 24, 49, 60, 75, 80, 83–5, 90, 107, 110–1, 119–20, 128–9, 131, 133, 135, 179
triunity 175, 182
truth xi, 4–12, 14, 16–19, 21–2, 24–5, 28–9, 32–4, 38–40, 43, 45–6, 49, 51–2, 54–6, 62, 65, 67–70, 74–5, 77, 80, 94–6, 98–9, 101–6, 108–10, 114–15, 117, 121, 123–4, 129, 141, 143, 166, 173, 176, 180–1, 186–91

vicarious humanity see Christ, Jesus
voluntarism 6

"wholly Other" x, 103, 105, 190
Wisdom 87, 89
worship 55, 64, 79, 116